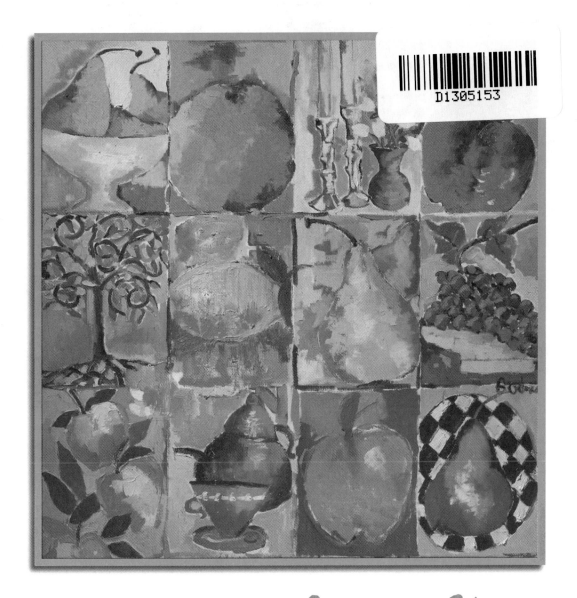

SEASONED *Love*

WITH

CULINARY TREASURES FROM THE BREMAN

The William Breman Jewish Heritage Museum
Atlanta, Georgia

First Printing   October 2006   5,000 copies

ISBN: 0-9761534-1-6

To order additional copies, use the order forms in the back of the book.
For additional information about recipes
and about The Breman, visit www.thebreman.org.

WIMMER
COOKBOOKS

A CONSOLIDATED GRAPHICS COMPANY

800.548.2537   wimmerco.com

TABLE OF CONTENTS

FOREWORD

Within the pages of *Seasoned with Love,* you will find delectable kosher dishes served up with southern charm, hospitality, history and hope for humanity. Food, whether simply prepared or part of a gourmet masterpiece, provides nourishment for the body and soul. Eating is life affirming in every possible way. Food is essential to Jewish life, culture, community and continuity. In the South, food is taken, by many, as seriously as religion.

From Augusta to Atlanta, from Macon to Moultrie, and from Columbus to Cartersville, The Breman celebrates, commemorates, documents and preserves Jewish life in Georgia. The museum's archive holds recipe books, newspaper articles, oral histories and photographs, including all those featured in this book, that trace the tastes of southern Jewish life. Holocaust survivors who made their homes in Atlanta share their personal perspectives. "I was a girl when I went to the camps. I never knew if I would be alive at the end of the day. I was hungry always. I dreamt of making the dishes I had helped my mother and grandmother make. It is my great fortune that I survived. I have been able to pass those dishes on to my children and grandchildren."

Today, Jewish individuals from communities around the world have settled in Georgia, bringing with them traditions of religious observance and cultural heritage, including special foods. Many, having been here for generations, adopted uniquely southern customs. *Seasoned with Love* illuminates Georgia's rich Jewish history and allows you to savor the down home flavors of southern Jewish kitchens and distinct culinary customs. The Breman is pleased to present a spectacular collection of outstanding recipes that reflect Georgia's diverse Jewish community.

We invite you to try these recipes and then make them your own. Enliven your table with new menus, jazz up traditional meals with contemporary dishes and create new delicacies.

Our heartfelt thanks to all the donors and volunteers who made this book possible. Special thanks to The Breman staff who worked many, many hours, both on and off the job, to realize this project. It has taken three years and many thousands of hours to produce *Seasoned with Love.* Thus, it is with great appreciation and pleasure that we, the three presidents of the Board of Trustees of The Breman, during whose tenure this book was developed, present this cookbook.

Coming to America, the S.S. George Washington, c.1928

L'chaim y'all!

Thomas J. Asher	Carole Goldberg	Valerie Needle
President, 2002-2004	President, 2004-2006	President, 2006-2008

Kosher Basics

Seasoned with Love is for everyone. *Seasoned with Love* is a collection of delicious kosher recipes that comply with the Jewish dietary laws, the laws of *kashruth*. The laws of *kashruth* are an integral component of Jewish heritage. However, interpretations of the laws of *kashruth* are plentiful. For questions about a particular recipe, consult your rabbi or *kashruth* authority.

For the purpose of this cookbook, recipes comply with standards set forth by the Orthodox Union. The volunteers involved with this project, including many who keep strictly kosher, have screened, edited and categorized these recipes as dairy, meat, pareve and appropriate for Passover for your convenience. *Every effort has been made to ensure the accuracy of the information; we apologize for any errors.*

Cooks who are learning about the laws of *kashruth* or striving to make a kosher meal may find the laws to be varied and complex. From preparation to presentation, the laws deal not only with the ingredients of each recipe, but the utensils, cookware and dishes used to prepare and serve food.

What is different about kosher recipes?

- Certain food is *treif,* or forbidden, such as pork, ham, birds of prey or shellfish, swordfish, eel, catfish and other scavenger species.

- Meats must be purchased from a kosher butcher. Certain cuts of meat (from the rear portion of an animal) are prohibited.

- Dairy products are not used with meat or poultry.

- *Pareve* products and ingredients do not contain milk, meat or their derivatives and can be used when preparing dishes with meat, poultry or dairy. *Pareve* foods include eggs, fruits, vegetables and grains, as well as fish with fins and scales.

Only kosher-for-Passover ingredients are permitted when cooking for Passover. Many products must be marked "Kosher for Passover" on the label to be suitable for use during the holiday.

Please note, traditions vary and this is not a comprehensive representation of the laws of *kashruth,* but rather a quick overview of some of the basics.

THE WILLIAM BREMAN JEWISH HERITAGE MUSEUM

Jewish immigrants from all over the world have been welcomed in communities throughout Georgia. Jewish cuisine in Georgia, as in all other places Jews have settled, has been shaped both by kosher dietary laws as well as the many cultures in which Jews have lived and traveled. As Georgia's Jewish heritage museum, The Breman collects, preserves and interprets material culture reflecting the backgrounds, ethnic and religious traditions that, when woven together, form the fabric of Georgia's Jewish community.

Founded in 1996 at The Selig Center, The Breman is the largest repository for the archival material related to Jewish life in Georgia with collections dating back to the 1850s. The Breman features:

- The Blonder Family Heritage Gallery which houses *Creating Community: The Jews of Atlanta from 1845 to the Present*

- The Holocaust Gallery which houses *Absence of Humanity: The Holocaust Years, 1933-1945*

- The Marlene J. and William A. Schwartz Special Exhibitions Gallery

- The Ida Pearle and Joseph Cuba Community Archives and Genealogy Center

- The Lillian and A.J. Weinberg Center for Holocaust Education

- The Elinor Rosenberg Breman Museum Shop

- The Pola and Sam Arbiser Family Theater

- The Reference Library

Elinor and Bill Breman celebrate the museum's opening, Atlanta, Georgia, June 1996

Personal stories and historical memorabilia provide a springboard for discovery and dialogue from generation to generation. The Breman attracts diverse audiences with exhibitions, programs and educational opportunities. The museum educates visitors about universal themes such as personal responsibility, community building, cross-cultural understanding, *tzedakah* (righteousness and benevolence) and *tikkun olam* (repairing the world and social action). The Breman's archives holds documentation of Jewish life in Georgia communities, synagogues and organizations. It sheds light on how Jewish people have lived, organized and participated in communities throughout the state.

Education is at the heart of The Breman. Its galleries, programs, archives, library and exhibitions share stories of Jewish history, culture and values.

Each year more than 40,000 individuals benefit from The Breman's resources. More than half of the museum visitors are students. At The Breman, student groups hear stories directly from Holocaust survivors about man's inhumanity, human resilience, resourcefulness and rescue. Educators from religiously and culturally diverse teaching institutions are trained to teach in their classrooms about the Holocaust. Hundreds of thousands of students benefit from this specialized education each year. The Breman's message to each individual is one of respect for difference and dignity for all.

The leadership of The Breman is committed to strengthening its offerings and developing new initiatives to meet the educational needs of the multi-faceted Jewish and general communities. At a time when the Holocaust survivor community is aging, the physical evidence of Jewish life in small southern towns is disappearing and antisemitic acts are taking place around the world, The Breman's mission is vital and your support makes a difference. You can strengthen The Breman's educational programs by purchasing one or more cookbooks today, becoming a museum member online at www.thebreman.org, visiting The Breman at 1440 Spring Street, Atlanta, GA, and/or contributing your family's Georgia Jewish memorabilia to The Breman archives.

Ben Walker (center), a Holocaust survivor who resides in Atlanta, Georgia, shares his story with students at The Breman, c.2005.

Special Thanks
The Breman Staff

While volunteers and sponsors were key ingredients for *Seasoned with Love*, the staff of The Breman was essential as well. Without the time and talent of the museum staff, this book would not have been possible. The staff took the material provided by the volunteers polished it, dressed it up and put on the finishing touches. Every picture shown throughout this book was hand-picked from the archives, captioned and digitized by the staff. This book is what it is, an amazing tribute to Jewish life in Georgia, in large part because of their efforts. And we thank them.

Judi Ayal

Liliane Kshensky
Baxter, Ph.D

Sandra Berman

Jennifer Campbell

Ruth Einstein

Cherryl Goldstein

Haven Hawley, Ph.D

Debbie James

Phyllis Lazarus

Jane Leavey

Maureen MacLaughlin

Janie Morgan

Katherine Smith

Featured Artist

Seasoned with Love's vibrant cover art and its chapter dividers were created by Atlanta resident Gary Bodner, a practicing physician specializing in obstetrics and gynecology. These works, done especially for the book, represent Dr. Bodner's passion and talent for art as well as his Jewish roots.

The Breman expresses heartfelt gratitude to Dr. Bodner for his joyous interpretations of Jewish culinary themes. His lively artwork adds a dimension of festivity, reverence and love to our cookbook.

Dr. Bodner's art is represented by Anne Irwin Fine Art (www.anneirwinfineart.com). His work has been included in group and solo exhibitions in Atlanta, Nashville and Highlands, North Carolina. As the featured artist for Northside Hospital's Foundation Ball in 2000, Dr. Bodner has also had his work reproduced on several covers of the *Georgia Pharmacy Journal*.

Sponsors

The Breman is grateful to the generous donors at all levels who made publishing Seasoned with Love possible. Their gifts represent an investment in the museum and in our community. This book is a gift to all who love learning and eating.

Ruby Spoon

Elinor Breman

Beverlee Shere

Platinum Spoon

Laura & Marshall Dinerman

Charles A. Henderson

Judith & Mark Taylor

Bo Waddell & Tim Bacon

Gold Spoon

Spring & Tom Asher

Shirley Blaine

Mark Gronsbell

Susan & Leon Gross

Barbra Morganstern

Carol & Bob Nemo

Johanna & Rabbi Hillel Norry

Betty T. Schiff

Jane Schiff & Lon Gratz

Susan & Ray Schoenbaum

Silver Spoon

Marilyn & Sam Eckstein

Viki & Paul Freeman

Corky & Roger Gelder

Elliott Goldstein

Etta Raye Hirsch

Barbara & Alan Kaplan

Lawrence & Leona Krevat

Jeff Krevat

Lois & David Kuniansky

Peter Mallen

Twom Mallen

Valerie & Bill Needle

Barbara Weinberg-Riff
    & Maury Riff

Len Buccellato & Ken Spooner

Joan & Stanley Srochi

Irene & Howard Stein

Bronze Spoon

Toni & Joel Adler
Ruth Arnovitz
Millie & Norman Asher
Penny Berk
Sandy & Ozzie Berman
Judith & Elliott Cohen
Sally & Sammy Coolik
Ina & Harold Enoch
Carole & Joel Goldberg
Bernie Goldstein
Judy & Hank Greenstone
Carol & Alan Grodin
Sherry & Ike Habif

Barbara & Jay Halpern
Edythe & Larry Hecht
Lila Herbert
Gene Hirsch
Nancy & John Hirsch
Cheryl & Russell Kramer
Phyllis & Wayne Lazarus
Jane & Bob Leavey
Joel & Irwin Lowenstein
Donna & Philip Newman
Susan & Michael Plasker
Helen & John Plous
Ruth Rauzin

Brenda & Paul Raymon
Jodi Ann & David Schiff
Joyce & Henry Schwob
Marlene Schwartz
Ray Ann Kremer &
    George Shapiro
Joyce & Sonny Shlesinger
Sue & Dick Stern
Susan & Sidney Tourial
Sue & Jon Winner
Judy & Erwin Zaban
Harriet & Norman Zoller

Brass Spoon

Sheryl Adair
Eliot & Ellen Arnovitz
Kimberly & Hugh Asher
Johanna & Joey Asher
Juliet Asher-Golden
Betsy & David Baker
Sally Beer
Candy & Steve Berman
Annie & Bernard Birnbaum
James Blanc
Joyce & Donald Block
Mona Blumenthal
Christine & Jeffrey Bogart
Jim Breman
Jeffrey Cohen
Anita & Max Eidex
Barbara & Steven Eisenberg
Katherine & Alan Elsas
Judith Finkel
Barbara & Pete Fishman
Gloria & Geoff Frisch
Elsa & Jay Goldberg

Penny & Jerry Goldwasser
Bea & Robert Grossman
Sherry & Alvin Halpern
Stuart Handelsman
Pearlann & Jerry Horowitz
Marice Katz
Rosanne & Andy Kauss
Joyce Kinnard
Carole & Sid Kirschner
Cathy Selig-Kuranoff &
    Steve Kuranoff
Renay & Alan Levenson
Ruth & Gary Levison
Meryl & Richard Levitt
Renee & Alan Levow
Suzie & Bill Lowenstein
Jackie & Tony Montag
Janet Page
Judi & Richard Pawliger
Deborah & Hank Payne
Paul Rabinowitz
Anta & Mendel Romm

Barbara & Dukie Roos
Flora & Bernard Rosefsky
Judy & Phillip Rosenberg
Robin & Fred Rosenberg
Peggy & Manny Roth
Virginia & Milton Saul
Fran & Jerry Scher
Francie & Barry Schwarz
Joyce & Henry Schwob
Denise Shaw
Doris & John Sherman
Madelyn & Herb Shessel
Diana & Mark Silverman
Jill & Herbert Spasser
Andrea & Steve Steinman
Arlene & David Taylor
Lisa & Chuck Taylor
Margaret & Bill Weiller
Julie & David Weinstein
Deanne & Morris Whitlock
Jackie & Dave Wolf

*Special thanks to our in-kind sponsors: Added Touch Catering, Binders Art Supplies
and Frames, Dr. Gary Bodner, Dobel Salon and Spa, D'Vine Wine Bar and Shop, Eve Mannes,
National Distributing Company, Return to Eden, Saks Fifth Avenue, Phipps Plaza, and Young Chef's Academy.*

*Every effort was made to ensure the accuracy of the acknowledgments.
We apologize for any unintentional errors or omissions.*

VOLUNTEERS

For more than three years, the following individuals have tirelessly worked on testing, sorting, rewriting, editing and putting this book together. The combination of each of their efforts has resulted in this extraordinary tribute to our community that will benefit educational programs at The Breman for years to come. There are no words to adequately thank them for the hours and energy it took to produce this book, however, we wish to acknowledge them for all their hard work and accomplishment! *Yasher Koach!*

Jane Schiff, Project Chair

Elaine Skibell, Chair
Recipe Collection, Testing and Selection

Betsy Lurey, Chair
Copy Writing and Editing

COMMITTEE MEMBERS

Sylvia Becker	Maggie Glezer	Barbra Morganstern
Penny Berk	Bea Grossman	Phyllis Napoli
Shirley Brickman	Ruth Hackner	Donna Newman
Suzi Brozman	Jill Harrison	Pat Pugrant
Laura Dinerman	Nancy Hirsch	Gloria Smiley
Karen Lansky Edlin	Carol Sue Legum	Judy Sobel
Helen Freed		

SPECIAL CONSULTANTS

Rebbetzin Dassie New	Roberta Scher
Rabbi Yossi New	Rabbi Julie Schwartz

Hundreds of individuals volunteered their recipes, time, kitchens, homes, taste buds, memories, creativity, ideas, enthusiasm, talent and skills to fill the pages of *Seasoned with Love*. Thousands of recipes and hundreds of memories, together with the reality of limited space, meant many wonderful submissions needed to be saved for another day. The Breman is extremely grateful to and proud of everyone who participated in bringing this cookbook to fruition. *Every effort was made to ensure the accuracy of the acknowledgments. We apologize for any unintentional errors or omissions.*

Barbara Abend

Sarah Abend

Stephanie Abes

Lillian Abramowitz*

Marci Abrams

Sandra Adair

Cantor Benjamin Adler

Toni Adler

Affairs to Remember

Hank Aldorf

Marlyne Israelian
    Alembik

Ali Allen

Helen Alperin

Sara Alterman

Harryette Altman*

Emily Amato

Arlene Applerouth

Marla Arbet

Dorita Arnold

Ruth Arnovitz

Spring Asher

Thomas Asher

Judi Ayal

Rebecca A. Azran

Susan Backer

Sandra Bank

Nancy Banks

Betsy Baker

Regina Barah

Jimmy Baron

Lisa Baron

Arline "Cookie" Bashuk

Holly Bashuk

Louise Baum

Dora Becker*

Mary Jane Becker

Saul Becker

Sylvia Becker

Sally G. Beer

Harriett Behr

Rita Benamy

Asher Benator

Shoshana Ben Yoar

Susan Berch

Lois Berch

Carole Berenson

Robyn Berger

Penny Berk

Susan Berkowitz

Lesley Berman

Goldie Bertone

Sheila Biales

Anne Birnbaum

Lois Blonder

Rita Bloom

Bloomingdales Restaurant
    - 59th and Lex

Dot Blum

Rita Bodner

Eleanor Borneman

David Boucher

Penina "Penny" Bowman

Rose Bowman*

Nancy J. Brant

Elinor Breman

Joe Breman

Sylvia G. Breman*

Shirley Brickman

David Brooks

Lauren Brooks

Joan Brown

Suzi Brozman

Aline Brusman

Michelle Buckingham

Renee Buckler

Frances B. Bunzl

Jennifer Bushman

Bea Caine

Janet Camhi

Miriam Campbell

Lucille N. Canter

Julie Ann Caper

Rachelle Capes

Mary Capelito

Harriette Carter

Catherine "Cadena" Cohen*

Helen Cohen
Judy Cohen
Sandy Cohen
Sharon Polstein Cohen
Shirley Cohen
Stephanie Cohen
Terri Cohen
Walter Cohen
Gail Cohn
Sylvia Zanville Cohn
Nancy Cole
Bill Collins
Norma Conrad
Carole Cooper
Julie Ann Cooper
Nelma Ann Cowser
Vickie Cox
Jackie Crainen
Allison Cuba
Goldie Curley*
Tracy Dankberg
Bonnie Dannen
Linda Danzig
Mina Davidson
Marilyn Davidson
Patti Davidson
Christa Davis
Jon Davis
Pam Friedberg Davis
Sara Deitch
Laura Delong
Bobi Dimond
Laura Zaban Dinerman
Gary Donlick
Eileen Donner
Ruth Dubin

Elaine Dushoff
Marilyn Ginsberg Eckstein
Sam Eckstein
Karen Lansky Edlin
Rita Edlin
Anzonetta Edwards
Anita Eidex
Jeanne Eidex
Ruth Einstein
Vicky Alembik Eisner
Fred Ellman
Yetta Ellman
Lynn Elson
Sandra Epstein
Sue Epstein
Robyn Estroff
Sharon Fagin
David Farrell
Marilyn Feingold
Allison Fellner
Lori Fierman*
Laraine Fine
Stella Alhadeff Firestone
Barbara Fishman
Jeanne Fitterman
Elissa Fladell
Sharon Flexner
Lynn Kurtz Floum
Sylvia Fogel
Carol Fradkin
Sara Franco
Mary P. Franklin
Helen Freed
Phyllis Freedman
Marsha Zanville Friedberg
Brook Friedlander

Mark Friedlander
Steven Friedlander
Boni Friedman
Lynn Friedman
Lynne Friedman
Murray D. Friedman
Shirley Friedman
Betty Furst
Arlene Gabor
Lenora Galanti
Rachel Galanti
Nancy Gallant
Michelle Gary
Rosie Gates
Helen Gerson
Micheline Gerson
Sara Ghitis
Jessie Gladden
Sandy Zalbowitz Gladstone
Judy Glassman
Maggie Glezer
Carole Goldberg
Elsa Goldberg
Hannabelle H. Goldberg*
Sara Goldberg
Vida Goldgar*
Ginger Goldhammer
Janice Goldman
Carolyn Goldsmith
Cherryl Goldstein
Doris Goldstein
Judy Goldstein
Maria Gomez
Hilda Haver Goodelman
Betty Goodfriend
Frances Goodman

Marilyn Goodrich

Sonia Gordon

Heather Gottlieb

Frieda Gottsegen

Carvel Grant Gould

Rhoda Gould

Ida Gouscher

Karen Grablowsky

Jacqueline Granath

Jody Greenberg

Marjorie W. Greenberg

Aline Greenblatt

Gail Greenblatt

Judy Greenstone

Paula Neuman Gris

Susan Gross

Sylvia Gross

Traci Gross

Linda Grossbart

Bea Grossman

Bob Grossman

Betty Grus

Gertrude Gulden

Diane Gup

Billie Guthman

Mildred Gwinn

Jan Haber

Clare Habif

Sharon Habif

Sherry Habif

Ruth Hackner

Michele Halter

Lynn Halpern

Lynne Halpern

Rachel Dannen
    Hammel

Jennifer Hancock

Tamar Harel

Susan Harkavy

Amy Harris

Jack R. Harris

Jill Harrison

Trina Harrison

Renee Hartman

Blanca Hartstein*

Elice Haverty

Gloria Hecht

Mary Kae Heller

Jennifer Hendrix

Madelyn Herman

Ellen Herold

Esther Hersh

Reba Kreisberg Herzfeld

Saundra Higgins

John Hirsch

Nancy Hirsch

Reavena Miller Hirsch

Bertha Hirsh*

Ellen Holland

Margie Holland

Sheila Holtz

Yvonne Horesh

Dana Horowitz

Michelle Horowitz

Pearlann Horowitz

Sandra Horowitz

Jackie G. Howard

Blanchette Ichay

Sondra Ilgenfritz

Leslie Isenberg

Phyllis Isenberg

Betty Israel

Eva Iteld

Candy Jackson

Dee Dee Jackson

Diane Jacobi

Betty Ann Jacobson

Margaret Jaffee

Dana Joffe

Elizabeth Jump

Carolyn Kahn

Ralda Kahn

Robin Kalent

Marsha Kalison

Marcy Scher Kalnitz

Sally Kaplan

Renee Karchmer

Ruth Karlebach

Betty Karp

Hazel B. Karp

Barbara Katinsky

Mandy Katz

Ada Kaufman

Barbara Kaufman

Marilyn Maisel Kiang

Sherry King

Beverly Kingsley

Phyllis Klain

Betty Klein

Rachel Kleinman

Barbara Kluka

Randy Knopf

Margaret Kokotow

Sandy Kole

Minnie Kolodkin

Doris Koplin

Ida Koplin*

Sandi Friedberg Kornblum

Lee Kout
Amy Krafchick
Cheryl Kramer
Barbara Krasnoff
Robin Kreines
Estelle Kreisberg
Jana Kreisberg
Ray Ann Kremer
Mickie Eisenberg Krinsky
Patti Kroness
Courtney Kuriger
Gail Kuriger
John Kuriger, Jr.
John Kuriger, Sr.
Donna Kurtz
Bernice Kyles
Rhona Landis
Shari Landon
Lilo Lange
Robin Lapins
Sharyn Lazarnick
Phyllis Lazarus
Ann Le
Eileen Leader
Bob Leavey
Jane Leavey
Nikki Skibell Lebo
Cathy Lee
Liz Lee
Carol Sue Legum
Pamela Levenstein
Rachel Lehmann
Juliana Wolf Lerner
Renay Levenson
Doris Leverton
Phyllis Levin

Rose Levin
Wendy Levin
Evelyn Levine
Phyllis Levine
Pamela Levenstein
Jenny Levison
Renee Levow
Donna Levy
Meredith Levy
Valerie Hartman Levy
Rebbetzin Shternie Lew
Shera Lyn Lippman
Ron Lipsitz
Paulette Lovitz
Lisa Lubel
Betsy Bennett Lurey
Sharon Lusk
Roseanne Lutz
Eve Mannes
Annette Marcus
Marge Markowitz
Rose Markowitz *
Randi Mazer
Chris McHenry
Katie McLoughlin
Tracey Medeiros
Gail Medwed
Ronnie Seiden Melnick
Florence Melvin
Esther Mendel
Eva Mendel
Lee Mendel
Gary Mennie
Jacqueline G. Metzel
Julius "Mac" Meyer
Shirley Michalove

Karin Miehl
Annette Miller
Harriette Miller
Shirley Miller
Shirley Plous Miller*
Sissy Toronto Miller
Kim Mitchell
Yelena Moldovan
Julie Moradi
Jennie Moret
Barbra Morganstern
Anita Morris
Andi Morse
Lucy Moses
Shirley Yudelson Mosinger
Elyne Moss
Mira Naor
Phyllis Napoli
Valerie Needle
Melanie Nelkin
Carol Nemo
Roberta Nemo
Barbara Nesin
Rebbetzin Dassie New
Rabbi Yossi New
Richard Newfield
Donna Newman
Rosalie Newman
Janice Nodvin
Rebbetzin Johanna Norry
Rabbi Hillel Norry
Sharon Singer Norry*
Connie O'Neal
Jeanette S. Oppenheimer
Or VeShalom Sisterhood
Susan N. Schreiber Orloff

Anne Overstreet
Marilyn Donsky Pailet
Eleanor Parks
Judi Pawliger
Rita Pearlman
Nancy Peck
Sara Pichulik
Sarah Piha
Edith Pilzer
Debbie Pinsky
Barbara Planer
Susan Plasker
Amy Plous
Helen Cohn Plous
John C. Plous
Alyson Pollack
Chuck Pollack
Elaine Pollock
Andy Price
Bob Pugrant
Pat Pugrant
Esther Pugrant*
Jennifer Rae
Vernice Rae
Ruth Rauzin
Brenda Raymon
Ray's On The River
Lora Reed
Tom Reed
Gail Reid
Ilse Reiner
Susan Remson
Barbara Weinberg Riff
Marlene Rinzler
Karen Rittenbaum
Inge Robbins

Ozna Robkin
Joan Rocamora
Mary Ann Rogers*
Barbara Roos
Flora Rosefsky
Dulcy Rosenberg
Dorothy Rosenblum
Kimberly Rosenthal
Michelle Rosinek
Dorothy Roth*
Bertha Rubin
Barbara Rucket
Selma Ruda
Dalia Rudich
Lauren Rudick
Betsy Howard Russell
Ellen Sadiky
Nina Salkin
Adelle Salmenson
Sue Sandalon
Victoria Saranga
Yves Saranga
Amy Schatten
Barbara Schatten
Betty Schear
Rachel Schein
Roberta Scher
Madeline Schessel
Annie Schiff
Cathy Schiff
David Schiff
Evelyn Schiff
Fay Schiff
Hal Schiff
Hannah Schiff
Herb Schiff

Jane Schiff
Jodi Schiff
Arlene Shmerling
Barbara Schneider
Ray Schoenbaum
Susan Schoenbaum
Ann Schoenberg
Florence Schwartz
Rabbi Julie Schwartz
Marlene Schwartz
Terry Schwartz
Marcia Schwarz
Jean Schweikher
Sara Seelke
Zelda Seigel
Janet Selig
Linda Selig
Linda Selsberg
Amanda Shams
Andee Shapiro
Elaine Shapiro
Gail Shattah
Beverlee Shere
Joyce Shlesinger
Sarah Shlesinger
Ruth Siegel
Ann Silver
Diana Silverman
Saba Silverman
Bert Silverstein
Marci Abrams Silverstein
Rosie Singer
Ruth Singer*
Sol Singer*
Cathy Sinsheimer
Elaine Cohn Skibell

Erwin Skibell

Karyn Slovin

Gloria Smiley

Minette Smith*

John Smith*

Barbara Snow

Rose Schoen Snyder

Judy Sobel

Bonnie Sobelson

Sheila Sofsky

Cooper Speaks

Luther Alvin Speaks*

Elsie Branch Speaks*

Betty Jo Speight*

Helen Spiegel

Sylvia Werner Spiegel

Edna Spindel*

Robyn Freedman Spizman

Andrea Steinman

Margie Stern

Sunny Stern*

Tamar Stern

Hope Straney*

Arlene Strauss

Adele Tanenbaum

Tilly Tannebaum

Roz Taranto

Arlene Taylor

Judith Taylor

Darlin Tolpin

Shirley Tolpin

Maryann Toub

Michael Touhy

Regina Tourial

Doug Turbush

Anne Van Prooyen

Alice Verner

Lisa Vivori

Leslie Vogelman

Beverly Wainer

Ronit Walker

Carolyn Wallace

Jennifer Walters

Cecile Waronker

Gail Warren

Rose Washington

Lorraine Watkins

Camilla Watson

Glenda Watters

Margaret Weiller

Rona Weinberg

Lil Weinberg*

Lynne Weiner

Josephine Weinstein

Shirley Weinstein*

Shirley Romm Wender

Lisa West

Jerry Westbrooks

Marilyn Westbrooks

Marci Mendel White

Teresa White

Deanne Whitlock

Betty Hodges Williams*

Claire Wilson

Craig Wilson

Ida Wise*

Rachel Wise

Jodi Wittenberg

Hermina "Hum" Wolf *

Jackie Wolf

Rina Wolfe

Barbara Wolff

Terri Wruck

Carrie Wynn

Louis Yakrus

Jennifer Yaffe

Mary Sue Younce

Helen Breman Zageir*

Stephen Zanville

Edythe Adelstone Zanville*

Sheila Zeitzer

Beverly Zoblotsky

Harriet Zoller

of blessed memory

17

JEWISH HOLIDAYS

Food and family are central to the Jewish lifestyle. Holidays create the rhythm of Jewish life throughout the year. Most holidays are associated with special meals or traditional fare. On this page is a very brief outline of the Jewish holidays mentioned in *Seasoned with Love*. Many recipes featured throughout *Seasoned with Love* are perfect for holidays and simchas, joyous occasions. For detailed menu suggestions, check our website, www.seasonedwithlovecookbook.com.

Shabbat is the Sabbath or "Day of Rest". It is a weekly holiday celebrated from sundown Friday night to sundown Saturday night. Work is completely suspended.
Food Traditions: A joyful feast on Friday night and *cholent*, a slow cooking stew, for lunch on Saturday.

Rosh Hashanah is translated as "Head of the Year." This is the traditional Jewish New Year and beginning of the High Holy Days.
Food Traditions: Preparing a feast, dressing and decorating in white, serving sweet dishes, especially ones that include apples and honey.

Yom Kippur is the Day of Atonement. It follows 10 days after *Rosh Hashanah* and is a fast day.
Food Traditions: The Break the Fast meal is a dairy feast, often celebrated as a community.

Sukkot is the Festival of Tabernacles. It is an 8-day fall harvest holiday. Meals for the week are traditionally eaten in a *Sukkah*, a temporary hut, with family and friends.
Food Traditions: Seasonal vegetables, grains and sweet dishes.

Chanukah, also known as the Festival of Lights, is an 8-day winter holiday that celebrates the story of the Maccabees and the miracle of a little oil that lasted for eight days.
Food Traditions: Foods prepared in oil such as *latkes* (potato pancakes), *sufganiyot* (donuts), and in Georgia, fried chicken.

Purim commemorates the narrow escape by the Jews of Persia from annihilation thanks to the bravery of Queen Esther. It is a winter holiday that includes dressing up in costume, merriment and bringing sweet treats to friends.
Food Traditions: Hamantaschen, candy and lots of other sweets.

Passover celebrates the Jews' liberation from slavery and the Exodus from Egypt. It is an 8-day spring holiday, which commences at a home service, called a *seder,* that includes a meal. This meal is a special highlight for cooks as many traditional dishes are served.
Food Traditions: Unleavened bread *(matzah), charoset,* eggs, bitter herbs, and a plethora of family favorites.

Shavuot is holiday that commemorates the day the *Torah* was given to Moses at Mount Sinai and recognizes the covenant between God and the Jewish people. It is a spring harvest holiday.
Food Traditions: A dairy feast, especially cheese *blintzes.*

IN THE *Beginning*

APPETIZERS

SALMON STUFFED NEW POTATOES

New potatoes, salmon and capers are a sensational flavor combination.

Dairy / Pareve / Passover   *Serves 12*

12   small red new potatoes

1   tablespoon olive oil

4   ounces smoked salmon, divided

2   tablespoons dairy or pareve sour cream

2   teaspoons minced onion

1   teaspoon capers

½   teaspoon prepared horseradish

¼   teaspoon pepper

Preheat oven 400°. Cut potatoes in half, toss with oil. Place potatoes, cut side down, on baking sheet. Roast 25 minutes until just tender, cool. Finely dice 3½ ounces salmon. Add diced salmon to remaining ingredients, except reserved salmon. Using demitasse spoon or small melon baller, scoop out center from cut side of each potato half. Slice tiny piece from potato bottoms to stabilize. Spoon 1 teaspoon filling into each potato half. For garnish, chop remaining ½ ounce salmon. Place on top of each stuffed potato.

As a variation, top these potatoes with sautéed onion, fresh herbs, grated cheese or finely chopped walnuts.

Potato relay team, Crew Street School, Atlanta, Georgia, 1931.

ENDIVE WITH CRANBERRY ORANGE CHICKEN SALAD

Annette Marcus' culinary reputation spread as she entertained friends in her own home. Try this colorful finger food when hosting guests.

Meat / Passover   *Yields 16 pieces*

1	cup cubed cooked chicken	¼	cup mayonnaise
2	tablespoons chopped green onions	16	endive or red lettuce leaves
½	teaspoon grated orange zest	⅓	cup cranberry orange relish
¼	teaspoon salt	16	cashews
¼	teaspoon ground ginger		Orange zest, for garnish

Combine first 6 ingredients until well blended. Spoon about 1 tablespoon chicken mixture onto each lettuce leaf. Top with 1 teaspoon cranberry orange relish and 1 cashew. Garnish with additional orange zest.

Annette Marcus Catering, Atlanta, Georgia

Plan on 12 hors d'oeuvre per person for a cocktail buffet or 5 per person for cocktails before dinner.

Astound guests with this special salad.
Dinner party, Atlanta, Georgia, c.1925.

Appetizers

20

ENDIVE STUFFED WITH GOAT CHEESE AND WALNUTS

The best appetizers are those that can be prepared in advance.

Dairy   *Serves 8*

⅓ cup coarsely chopped walnuts	⅓ cup crumbled goat or blue cheese, about 1½-ounces
2 tablespoons honey, divided	⅓ cup dried cranberries, optional
¼ cup balsamic vinegar	1 tablespoon minced fresh chives
3 tablespoons orange juice	¼ teaspoon pepper
16 Belgian endive leaves, 2-3 heads	
16 small Mandarin orange slices, or Clementines	

Preheat oven to 350°. Combine walnuts and 1 tablespoon honey. Spread on rimmed baking sheet coated with nonstick spray. Bake about 10 minutes, stirring after 5 minutes, watching carefully to avoid burning. Combine remaining honey, vinegar and orange juice in small saucepan. Bring to boil over high heat, simmer until reduced to 3 tablespoons, about 5 minutes.

To assemble, fill each endive leaf with 1 orange section, top with 1 teaspoon goat or blue cheese, 1 teaspoon walnuts, and some cranberries. Arrange on serving plate. Drizzle vinegar mixture evenly over leaves. Sprinkle with chives and pepper.

Endive leaves are a popular and elegant base for favorite fillings of soft cheeses and toasted nuts. The leaves may be trimmed in the morning, refrigerated, wrapped in a damp towel and sealed in a plastic bag until served.

Party Platter Niçoise

Favorite vegetables, with a French accent.

Pareve/Passover   *Serves 24*

3	(14-ounce) cans solid white albacore tuna, drained, flaked	1	(5-ounce) jar pimiento stuffed green olives, drained
1	(14-ounce) can artichoke hearts, drained, quartered	1	(8-ounce) jar pickled pearl onions, drained
1	(8-ounce) can button mushrooms, drained	1	cup grape tomatoes
1	(8-ounce) can black olives, sliced, drained	1	(8-ounce) bottle red Russian or French dressing
		¼	cup white vinegar
		½	cup mango chutney

Combine tuna, artichoke hearts, mushrooms, olives, pearl onions and tomatoes in large bowl. Whisk together dressing, vinegar and mango chutney. Toss with vegetables. Refrigerate 24 hours, stirring 2 or 3 times. Drain excess liquid. Arrange on platter.

The olive tree dates to ancient times in both biblical and classical writings. It was an olive branch that a dove brought back to Noah as a sign that the flood was finally over. The olive tree and branch are universal symbols of peace and harmony.

SOUTHWEST CHEESECAKE

Dairy   *Serves 18 to 20*

1½ cups crushed tortilla chips
4   tablespoons butter, melted
1   cup cottage cheese
3   (8-ounce) packages cream
    cheese, softened
4   large eggs
2½ cups shredded Monterey
    Jack cheese with peppers

1   (7-ounce) can chopped
    green chilies or jalapeños
8   ounces sour cream
1   cup chopped tomatoes,
    drained
½-1 cup chopped green onions
¼-½ cup sliced black olives

Preheat oven to 325°. Combine tortilla chips with butter. Press into the bottom of 9-inch springform pan. Bake 15 minutes. Beat cottage cheese until smooth. Add cream cheese, mix until silky. While beating, add eggs, 1 at a time. Fold in Monterey Jack cheese and chilies. Pour mixture into crust. Bake 1 hour or until cheesecake begins to crack on top. Remove from oven, cool on rack. Freeze at this point, if desired.

Spread with sour cream. Garnish in circles with tomatoes, green onions and olives.

Cut into small wedges or serve as dip with crackers or tortilla chips.

For 2 small cakes, make 2 crusts and divide the filling between each crust.

Cowpokes and cowgirls alike love this Southwest Cheesecake.
Sign at Cross Roads Restaurant, Atlanta, Georgia, c.1950.

DATE NUT CHEESE ROLLS

Dairy/Passover   *Yields 10 to 15 pieces*

2   (8-ounce) packages cream
    cheese, softened
2   ounces crumbled blue
    cheese
½   cup shredded sharp Cheddar
    cheese

4   ounces chopped dates
½   cup golden raisins
2   cups finely chopped pecans,
    toasted

Dates play a prominent role in Jewish tradition. The "land flowing with milk and honey" refers to date honey which dates produce when overripe.

Combine cream cheese, blue cheese, Cheddar cheese, dates and raisins, mix well. Pinch off pieces to form into ¾-inch balls. Roll in chopped pecans. Chill until ready to serve.

To prevent dates from sticking while chopping, lightly oil the knife or scissors.

Date Nut Cheese Rolls are the perfect appetizer for a club meeting. Study group, Atlanta, Georgia, c.1900.

Apricot Blue Cheese Kisses

Everyone is nuts about these kisses.

Dairy/Passover   Yields 15 pieces

2   ounces cream cheese,
    softened
2   ounces blue cheese,
    softened

15 dried apricots
15 toasted pecan halves

Up to 1 day in advance, combine cheeses stirring until well blended. Cover, refrigerate until ready to use. Top each apricot with ½ teaspoon of cheese mixture and 1 toasted pecan. Cover tightly, refrigerate up to 8 hours. Serve at room temperature.

Roasted Garlic and Feta Spread

A favorite for summer entertaining and a popular menu item shared by one of Georgia's premier caterers, Affairs to Remember.

Dairy/Passover   Serves 6 to 8

1   head garlic, unpeeled
1   tablespoon olive oil
3   tablespoons water

6   ounces cream cheese,
    softened
6   ounces feta cheese, softened

Preheat oven to 350°. Cut garlic head in half horizontally. Place unpeeled garlic halves cut side up on baking sheet lined with foil. Drizzle with olive oil, sprinkle with water and cover tightly with foil. Bake 45 minutes to 1 hour, depending on size. Squeeze the cloves out of their papery husks into bowl of food processor. Process cream cheese, feta and roasted garlic until smooth. Add just enough olive oil to make smooth purée. Serve chilled with crackers, bagel chips or matzahs for Passover.

Affairs To Remember, Atlanta, Georgia

A head of garlic is a large bulb made up of many smaller cloves.

THREE CHEESE WAFERS

Delicate and crisp, these are always a favorite.

Dairy   *Yields 12 to 15 wafers*

4 ounces butter	Dash of hot pepper sauce
1¼ cups grated Cheddar cheese	1 cup flour
2 ounces Boursin cheese	1 cup crispy rice cereal
8 ounces Gorgonzola cheese	1 cup toasted slivered
⅛ teaspoon salt	almonds, optional

In electric mixer bowl, beat butter until soft, add cheeses, salt and hot sauce until well blended. Slowly add flour, continuing to beat, until thoroughly blended. Fold in rice cereal and almonds. Form into 2 logs. Refrigerate 30 minutes. At this point, logs may be wrapped in wax paper and frozen. Preheat oven to 325°. Slice logs into ⅛-inch slices. Place slices on parchment lined cookie sheet. Bake 30 minutes or until lightly browned. Cool to serve.

Vick's Delicatessen, Atlanta, Georgia, 1943.

FIG AND WALNUT TAPENADE

From Affairs to Remember, a spread to remember.

Dairy/Passover   *Serves 10 to 12*

1¼	cups chopped dried figs	1¼	teaspoons chopped fresh thyme
5	tablespoons water		Salt and pepper
5	tablespoons premium brine cured black olives	11	ounces goat cheese
2	tablespoons olive oil	1	cup chopped walnuts
1	tablespoon balsamic vinegar	12	walnut halves to garnish Thyme sprigs

Combine figs and water in saucepan. Cook over medium high heat until liquid evaporates and figs are soft, about 5 to 8 minutes. Transfer to medium bowl. Pit and chop olives. Add olives, olive oil, vinegar and thyme to figs. Season tapenade with salt and pepper. Cut goat cheese into ½-inch rounds, arrange on platter. Stir chopped walnuts into tapenade, spoon mixture onto cheese rounds. Garnish with walnut halves and thyme sprigs. Serve with crackers or matzahs.

Tapenade can be made up to 3 days ahead. Bring to room temperature before serving.

Affairs To Remember, Atlanta

SHERRY MUSHROOM PÂTÉ

This vegetarian pâté is easy to prepare. Serve with homemade pita chips.

Dairy/Pareve/Passover   *Serves 6 to 8*

⅓	pound mushrooms	1	tablespoon sherry
¼	cup butter or pareve margarine	6	ounces dairy or pareve cream cheese, softened
⅓	cup finely chopped onions	¼	cup minced parsley

Coarsely chop mushrooms. In large skillet, melt butter or margarine over medium heat. Sauté mushrooms and onions, stirring often until mushrooms are brown, about 15 minutes. Remove from heat, stir in sherry and cool slightly. In medium bowl, beat cream cheese and parsley until blended, add mushrooms, spoon into serving dish. When preparing in advance, cover and refrigerate up to 3 days. Serve at room temperature.

For homemade pita chips, slice pita crosswise into 2 thin rounds. Brush 1 side with butter, pareve margarine or olive oil. Top with crushed garlic and rosemary, or sprinkle with Parmesan, coarse salt and ground red pepper. Stack the rounds, cut into wedges. Toast in a single layer on a cookie sheet in oven at 250°, 15 to 20 minutes until golden.

VEGETARIAN CHOPPED LIVER

So good, even Grandma would approve!

Pareve   *Serves 8 to 10*

2	large onions, sliced
2	tablespoons canola oil
2	garlic cloves, minced
4	large eggs, hard-cooked
¾	cup walnuts
1	tablespoon soy sauce or tamari

¼	teaspoon salt
¼	teaspoon pepper
1	(8-ounce) can small green peas, drained or string beans

Sauté onion in oil until lightly browned. Stir in garlic, sauté for 1 minute, cool. In food processor blend all ingredients, pulsing until just blended, not puréed. Cover, chill at least 1 hour or up to 4 to 5 days. Do not freeze.

If too much oil is used, the "liver" will separate when processed.

ZAIDE'S CHOPPED LIVER

Pâté and chopped liver are first cousins.

Meat / Passover   *Serves 10 to 12*

6	large hard-cooked eggs, peeled, divided
¼	cup melted chicken fat, divided

1	pound chicken livers, drained
1	large onion, sliced Kosher salt and pepper

Cut eggs into quarters, setting aside ½ egg for topping. Lightly grease broil pan with melted chicken fat. Broil livers until no longer pink, drain and cut into small pieces. In large skillet, sauté onion in ½ of the remaining chicken fat. Remove onions. Sauté livers for 1 minute. Transfer onions, liver, pan juices and eggs to processor. Pulse only until chopped. Transfer to large bowl. Stir in reserved chicken fat, season with salt and pepper. Grate reserved egg on top. Serve immediately or refrigerate to serve cold. Serve with crackers or matzahs.

Chopped liver is generally made using either calves' liver or chicken liver. Traditionally, a key ingredient is schmaltz, rendered chicken fat. Shortening or oil may be substituted for schmaltz. The liver itself is high in protein, fat and cholesterol; thus creative cooks have developed low-fat mock and even vegetarian versions.

Schmaltz is melted, or rendered, chicken fat. To make homemade schmaltz, purchase 1 pound of chicken fat or save fat from chickens used in other recipes and freeze. Place chicken fat in a frying pan on low heat. Stir the pieces of fat frequently. Most of the fat will slowly melt down. Discard solids, the rendered fat is schmaltz. Strain and store in a glass jar in the refrigerator.

LAYERED SALMON TERRINE

Pretty as a picture and well worth the time. Served
on a bed of Boston lettuce, this makes a fabulous first course.

Dairy / Pareve / Passover   *Serves 18 to 24*

FIRST LAYER

8	ounces dairy or pareve cream cheese, softened	1	green onion, finely chopped
½	cup mayonnaise	1	teaspoon Dijon mustard
1	teaspoon kosher gelatin	1	teaspoon horseradish
4	teaspoons lemon juice		Pepper
¼	cup boiling water	1	tablespoon chopped parsley

SECOND LAYER

1	tablespoon kosher gelatin	½	cup mayonnaise
¼	cup lemon juice	½	pound Nova or canned smoked salmon
¼	cup boiling water		
2	green onions, chopped	1	teaspoon horseradish
8	ounces dairy or pareve cream cheese, softened	½	teaspoon dill weed

Line 9x5-inch loaf pan with plastic wrap. Blend cream cheese with mayonnaise, set aside. Soften 1 teaspoon gelatin in lemon juice 5 minutes, stir into boiling water, until dissolved. Stir into cream cheese. Fold in remaining first layer ingredients. Spoon mixture into prepared loaf pan. Refrigerate at least 2 hours, until completely set before adding second layer.

To prepare second layer, soften 1 tablespoon gelatin in lemon juice 5 minutes. Add to boiling water, stir until dissolved. Place remaining ingredients in food processor, blend well. Add gelatin mixture, process completely. Pour mixture on top of first layer. Cover, refrigerate at least 2 hours until firm. To serve, uncover, hold plate over pan, invert and slice.

BAKED BRIE WITH HONEY NUT SAUCE

An elegant way to welcome hungry guests.

Dairy   *Serves 10 to 12*

1	(2.2-pound) round Brie cheese	5	tablespoons honey
2	sheets frozen puff pastry, thawed	2	teaspoons minced garlic
1	large egg, beaten	1/4	cup chopped walnuts or pecans
4	tablespoons unsalted butter	2	tablespoons chopped fresh parsley

Preheat oven to 400°. Place Brie on 1 sheet puff pastry, top with second sheet of pastry. Seal cheese between pastry sheets, cutting off excess at corners. Transfer to greased baking sheet. Brush with egg. Bake until pastry is golden, 10 to 15 minutes. Place on serving plate.

Melt butter with honey and garlic in small saucepan over low heat, stirring until butter melts. Pour sauce over baked Brie. Sprinkle with nuts and parsley. Serve with crackers or French bread.

For extra flair, cut Brie in half horizontally. Place ½ rind side down on puff pastry. Spread with generous ½ cup diced fresh fruit, apples, pears, dried cranberries and/or raisins that have been tossed with ½ tablespoon melted butter, 1½ teaspoons firmly packed brown sugar and dash of cinnamon. Place top ½ of Brie rind side up over fruit mixture. Top with second pastry sheet, seal and continue with recipe.

Honey is essential to this Baked Brie recipe. Dance recital, Augusta, Georgia, c.1928.

GOAT CHEESE CROSTINI

My mama once told me, "If you like to eat and you can read, you can learn to cook!"
This is easy to make and a crowd pleaser.

Dairy   *Serves 6 to 8*

11   ounces goat cheese
2   large garlic cloves, minced
24   crostini slices
2-3 plum tomatoes, thinly sliced

Fresh basil leaves, cut
   chiffonade
Asiago or Parmesan cheese,
   shredded
Olive oil

Preheat oven to broil. Mix goat cheese and garlic, spread on crostini. Top each with 1 tomato slice, fresh basil and shredded Asiago or Parmesan cheese. Sprinkle with olive oil. Broil until golden brown.

Chiffonade is an effective technique to thinly slice herbs and large leafed vegetables, such as spinach or lettuce. Stack the leaves and roll them tightly, slice into fine strips.

Goat cheese, the key ingredient!
Goat cart, Atlanta, Georgia, 1923.

Artichoke Cheese Bread

Simple and simply sensational.

Dairy

Serves 8 to 10

¼ cup butter	1 cup shredded Parmesan cheese
2 garlic cloves, minced	
2 teaspoons sesame seeds	½ cup sour cream
1 (14-ounce) can chopped artichoke hearts, drained	1 loaf French bread
	1 cup shredded Cheddar cheese
1 cup shredded Monterey Jack cheese with peppers	

Preheat oven to 350°. Melt butter in large skillet. Sauté garlic and sesame seeds until lightly browned, remove from heat. Stir in artichokes, cheeses and sour cream, transfer to bowl. Cover, refrigerate until ready to assemble. Cut French bread in ½ horizontally, scoop out bread leaving 1-inch thick shells, set aside. Crumble removed bread, stir into artichoke mixture. Spoon mixture into bread shells, sprinkle with Cheddar cheese. Place on foil lined baking sheet. Cover with foil, bake 25 minutes. Uncover, bake an additional 5 minutes until cheese melts. Cut in slices to serve.

Artichoke and Goat Cheese Bruschetta

Dairy

Serves 4

4 tablespoons olive oil, divided	½ teaspoon finely grated lemon zest
2 garlic cloves, minced	¼ teaspoon finely grated orange zest
1 shallot, minced	
1 bay leaf	½ cup goat cheese, softened
5 thyme sprigs	1 teaspoon lemon juice
1 (10-ounce) package frozen artichoke hearts, thawed, squeezed dry	1 teaspoon orange juice
	Salt and pepper
	1 baguette, thinly sliced

Preheat broiler. Heat 2 tablespoons olive oil in skillet. Sauté garlic and shallot until soft and light brown. Add bay leaf and thyme, stir 1 minute. Add artichokes and zests, stir 4 minutes. Remove from heat, discard bay leaf and thyme. In food processor, pulse artichoke mixture with goat cheese and juices. Season with salt and pepper. Turn into small serving bowl, cover to keep warm while preparing bread. Brush bread slices with remaining olive oil. Broil 1 minute until golden and crisp, turning once. Serve artichoke spread with baguette slices.

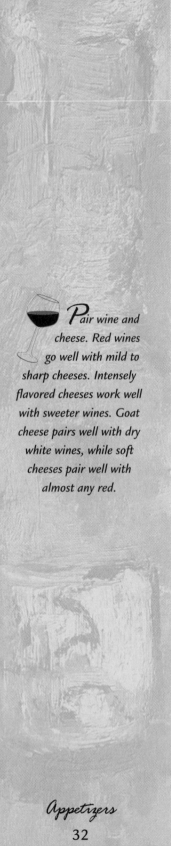

Pair wine and cheese. Red wines go well with mild to sharp cheeses. Intensely flavored cheeses work well with sweeter wines. Goat cheese pairs well with dry white wines, while soft cheeses pair well with almost any red.

WILD MUSHROOM BRUSCHETTA

Enjoy the delicious woodsy flavor of exotic mushrooms.

Dairy   *Serves 8 to 12*

4   ounces oyster mushrooms
8   ounces Shiitake mushrooms
10   ounces Portobello mushrooms
3   tablespoons olive oil
3   tablespoons unsalted butter
4   large garlic cloves, minced
2   shallots, minced
1   green onion, finely chopped
½   cup dry sherry
½   cup vegetable stock
2   teaspoons dried thyme

1   teaspoon dried basil
   Kosher salt
   Red pepper flakes
6-8   ounces goat cheese, softened
½   teaspoon finely grated lemon zest
½   teaspoon finely minced chives
   Minced lemon zest
   Minced chives
32   thin slices French sourdough baguette

Preheat broiler. Trim ends off mushroom stems, discard. Coarsely chop mushrooms. In large skillet, heat olive oil and butter over medium heat. Sauté garlic, shallots and green onion 1 to 2 minutes, stirring constantly. Increase heat slightly, add mushrooms, sauté 7 to 8 minutes. Stir in sherry, vegetable stock, thyme and basil. Simmer until liquid evaporates. Season with salt and red pepper flakes. Keep warm.

Blend goat cheese, ½ teaspoon lemon zest and ½ teaspoon chives. Prepare garnish by combining additional lemon zest and minced chives. Brush bread slices with olive oil, broil 1 minute until golden, turning once. Transfer to cookie sheet. Spread each bread slice evenly with cheese mixture, then mushroom mixture. Broil 3 to 4 minutes until mushrooms just begin to brown. Remove from oven, place on serving dish. Garnish each piece with sprinkling of lemon zest and chives.

Kosher salt gets its name from its primary function. It is used in the process of making meat kosher. Kosher salt is an additive-free coarse-grained salt. Many cooks prefer to use it in their cooking, as the flavor is distinct from ordinary salt. It has big crystals with large surface areas, thus it absorbs more moisture than other salts.

GRUYÈRE ONION TART

This is a scrumptious beginning to a dairy meal.

CRUST

1⅓ cups flour	¼ cup ice water
¼ teaspoon salt	2 tablespoons Dijon mustard
½ cup unsalted butter, cut into pieces	2 tablespoons shredded Gruyère cheese

CARAMELIZED ONIONS

2 tablespoons unsalted butter	1 tablespoon sugar
¼ cup olive oil	½ teaspoon salt
6-7 large yellow onions, cut into quarters, thinly sliced	Pepper

FILLING

2 large eggs	1 cup shredded Gruyère cheese, divided
⅓ cup cream	
1½ teaspoons finely chopped fresh thyme or ½ teaspoon dried thyme	

"As a new bride, I thought the kitchen was just a room to go through to get to the garage."

Combine flour and salt in food processor, pulse to blend ingredients. Add butter, process to resemble coarse meal, 5 to 10 seconds. With motor running, slowly add ice water, just enough for dough to come together in a ball. Transfer dough to floured work surface. Press into shape to fit 9-inch round tart pan or 11x8-inch rectangular tart pan with removable bottom. Place in pan, pressing against sides without stretching. Trim excess dough, pierce dough with fork at 1-inch intervals. Refrigerate until firm, about 30 minutes.

In large, deep skillet, melt butter with olive oil. Add onions, sugar, salt and pepper. Simmer very slowly over low to medium low heat. Stir often, cook until onions are a rich brown color.

Preheat oven to 375°. Place tart pan on baking sheet. Cut parchment paper to fit over dough, fill with pie weights, raw rice or dried beans. Bake uncovered 20 to 25 minutes, until lightly browned, cool completely on wire rack. Remove weights and paper. Brush crust with mustard, sprinkle with Gruyère cheese. Return to oven, bake until cheese melts, about 7 minutes. Cool completely. Reduce temperature to 350°.

CONTINUED ON NEXT PAGE

In bowl, beat eggs, cream, thyme and ¾ cup cheese. Add caramelized onions, stir well. Spoon mixture into crust, sprinkle with remaining cheese. Bake until filling is set, 30 to 35 minutes. Cool for 15 minutes. Remove sides of pan, transfer to serving plate. Serve warm or at room temperature.

TOASTED MUSHROOM TURNOVERS

Sautéed mushrooms and onions wrapped inside a smooth cream cheese pastry will delight guests.

Dairy/Pareve   *Serves 12*

CREAM CHEESE PASTRY

2	sticks butter or pareve margarine, softened	½	teaspoon salt
8	ounces dairy or pareve cream cheese, softened	2	cups flour

FILLING

½	pound finely chopped mushrooms		Dash of ground nutmeg
½	cup chopped onion	1	teaspoon lemon juice
2	tablespoons butter or pareve margarine	2	teaspoons flour
½	teaspoon salt	½	cup dairy or pareve sour cream
	Dash of pepper	1	teaspoon dill weed

EGG WASH

1	egg yolk	2	teaspoons milk or pareve soy milk

Beat together pastry ingredients, chill overnight. Sauté mushrooms and onions in butter or margarine until softened, add salt, pepper, nutmeg and lemon juice. Blend in flour until smooth and slightly thickened. Stir in sour cream and dill weed. Remove from heat, cool. In small bowl, beat egg yolk with milk.

Preheat oven to 350°. Break off part of dough, keep remainder chilled until ready to use. Between sheets of floured wax paper, roll dough until paper thin. With cookie cutter make 2-inch or 3-inch circles. Place 1 scant teaspoon filling on each pastry round. Fold pastry in half and crimp edges with fork tines. Repeat with remaining dough. Freeze at this point, if desired. Baste tops of turnovers with egg wash. Place on ungreased baking sheet, bake 20 minutes until light brown.

"I remember as a child helping my bubbe wipe the glasses with a tea towel for Shabbos. I was the worker. She was the chief inspector."

Sweet Potato Blinis

These Sweet Potato Blinis are a winner!

Dairy   *Serves 4 to 6*

1	cup heavy cream	3	eggs, separated
6	tablespoons cornstarch	1	pound sweet potatoes, cooked
1	tablespoon grated fresh ginger		Salt and pepper

In mixing bowl, combine cream, cornstarch, ginger and egg yolks. Press potatoes through ricer, into cream mixture. Whip egg whites into soft peaks. Fold into potato mixture, season with salt and pepper. Place small dollop of batter onto hot nonstick griddle or pan, turning over when golden brown. Serve warm.

Executive Chef Gary Donlick, Pano's and Paul's Restaurant, Atlanta, Georgia

Fresh gingerroot keeps well in the freezer. When frozen, it is very easy to peel and grate.

Mah jongg game, Valdosta, Georgia, 1962.

LOADED SMOKED SALMON QUESADILLAS

QUESADILLAS

½ pound smoked salmon, cut julienne	1 tablespoon chopped fresh thyme
1 Fuji apple, cut julienne	¼ cup diced red onion
½ pound mozzarella or Monterey Jack cheese, shredded	Juice of 1 lemon
	4 flour tortillas
1 tablespoon chopped cilantro	2 tablespoons vegetable oil

HORSERADISH CREAM

1 cup sour cream	¼ cup heavy cream
1 cup mayonnaise	2 tablespoons minced shallot
3 tablespoons bottled white horseradish	Juice of 1 lemon
	Salt

FUJI APPLE JICAMA SALSA

1 Fuji apple, peeled, cored, diced	1 tablespoon minced jalapeño pepper
1 cup peeled, diced jicama	Juice of 1 lime
¼ cup diced red onion	1 tablespoon chopped cilantro
	1 tablespoon honey

Combine salmon, apple, cheese, herbs, red onion and lemon juice. Spread mixture on tortillas, fold in half. Heat oil in large skillet. Carefully transfer quesadilla to skillet, sauté 2 minutes on each side until golden brown and hot inside. Slice in wedges. In separate serving bowls, combine Horseradish Cream ingredients and Apple Salsa ingredients. Serve quesadilla wedges with dollop of Horseradish Cream on top and Apple Salsa on the side.

Executive Chef Doug Turbush, Nava Restaurant, Atlanta, Georgia

To julienne any vegetable, cut a piece off each end so it will sit firmly on the work surface. Cut vegetables into long thin slices. Stack slices and cut uniform match stick-sized strips.

This salsa calls for one big apple!
Big Apple Supermarkets, Atlanta, Georgia, c.1960.

Barbequed Drumettes

These little gems are sure to be snapped up the minute they are served.

Meat   *Serves 8 to 10*

1	(6-ounce) can frozen orange juice concentrate	6	ounces prepared mustard
6	ounces soy sauce	2	pounds chicken drumettes

Preheat broiler. Combine orange juice, soy sauce and mustard. Place drumettes in single layer in 2 shallow pans. Baste chicken with liquid mixture. Broil until brown, turning when necessary. Reduce oven to 300°. Turn drumettes occasionally to coat. Bake about 1 hour. Refrigerate overnight or at least 6 hours. Reheat in 350° oven 20 minutes to serve.

Coconut Chicken Bites

Kick the party up a notch with these tropical morsels.

Meat / Passover   *Yields 20 pieces*

3½	cups sweetened coconut flakes		Salt and pepper
2	teaspoons ground cumin	2	large eggs, beaten
¾	teaspoon ground coriander	2	pounds skinless, boneless chicken breasts
¼	teaspoon cayenne pepper		

Dipping Sauce

½	cup Dijon mustard	½	cup orange marmalade

Preheat oven to 325°. Bake coconut on heavy baking sheet until golden brown, stirring frequently, about 15 minutes, cool. Coarsely grind in food processor or blender. Grease 2 heavy rimmed baking sheets. In large bowl, combine cumin, coriander, cayenne, salt, pepper and eggs. Cut chicken breasts into 1-inch pieces. Add to spice mixture, turn to coat. Dredge chicken in coconut, coating completely, transfer to prepared baking sheets. Refrigerate 1 hour. Increase oven to 400°. Bake chicken until crisp and golden brown, about 12 minutes. In small serving bowl, combine mustard and marmalade. Arrange chicken on platter. Serve warm or at room temperature with dipping sauce.

Fresh frozen sweetened coconut flakes packs lots of flavor, thus is preferred over coconut in cans or plastic bags.

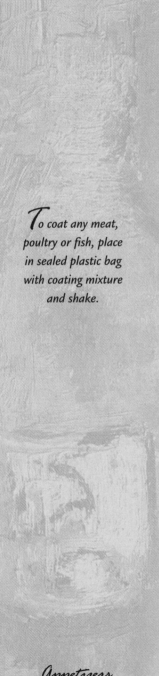

To coat any meat, poultry or fish, place in sealed plastic bag with coating mixture and shake.

THAI CHICKEN SATAY

Either on a buffet or passed on trays, this hors d'oeuvre will thrill guests.

Meat   *Serves 10 to 15*

Wooden skewers

MARINADE

2	garlic cloves, chopped	¾	cup tomato juice
2	tablespoons minced fresh ginger	1½	cups sweetened pineapple juice
¼	cup soy sauce	¼	cup olive oil

CHICKEN

2   pounds chicken breast cutlets

DIPPING SAUCE

2	tablespoons peanut oil	12	ounces coconut milk
6	garlic cloves, minced	¼	cup lemon juice
2	medium onions, finely minced	¼	cup soy sauce
1	pound chunky peanut butter	2	tablespoons honey
12	ounces chicken or vegetable stock		Cayenne pepper or hot pepper sauce

Soak skewers in water 30 minutes. Combine marinade ingredients, pour into large plastic bag. Cut chicken into 1 to 2-ounce strips. Thread chicken strips on skewers. Place chicken in plastic bag with marinade, close tightly. Marinate at least 3 hours but not more than 12, turning bag several times to coat all strips with marinade.

To prepare dipping sauce, heat peanut oil in 4-quart saucepan. Sauté garlic and onion until cooked, not browned. Add remaining ingredients except cayenne pepper. Cook over medium heat, stirring constantly until sauce thickens, about 15 minutes. Add cayenne pepper sparingly, 1 pinch at a time, for desired spiciness.

Preheat oven to 350°. Remove chicken skewers from marinade, place on baking sheet. Bake 10 to 12 minutes or until chicken is no longer pink. Serve with warm Dipping Sauce.

Marinade may be prepared up to 7 days in advance. The Dipping Sauce may be prepared up to 5 days in advance or frozen up to 30 days. Chicken may be prepared, cooked and refrigerated early in the day. Reheat chicken and sauce before serving.

Spray the measuring cup with nonstick cooking spray before pouring in honey, molasses or peanut butter. The ingredient will slip right out of the cup.

HOT GINGER CHICKEN ROLL

PAREVE CREAM CHEESE PASTRY

8	ounces pareve margarine, softened	½	teaspoon salt
8	ounces pareve cream cheese, softened	2	cups flour

FILLING

1	pound ground chicken	½	teaspoon ground ginger
1	tablespoon olive oil	2	tablespoons soy sauce
1	teaspoon salt	1	small garlic clove, crushed
½	cup diced water chestnuts, drained	1	large egg
2	green onions, minced	¼	cup fine dry breadcrumbs

EGG WASH

1	egg yolk	2	teaspoons pareve soy milk

In electric mixer, beat all pastry ingredients to form soft dough. Chill overnight.

Cook chicken in olive oil until it loses its pink color. Mix chicken with remaining filling ingredients, cool.

Beat egg yolk with milk. Roll pastry into four 12x9-inch rectangles between sheets of wax paper. Spread each with ¼ of the filling. Roll up, beginning at long side. Moisten edges with a little water, press to seal. Chill 1 hour or freeze for later use.

Preheat oven to 375°. Baste tops of roll with Egg Wash. Bake on an ungreased baking sheet 30 to 35 minutes, cool slightly. With serrated knife, carefully cut into 1-inch slices to serve.

Fresh breadcrumbs are far superior to commercially made products. Any good quality bread can be made into fresh crumbs. Slightly stale bread is preferred. Remove crusts, cut into small cubes then chop or pulse in food processor. Freeze in tightly sealed plastic bags.

CHINESE CHICKEN LETTUCE WRAPS

"Lettuce" share this modern take on an Asian favorite.

Meat — *Serves 8 to 10*

2 tablespoons dark Asian sesame oil	1 tablespoon finely grated fresh ginger
1 cup soy sauce	½ cup coarsely chopped water chestnuts, drained
2 tablespoons chicken stock	2 teaspoons cornstarch, mixed well in ¼ cup cold water
3 tablespoons dry white wine	
1 pound skinless, boneless chicken breasts, cut into ½-inch cubes	2 heads of Boston lettuce or other soft lettuce
¼ cup peanut or vegetable oil	Chili paste, optional
3 green onions, minced	Snipped green onions, optional
1 tablespoon minced garlic	

In medium bowl, whisk together sesame oil, soy sauce, chicken stock and wine. Add cubed chicken, marinate 30 minutes. Pour oil in skillet or wok, heat until just smoking. Sauté green onions and garlic until fragrant, less than 1 minute. Remove chicken from marinade, reserving liquid. Stir fry chicken 4 to 5 minutes until chicken loses pink color.

Add ginger and water chestnuts, stir fry 2 minutes. Add reserved marinade, simmer 1½ minutes. Stir in cornstarch, bring to boil and cook 1 minute to thicken. Place several tablespoons of chicken mixture along center of each lettuce leaf and roll up. Place seam side down on serving dish.

Concentration is the key to rolling wraps.
Religious school students, Savannah, Georgia, 1952.

STEAMED CHICKEN DUMPLINGS

Kreplach with a Far East twist.

Meat   *Yields 30 pieces*

FILLING

1	pound skinless, boneless chicken breasts	2	green onions, finely minced
2	tablespoons pareve margarine, melted	2	teaspoons finely minced fresh ginger
2	tablespoons cold water	¾	teaspoon salt
1	tablespoon rice wine or dry sherry	½	cup minced water chestnuts
		½	cup minced red bell pepper or minced cilantro

WRAPPERS

30 (3½-inch) round shao mai wrappers, or wonton wrappers, cut into (3½-inch) rounds

DIPPING SAUCE

2	tablespoons soy sauce	½	teaspoon minced fresh cilantro
2	tablespoons rice vinegar		

Finely chop chicken in food processor. In large bowl, combine chicken with remaining ingredients, except bell pepper. Place 1 tablespoon chicken mixture in the center of each wrapper. Gather edge of wrapper around filling leaving some filling exposed at the top. Press corners of wrapper into filling. Sprinkle exposed chicken filling with bell pepper or cilantro. Lightly oil steamer rack, arrange dumplings on rack 1-inch apart. Add 1-inch water to steamer, keeping water from reaching bottom of rack, bring water to boil. Set rack in place, cover pot. Steam until wrappers are supple, about 15 minutes.

Combine dipping sauce ingredients in small serving bowl. Serve dumplings warm with dipping sauce.

Steamers come with 2 or more compartments. They are sold in kitchen supply stores. Stainless steel steamers last longer than bamboo and are easier to clean. Select a steamer that has holes about ⅛-inch in diameter.

CHATTAHOOCHEE COCKTAIL

Pareve   Serves 4

4	ounces vodka	1	banana
6	ounces pineapple juice	1	cup crushed ice
2	ounces coconut cream		

Place all ingredients in blender. Blend until puréed.

Coconut milk should not be substituted for coconut cream, as cream is richer.

ST. SIMON'S SWINGIN' PUNCH

Pareve   Serves 20

8	bananas	1⅔	cups dark rum
1	cup lime juice	18	ounces pineapple juice
1	cup sugar	12	ounces apricot nectar
1	(fifth) bottle light rum	2	limes, sliced

In blender purée bananas, lime juice and sugar. Add rum, pineapple juice and apricot nectar. It may be necessary to blend in batches. Chill for 1 day before serving. Garnish with slices of lime.

Friends hamming it up, Atlanta, Georgia, c.1910.

SOUTHERN SUMMER PEACH LIQUEUR

*This peach liqueur, **six months in the making**, is amazing. Prepare
and serve this to very good friends or package it in a wonderful bottle to give as a gift.
Better yet, do both. This liqueur is the base ingredient for the next 3 recipes.*

Pareve   *Serves 40*

12	soft ripe peaches	2	cups sugar
1-2	bottles good quality dark rum		

Pierce numerous holes in unpeeled peaches with a fork. Put into 4-quart glass, widemouth jar with rubber seal. Fill with good quality dark rum. Cover with sugar, close jar. Let stand at least 6 months before serving as a liqueur. As rum level drops, replenish rum to keep peaches covered.

Peachy Peach Bellini

Pareve   *Serves 4*

1	cup peeled, chopped peaches, frozen	1	cup small ice cubes
1/4	cup Southern Summer Peach Liqueur	1/2	cup peeled, chopped peaches
2	tablespoons superfine sugar	1 2/3	cups Champagne, chilled

Blend frozen peaches, liqueur, sugar and ice in blender until smooth. Divide mixture into 4 glasses. Top off each glass with 1/3 cup champagne. Garnish with peaches.

To prepare superfine sugar, place sugar in food processor and blend at high speed for 30 seconds.

Pineapple "Peachtree-tini"

Pareve   *Serves 2*

2 1/2	ounces white grape juice	1	ounce vodka
2 1/2	ounces pineapple juice	1	ounce cranberry vodka
1	ounce Southern Summer Peach Liqueur		

Combine juices, chill for 4 hours. Pour all ingredients in a cocktail shaker, fill with ice and shake well at least 1 minute. Strain, serve in cocktail glasses.

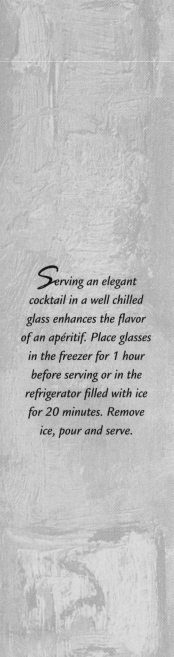

Serving an elegant cocktail in a well chilled glass enhances the flavor of an apéritif. Place glasses in the freezer for 1 hour before serving or in the refrigerator filled with ice for 20 minutes. Remove ice, pour and serve.

Appetizers

CONTINUED ON NEXT PAGE

Peach and White Wine Sangría

Pareve   *Serves 8 to 12*

1	cup frozen lemonade, thawed	1	(750-ml) bottle dry white wine
½	cup pineapple juice	¾	cup Southern Summer Peach Liqueur
¼	cup superfine sugar		
3	peaches, peeled, pitted, thinly sliced		

Place lemonade, pineapple juice, sugar and slices of 1 peach in blender, purée. Pour into pitcher, stir in wine and liqueur. Add remaining peach slices, mix well. Refrigerate at least 12 hours. Serve over ice.

MARIETTA MANGO DAIQUIRI

Pareve   *Serves 6*

8	ounces mango rum	½	cup pineapple juice, chilled
½	cup mango fruit slices, fresh or frozen	2	cups crushed ice, divided
½	cup orange juice, chilled		Orange slices

Purée rum, fruit and juices in blender. Remove ½ of mixture. Add 1 cup crushed ice to blender, purée. Pour mixture into pitcher. With remaining ingredients, repeat procedure. Serve in white wine glasses. Garnish with orange slices.

Affairs To Remember, Atlanta, Georgia

Fully stocked with mango rum.
Fulton Liquor Store, Atlanta, Georgia, c.1950.

Wine should be stored on its side in a cool, dark place with a temperature of less than 60 degrees. Chilling brings out the crisp flavor of white wines, while red wines are usually served cool at room temperature.

COOL SOUTHERN DREAM

Dairy/Pareve   *Serves 4*

¼   cup orange liqueur
½   cup vodka
½   cup heavy cream or pareve
       vanilla soy milk
1   (6-ounce) can frozen orange
       juice concentrate

3   scoops dairy or pareve soy
       vanilla ice cream
2   cups crushed ice
       Orange slices

Pour orange liqueur, vodka, cream or milk and orange juice concentrate into blender, blend well. Add ice cream and ice, process until smooth. Serve in wine or high ball glasses. Garnish each glass with ½ orange slice.

WILD WATERMELON MARGARITA

Pareve   *Serves 5*

3   cups cubed, seeded
       watermelon
       Lime wedges
       Salt
½   cup tequila

¼   cup triple sec liqueur
2   tablespoons fresh lime juice
2   cups ice cubes
       Watermelon slices

Place watermelon cubes in sealable plastic bag. Freeze 2 hours. Rub rims of martini glasses with lime wedges. Place salt in saucer and dip glass rims in salt. Process watermelon, tequila, triple sec and lime juice in blender until thoroughly combined. Add ice, blend again. Pour into martini glasses. Garnish with watermelon slices.

Garden PALETTE

SALADS

Fruit and Glazed Walnut Salad

This is a ladies' luncheon favorite, and men will love it, too.

Sugar Glazed Walnuts

¾ cup sugar
¼ cup water

2 cups walnut halves or pieces

Vinaigrette Dressing

2 tablespoons red wine
   vinegar
2 teaspoons Dijon mustard
½ teaspoon salt

½ teaspoon pepper
6 tablespoons olive oil
4 tablespoons water
2 garlic cloves, crushed

Salad

12 ounces fresh mixed baby
    greens
1 (11-ounce) can Mandarin
   oranges, drained
6 ounces feta or goat cheese,
   crumbled

6 ounces toasted pine nuts or
   glazed walnuts
½ cup dried or fresh
   blueberries
3 green onions, chopped
¼ cup diced dried apricots

Either lightly grease baking sheet or line with parchment paper. Dissolve sugar in water, pour over walnuts in glass bowl and stir. Microwave on high 6 to 8 minutes, stirring several times, until sugar is caramelized. Quickly pour onto prepared baking sheet, separating pieces. Cool completely. Prepared in advance, store in airtight container.

Combine dressing ingredients in closed jar, shake well. Combine salad ingredients, toss with dressing. Top with glazed walnuts when ready to serve.

Atlanta Jewish Federation Women's Division luncheon, Atlanta, Georgia, c.1975.

WINE-POACHED PEAR SALAD

TOPPINGS

2	pears, peeled	⅓	cup halved walnuts, toasted
	White wine, to cover pears		

BALSAMIC DRESSING

1	clove garlic, minced	½	cup olive oil
½	teaspoon mustard	1	tablespoon water
½	teaspoon honey		Salt and pepper
¼	cup balsamic vinegar		

SALAD

½	head leafy lettuce, such as red leaf	½	cup crumbled blue cheese

Place pears in saucepan, cover with white wine. Poach pears until tender, yet slightly firm and easily pierced with knife. Cool, cut in quarters lengthwise and remove core. Slice pears, set aside. Preheat oven to 375°. Place walnuts on cookie sheet. Bake 5 to 10 minutes until slightly dark and aromatic. Watch closely, to avoid burning.

Whisk together garlic, mustard, honey and vinegar. Slowly add oil, stirring until well combined. Slowly whisk in 1 tablespoon or more of warm water to adjust consistency and/or flavor. Season with salt and pepper. Place lettuce on plates. Top with pears, then cheese and walnuts. Serve with dressing on the side.

To ripen fruit, place in a loosely closed paper bag at room temperature until the fruit responds easily to gentle pressure. To shorten ripening time, add an apple or banana to the bag. Once ripe, refrigerate the fruit.

Poaching fruit means cooking the fruit in a boiling or simmering liquid.

Mango Green Bean Salad

Pareve   *Serves 7-8*

DRESSING

2	shallots	1	clove garlic, minced
⅓	cup olive oil	1	tablespoon honey
3	teaspoons orange juice	1	tablespoon firmly packed
1	(1-ounce) envelope Italian		dark brown sugar
	salad dressing mix	1	tablespoon Dijon mustard

SALAD

2	pounds green beans	½	cup pine nuts, toasted
1	large fresh mango, peeled,		
	diced		

In food processor, pulse all dressing ingredients. When smooth, pour into jar. Refrigerate up to 3 days. When ready to serve salad, blanch green beans until just tender. Plunge into ice water bath, drain. Bring dressing to room temperature, shake well. Pour dressing over green beans. Sprinkle with mango cubes and pine nuts, toss gently.

Check out this delicious salad!
Checking out at Vrono's Market, Atlanta, Georgia, 1954.

From the late 1800s to the 1960s, "Mom-and-Pop" grocery stores, many of which were Jewish-owned, dotted Atlanta neighborhoods. Often operated by immigrants, these small stores could be opened with little capital and new Americans, even with an uncertain command of the English language, could become entrepreneurs. Family living quarters were often above the store and there was always enough to eat. These stores succumbed to competition from large, national supermarket chains. Changing neighborhood demographics also led to the demise of many "Mom-and-Pop" groceries.

Strawberry Mango Spinach Salad

It will be hard to decide which dressing to try. Both are fabulous on this light, refreshing salad. No need to buy bottled dressing again!

Dairy/Pareve   *Serves 8*

Lemon Dressing

4	tablespoons balsamic vinegar	2	tablespoons lemon juice
½	cup canola oil	2	teaspoons dry mustard powder
½	cup olive oil	2	tablespoons brown or white sugar or sugar substitute
1	teaspoon salt		

Poppy Seed Dressing

½	cup sugar	1½	teaspoons minced onion
¼	teaspoon Worcestershire sauce	¼	teaspoon paprika
2	tablespoons sesame seeds, toasted	¼	cup white wine vinegar
1	teaspoon poppy seeds	¼	cup cider vinegar
		½	cup vegetable oil

Salad

2	(6-ounce) packages fresh spinach	1	mango, peeled, diced
1	avocado, peeled, pitted, sliced	½	cup praline almonds or honey roasted almonds
1	small bunch green onions, chopped	1	kiwi, peeled, sliced, optional
1	pint strawberries, sliced	¼	cup crumbled blue cheese, optional

Prepare Lemon Dressing by whisking ingredients until well blended. Prepare Poppy Seed Dressing by processing all ingredients except oil. With processor motor running, slowly add oil, process until well blended.

On large platter, layer all salad ingredients in order, except nuts, kiwi and cheese. Drizzle choice of dressing over salad. Sprinkle with nuts, kiwi and cheese.

Minted Watermelon Salad

This medley of flavors is sure to please family and friends.

Dressing

¼	cup red wine vinegar	2	tablespoons chopped fresh mint
	Salt and pepper		
½	cup olive oil		

Salad

1	(5-pound) watermelon	1	avocado, peeled, pitted, coarsely diced
1	Vidalia or other sweet onion	4	ounces feta cheese, crumbled

Combine vinegar, salt and pepper in small bowl. Whisk in olive oil. Add mint, adjust seasonings. Cut watermelon into bite size pieces. Slice onion into thin rings. Just before serving, combine watermelon, onion, avocado and feta cheese in serving bowl. Toss gently with dressing.

Willie Reisman Groceries & Meats, Atlanta, Georgia, c.1914.

ARUGULA AND FRESH FIG SALAD

A salad favorite from Souper Jenny's kitchen.

Dairy / Passover　　　　　　　　　　　　　　　　　　*Serves 8*

1 cup unsalted macadamia nuts	½ pound goat cheese, crumbled
2 teaspoons jerk seasoning	2 tablespoons fig vinegar or any fruit vinegar
½ pound arugula lettuce	Vegetable oil
2 pints fresh figs, each fig cut into 8 pieces	Salt and pepper

Preheat oven to 350°. Coat small roasting pan with nonstick spray. Sprinkle macadamia nuts with jerk seasoning, layer in roasting pan and toast for 15 minutes. Cool, toss with remaining ingredients in large serving bowl.

Jenny Levison, Souper Jenny, Atlanta, Georgia

The fig has been popular since biblical times. It is included in descriptions of the Garden of Eden and is a traditional food for many Jewish holidays.

Remember to wait one hour after eating before swimming. Swimming lessons at the Atlanta Jewish Community Center pool, Atlanta, Georgia, 1956.

POMEGRANATE APRICOT SALAD

This piquant vinaigrette enhances the flavor of any salad.

Pareve/Passover   *Serves 4 to 5*

RASPBERRY/MUSTARD VINAIGRETTE

½	cup canola or vegetable oil	½	teaspoon pepper
2	tablespoons raspberry vinegar	½	teaspoon salt
		2	packets sugar substitute
2	teaspoons Dijon mustard		

SALAD

1	head romaine lettuce, torn in pieces	½	cup coarsely chopped dried apricots
½	cup pomegranate seeds	½	cup pecan pieces or slivered almonds

Combine vinaigrette ingredients in closed jar, shake well. Combine salad ingredients. Toss with vinaigrette.

To obtain seeds from pomegranate, cut the crown off the fruit, score the rind in several places and immerse fruit in bowl of water for 5 minutes. Hold the fruit under water, separate seeds from bitter membrane. Discard membrane and rind, strain and dry seeds. When handling pomegranates, wear an apron and disposable gloves. Use plastic or glass utensils, as dark red stains are difficult to remove.

CHERRY TOMATO SALAD
WITH ARTICHOKE VINAIGRETTE

This dressing works well for any tossed or pasta salad.

Dairy/Pareve/Passover   *Serves 6 to 8*

2	(6-ounce) jars marinated artichoke hearts, drained, divided	2	teaspoons honey
¼	cup balsamic vinegar	5	tablespoons mayonnaise
2	tablespoons chopped fresh chives or green onion tops	½	cup olive oil
		12	cups torn romaine lettuce
1	tablespoon fresh lemon juice	1	small red onion, thinly sliced
1	tablespoon Dijon mustard	2	cups halved cherry tomatoes
			Parmesan cheese, freshly grated, optional

Mince 1 jar artichoke hearts in food processor. Add next 6 ingredients, process 5 seconds. With processor running, slowly add oil, process for 30 seconds. Cover and chill dressing at least 30 minutes or up to 3 days. Combine lettuce, onion and tomatoes in mixing bowl. Toss with just enough dressing to coat. Divide salad among plates. Top with remaining artichokes.

For a dairy meal, sprinkle with Parmesan cheese and serve with Lacy Parmesan Crisps (see below).

LACY PARMESAN CRISPS

A perfect complement to a fresh crisp salad. Always make extra as guests will ask for seconds, maybe even thirds.

Dairy   *Yields 15 crisps*

1½	cups finely shredded Parmesan cheese	3½	teaspoons flour
		3	dashes cayenne pepper

Preheat oven to 350°. Line lightly greased baking sheet with parchment paper. In small bowl, stir together ingredients. Spoon round tablespoons cheese mixture in mounds 4-inches apart. Spread gently into 4-inch ovals or circles. Bake until golden, 8 to 10 minutes. Cool completely. Carefully peel off parchment paper. These may be made 2 to 3 days in advance. Store between layers of wax paper in airtight container at room temperature.

Cornucopia Salad

The sweet, tangy melange of fruits and vegetables will satisfy any palate.

Dairy   *Serves 4*

Sugared Almonds

3 tablespoons sugar   ½ cup sliced or slivered
                almonds

Dressing

1 teaspoon salt   4 tablespoons cider vinegar or
1 teaspoon pepper   white wine vinegar
½ cup vegetable oil   2 tablespoons fresh chopped
4 tablespoons sugar   parsley, optional

Salad

1 (6-ounce) green leaf and 1 avocado, peeled, pitted,
  spring mix lettuce   sliced
¼ cup dried cranberries   1 (11-ounce) can Mandarin
3 green onions, chopped   oranges, drained
½ cup crumbled blue cheese ½ cup pomegranate seeds,
1 Granny Smith apple, sliced optional

For sugared almonds, coat sheet of aluminum foil with nonstick spray. Heat sugar and almonds together in small skillet over medium heat, stirring until sugar melts and almonds are brown. Spread on prepared foil. When cool, break nuts apart.

Combine all dressing ingredients in closed jar, shake well. Combine lettuce, cranberries, green onions and blue cheese. Just before serving, add apple, avocado, Mandarin oranges and pomegranate seeds. Toss with dressing, top with sugared almonds.

To prepare sliced apples in advance, add juice of 1 lemon to 1 cup of water. In sealable plastic bag add apples and lemon water. Seal, toss to coat and refrigerate. Drain and serve. To prepare avocado in advance, peel, slice and store in sealed plastic bag with pit, up to 1 day.

Entertaining troops from Fort Benning, Columbus, Georgia, c.1943.

Avocado Raspberry Spice Salad

Pareve/Passover   *Serves 4*

Raspberry Dressing

¼ cup seedless raspberry jam	¾ teaspoon lemon pepper
3 tablespoons vegetable oil	seasoning
2½ tablespoons white wine vinegar	¾ teaspoon seasoned salt

Avocado Salad

1 avocado	2 medium tomatoes, cut into wedges
2½ cups shredded Napa cabbage	½ medium cucumber, thinly sliced
1½ cups shredded red cabbage	2 tablespoons chopped onion

Combine all dressing ingredients in closed jar, shake well. Just before serving, peel and cube avocado. On 4 serving plates, arrange Napa and red cabbage. Decoratively arrange tomatoes, avocado and cucumber on top. Sprinkle with onion, drizzle each plate with dressing.

Strike up the band for this special salad!
Young Circle League of the Arbeiter Ring Lyceum,
Atlanta, Georgia, c.1935.

CARTERSVILLE CRISPY TWO-WEEK SLAW

Unless devoured at once, this slaw stays fresh for two weeks.

Pareve/Passover   *Serves 10 to 12*

SLAW

1	large head white cabbage, shredded	2	medium onions, halved, thinly sliced
1	green bell pepper, seeded, diced	3	carrots, peeled, grated
1	red bell pepper, seeded, diced	1½	cups sugar
		1	small jar chopped pimiento, optional

DRESSING

¾-1	cup vegetable oil	2	teaspoons celery seeds
1½	cups white vinegar		Zest and juice of ½ orange
1	teaspoon salt		

In large bowl, toss vegetables together. Mix well with sugar, cover tightly and refrigerate 2 hours. In small saucepan, boil dressing ingredients, stirring until salt dissolves. Remove vegetables from refrigerator, do not drain. Pour hot mixture over vegetables. Refrigerate at least 3 hours or up to 2 weeks.

SESAME LIME JICAMA SLAW

A crisp, crunchy, low calorie salad that is sure to please.

Pareve/Passover   *Serves 6*

DRESSING

⅓	cup vegetable oil	⅛	teaspoon pepper
1	tablespoon sesame oil	2	tablespoons orange juice
4	tablespoons fresh lime juice	1	tablespoon grated orange zest
½	teaspoon Dijon mustard		
½	teaspoon salt		

SALAD

¾	pound red cabbage	½	cup packed fresh cilantro leaves, chopped
2	pounds jicama, cut julienne		Sesame seeds, toasted, optional
½	pound carrots, about 2 large, peeled, cut julienne		

Whisk together dressing ingredients in medium bowl. Cut cabbage into very thin shreds, add to dressing. Add vegetables and cilantro. Toss to coat. Sprinkle with sesame seeds, if desired. Chill 2 to 8 hours.

If preparing vegetables in advance, chill separately.

Jicama is a root vegetable with a sweet nutty flavor.

Salads

CRUNCHY ASIAN SALAD

Dairy / Meat / Pareve　　　　　　　　　　　　　*Serves 12 to 15*

DRESSING

⅔	cup vegetable oil	1	seasoning packet from
¼	cup apricot syrup		(2.8-ounce) Oriental
½	cup cider vinegar		flavored ramen noodle soup
		¼	cup sugar

TOPPINGS

1	(2.8-ounce) package Oriental flavored noodle soup, noodles only	1	(11-ounce) can drained Mandarin oranges, optional
¾	cup toasted almonds		Grilled chopped chicken breast, optional

SALAD

2	(2.8-ounce) packages Oriental flavored ramen noodle soup, divided	1	package broccoli slaw
		1	cup shelled, cooked edamame beans
1	tablespoon unsalted butter or pareve margarine	1	small carrot, peeled, grated
1	tablespoon vegetable oil	2	green onions, chopped

Whisk together all dressing ingredients. Crush 1 package noodles. Sauté in butter or margarine and oil until golden brown. Remove, drain well and reserve for topping.

Boil remaining noodles according to package directions, drain. In mixing bowl toss while hot with some dressing, cool. Add broccoli slaw, edamame, carrot and green onion. Toss with additional dressing as needed, saving some dressing to use immediately before serving. Top salad with reserved noodles, almonds and chicken, as desired.

Apricot syrup can be found near the pancake syrups in your grocery store. As a variation, try substituting apricot syrup with duck sauce, honey or stir and press apricot preserves through a strainer.

Nuts last longer when stored in the refrigerator or freezer in an airtight container.

To toast nuts, spread on baking sheet, place in a 325° oven. Stir every few minutes. Nuts are done when they begin to brown. Remove from pan immediately to arrest the cooking process. Toasted nuts should be consumed within a few days or frozen.

TUSCAN BREAD SALAD

Serve with Roasted Tomato Soup (page 90)
or Tilapia Santorini (page 103) for a hearty meal.

Dairy / Pareve   *Serves 8 to 10*

DRESSING

12	tablespoons olive oil
4	tablespoons red wine vinegar, plus more to drizzle
4	garlic cloves, minced
	Salt and pepper

SALAD

4 cups day old, crusty, Italian bread, cut into ½-inch cubes

7 plum tomatoes, seeded, cut into ½-inch cubes

3 seedless cucumbers, peeled, cut into ½-inch cubes

1 large red onion, very thinly sliced

½ cup fresh basil leaves, cut julienne

½ cup shaved fresh Parmesan cheese, optional

Olive oil

Whisk all dressing ingredients together in medium bowl. Combine all salad ingredients, except cheese, in large bowl. Just before serving, slowly pour dressing over bread, toss to coat evenly. Drizzle with small amount olive oil. Garnish with shaved cheese for dairy serving.

All salads are best when served on cold plates. Refrigerate plates 2 hours before using.

They still had to go home and cook dinner.
Atlanta Jewish Welfare Federation, Women's Division, c.1949.

WIEUCA WILD RICE SALAD

SALAD

2⅓	cups water
1	(6-ounce) box long grain and wild rice mix
1	(12-ounce) can whole kernel corn, drained
1	small cucumber, peeled, seeded, diced
2	medium carrots, peeled, coarsely chopped
2	green onions with tops, thinly sliced
⅓	cup chopped fresh parsley

DRESSING

⅓	cup olive or vegetable oil
¼	cup lemon juice
2	garlic cloves, minced
1½	teaspoons minced fresh dill
¼	teaspoon dry mustard
¼	teaspoon pepper
½	cup dry roasted, shelled sunflower seeds
⅓	cup slivered almonds, toasted

In medium saucepan, bring water and contents of rice mix to boil. Cover tightly, simmer until all liquid absorbs, about 25 minutes. Transfer to large bowl, cool to room temperature. Add corn, cucumber, carrots, green onions and parsley.

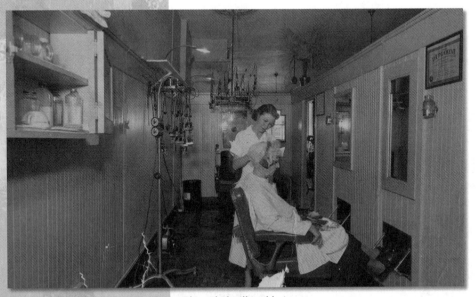

In small bowl, whisk together dressing ingredients, except sunflower seeds and almonds. Stir into rice mixture. Cover, chill several hours or overnight. Top with sunflower seeds and almonds.

This salad will curl hair.
Mackey Klein's Beauty Shop,
Atlanta, Georgia, c.1932.

Potpourri Pilaf

Pareve   *Serves 6*

Dressing

1	(8-ounce) bottle Italian dressing		1	tablespoon sugar
2	tablespoons soy sauce		1	teaspoon ground ginger

Salad

	White or pilaf rice for 6		1	(8.75-ounce) can baby corn on the cob, drained
4	green onions, sliced		1	red bell pepper, seeded, sliced in strips
½	pound snow peas, blanched 1 minute		1	(14-ounce) can quartered artichokes, drained
¼	pound green beans, blanched 1 minute		½	cup pine nuts, toasted
1	(5-ounce) can sliced water chestnuts, drained		¼	cup sesame seeds, toasted

In medium bowl, whisk dressing ingredients until blended. Prepare rice. Immediately add dressing, using entire quantity. Chill overnight. Before serving, combine vegetables and fold into cold rice. Toss in pine nuts and sesame seeds.

Refrigerate celery in aluminum foil to keep fresh for weeks.

Garden Vegetable Couscous

Doris Koplin is a past president of Les Dames d'Escoffier. She is an Atlanta culinary legend. This couscous is simply delicious.

Dairy / Pareve   *Serves 4*

1	(10-ounce) box couscous		½	cup prepared vinaigrette dressing, or more if needed
1	cucumber, seeded, diced			Crumbled goat cheese, optional
1	tomato, seeded, diced			
3	green onions, thinly sliced			
½	cup diced celery			
4	radishes, diced			

Prepare couscous according to package directions. Place in large bowl, cool and fluff. Add cucumber, tomato, onions, celery and radishes. Toss well with vinaigrette dressing, chill. Add crumbled goat cheese.

Adapted and reprinted with permission from The Quick Cook, by Doris Koplin

Sweet and Sour Chickpea Salad

Do more than throw chickpeas into a tossed salad.
This recipe showcases the nutritious, tasty, protein-packed chickpea.

Pareve   *Serves 6 to 8*

Sweet and Sour Dressing

½	cup vegetable oil	1	teaspoon paprika
¼	cup red wine vinegar	1	teaspoon salt
¼	cup ketchup	1	teaspoon pepper
¼	cup sugar		

Salad

2	(15-ounce) cans chickpeas, drained, rinsed	1	teaspoon salt
		1	teaspoon pepper
1	cup diced, seeded green pepper	½	cup mayonnaise
½	cup chopped pimiento	1-2	tablespoons white horseradish
1	cup diced celery		Red leaf lettuce

Combine all dressing ingredients in closed jar, shake briskly, chill well. Marinate chickpeas in ½ cup dressing at least 2 hours. Add green pepper, pimiento, celery, salt and pepper. Combine mayonnaise and horseradish, stir into chickpeas. Serve on bed of red leaf lettuce.

If desired, sprinkle with chives, dill or poppy seeds before serving.

Chickpeas, also known as garbanzo beans, originated in the Middle East, where this high-protein, high-fiber food is popular. Evidence of chickpeas being consumed dates back about 7000 years. The delicate nutlike flavor makes chickpeas suitable for all types of recipes.

HEARTY LENTIL SALAD

This healthy salad is packed with nutrients and dressed with an extraordinary vinaigrette.

Dairy/Pareve   *Serves 6 to 8*

SALAD

2	cups lentils	1	cup peeled, diced turnips or rutabagas
1	cup peeled, diced carrots		Butter or olive oil
1	cup diced celery		

VINAIGRETTE DRESSING

1	cup vegetable oil	1	clove garlic, minced
½	cup wine vinegar	1	teaspoon salt
¼	cup sliced green onion	1	teaspoon dried thyme, crushed
2	tablespoons chopped parsley	⅛	teaspoon cayenne pepper
1	tablespoon sugar		
1	tablespoon lemon juice		

Place lentils in saucepan, cover with water. Bring to boil. Immediately lower heat, gently simmer, partially covered, 20 to 25 minutes or until tender. Drain and cool. Sauté carrots, celery and turnips or rutabagas in butter or olive oil until tender. Cool, combine with lentils.

Whisk dressing ingredients in medium bowl, pour over vegetables. Toss salad and refrigerate. Serve cold or at room temperature.

In the book of Genesis, Jacob talked his older brother, Esau, into trading his birthright as oldest son for a bowl of lentil soup.

Hearty men will enjoy this hearty dish.
Freemasons, Elberton, Georgia, c. 1910.

SABRA SALAD

No Israeli meal, including breakfast, is complete without this traditional chopped salad.

Pareve/Passover   *Serves 6 to 8*

DRESSING

⅓	teaspoon garlic powder	¼	cup olive oil
1	teaspoon salt	¼	cup freshly squeezed lemon juice
½	teaspoon pepper		

SALAD

3	seedless cucumbers, peeled, finely diced	2-3	bunches green onions with tops, thinly sliced
1	large green pepper, seeded, finely diced	1	cup sliced green olives with pimientos
2	large tomatoes, finely diced	1	cup sliced black olives

There are two definitions of Sabra: the prickly pear fruit of a cactus that grows in Israel or a native born Israeli.

Whisk together all dressing ingredients and adjust seasonings. Place vegetables and olives in salad bowl. Toss with dressing.

Golda Meir, who became Israel's 4th Prime Minister in 1969, is shown raising money for the State of Israel, Atlanta, Georgia, 1949.

PRIZE WINNING BORSCHT SALAD

A "Best of Taste" award winner in Atlanta.
Who knew that beets and pineapple would be so good together?

Dairy / Pareve / Passover　　　　　　　　　　*Serves 8*

1	(20-ounce) can crushed pineapple	3	tablespoons white vinegar
1	(6-ounce) package kosher wild raspberry gelatin	1	teaspoon dried dill weed
1½	cups boiling water		Dash of salt
1	(15-ounce) can shoestring beets, including juice	1	cup chopped celery
			Dairy or pareve sour cream
			Dill weed

Drain pineapple, reserving syrup. Dissolve gelatin in boiling water. Stir in beets, juice, vinegar, dill, salt and reserved pineapple syrup. Chill until mixture thickens to consistency of unbeaten egg whites, possibly as long as 2 hours. Fold in celery and crushed pineapple. Pour into 6-cup mold. Refrigerate until firm. To serve, remove from mold, top with sour cream and sprinkle with dill weed.

Children's service, Adas Yeshurun Congregation,
Augusta, Georgia, c.1955.

SEARED TUNA VEGETABLE SALAD

Pareve   *Serves 4 to 6*

DRESSING

2	tablespoons olive oil
½	cup red wine vinegar
1	shallot, minced

Kosher salt
Pepper

SALAD

½   pound green beans, cut into 1-inch pieces

½   pound yellow wax beans, cut into 1-inch pieces

8   ounces shelled, raw edamame

2   tablespoons olive oil, divided

½   pound cremini mushrooms, sliced

1   pound tuna steaks, ½-inch thick

1   pint grape tomatoes, halved

1   cup fresh corn kernels, about 2 ears corn, uncooked

¼   cup fresh basil, torn into pieces

½   teaspoon sea salt
    Pepper
    Grated zest of 1 lemon

6   fresh basil leaves

Edamame is a soybean harvested at the peak of ripening. In East Asia, the soybean has been used for over 2000 years as a major source of nourishment.

Whisk together all dressing ingredients, set aside. Cook beans and edamame in large pot of boiling salted water for 6 to 8 minutes. Immediately immerse vegetables in bowl of ice water. Drain, pat dry. Heat large skillet over high heat, add 1 tablespoon olive oil and mushrooms, sauté 5 to 7 minutes until golden, tossing occasionally. Remove mushrooms, add remaining liquid in skillet to dressing. Heat same skillet until hot, add remaining olive oil. Sear tuna steaks over medium high heat. Turn once, sauté to desired degree of doneness, 4 to 6 minutes, depending on thickness of steaks. Add pan juices to dressing. Toss beans, edamame, mushrooms, grape tomatoes, corn and basil. Season with sea salt and pepper. Stir in enough dressing to coat, toss.

Cut tuna steaks into serving size pieces. Place in center of platter. Arrange salad around tuna, drizzle with remaining dressing. Garnish with zest and basil. Serve room temperature or cold.

Party Time "Crab" Salad

This is a great salad for lunch or brunch.

Pareve   *Serves 4 to 5*

Kosher Faux Crabmeat

1	pound kosher faux crabmeat	2	tablespoons olive oil
1	cup peeled, diced seedless cucumber	¼	cup finely slivered fresh basil
2	tablespoons fresh lime juice		Pepper

Lime Dressing

¾	cup canola or olive oil	⅛	teaspoon paprika
¼	cup orange juice	3	tablespoons minced fresh mint
3	tablespoons lime juice		
2	tablespoons cider vinegar		

Salad

1-2 (10- to 12-ounce) bags assorted lettuce

Garnish

	Flour tortilla shells, optional	1	cup Mango Salsa, see recipe for Pecan Tilapia with Mango Salsa (page 102)
2-3	tablespoons chopped fresh mint leaves	6	mint or basil sprigs

In large bowl, combine crabmeat, cucumber, lime juice, oil, basil and pepper. Set aside.

Briskly whisk dressing ingredients, set aside. Shortly before serving salad, toss lettuce with lime dressing. Place handful of lettuce in each tortilla shell or on each plate, top with scoop of crabmeat mixture. Fold chopped mint leaves into salsa. Top salad with 2 tablespoons mango salsa. Garnish with fresh mint or basil sprigs.

CHUTNEY CHICKEN SALAD

My mother always cooked two chickens for
dinner so we could enjoy her chicken salad the next day.

Meat   *Serves 8 to 10*

DRESSING

1½ cups mayonnaise

½ teaspoon curry powder

1 tablespoon soy sauce

¼ cup mango chutney

CHICKEN SALAD

¼ pound Chinese pea pods

4 cups cooked chicken breast, cut into bite size pieces

1 (8-ounce) can pineapple tidbits, drained

1 (8-ounce) can water chestnuts, drained, chopped

1 pound seedless green grapes

1 cup diced celery

1½ cups almonds, toasted

½ cup dried cranberries or raisins

Salt and pepper

Whisk together all dressing ingredients and set aside. Lower pea pods into boiling water until crisp tender, 1 to 2 minutes. Plunge into ice water. Cut each pea pod lengthwise into slivers. Place in large bowl with remaining salad ingredients. Toss with dressing. Chill several hours.

Minced fresh tarragon, chives or mint are pleasing substitutes for curry, in this recipe.

Only the plumpest bird will do for chicken salad. Vacationing in Los Angeles, California, 1915.

Apricot Chicken Salad

3   cups cooked chicken breast,
cut into bite size pieces

½   cup diced celery

⅔   cup dried mixed diced fruit,
or diced dried apricots

½   cup almonds, or other nut,
toasted

1   cup mayonnaise

5   tablespoons apricot syrup or
honey

Pepper

Glazed or toasted almonds

Combine chicken, celery, dried fruit and almonds. Whisk together mayonnaise, apricot syrup and pepper. Toss into chicken mixture. Garnish with glazed or toasted almonds.

Vacationing in Los Angeles, California, 1915.

Salads

Roasted Beet and Goat Cheese Salad

This elegant salad is sure to impress. Be prepared to share the recipe with everyone.

Beets

2	large beets, trimmed	1	branch rosemary
1	tablespoon rice wine vinegar	1	sprig thyme
1	teaspoon sugar		

Herb Goat Cheese

1	teaspoon each, chopped thyme, parsley and chives	¼	teaspoon pepper
		1	(6-ounce) log goat cheese

Hazelnut Citrus Vinaigrette

1¼	cups freshly squeezed orange juice		Grated zest of ¼ orange
1	tablespoon chopped shallots	2	tablespoons hazelnut oil
2	teaspoons chopped thyme	3	tablespoons olive oil
1	teaspoon balsamic vinegar		Salt and pepper

Salad

2-3	ounces mixed baby greens	¼	cup coarsely chopped hazelnuts, toasted

Preheat oven to 400°. Place each beet on square of heavy duty foil large enough to fully wrap. Sprinkle beets with vinegar, sugar, rosemary and thyme. Seal foil tightly, bake until tender, about 1½ hours. Cool, peel, cut into sixteen ¼-inch thick slices. Set aside.

Combine herbs and pepper on plate. Roll goat cheese in herbs to coat. Cut into eight ¼-inch thick slices. Preheat nonstick skillet, coat with cooking spray. Heat goat cheese slices in pan over low heat until just softened.

In nonstick pan, boil orange juice, reduce to ⅓ cup. Cool completely. Pour into small mixing bowl with shallots, thyme, vinegar and zest. Slowly whisk in oils. Season with salt and pepper.

To assemble, layer each goat cheese slice between two beet slices, pressing lightly. Cut each into 3 wedges. To serve, arrange wedges point side out around salad plates. Top with handful of mixed greens. Sprinkle with toasted hazelnuts, drizzle dressing on top.

Nut oils lend a lovely fragrance to all recipes. However, opened containers of nut oil can become rancid if not refrigerated. Keep unopened bottles in a cool dark place and use within 3 months.

VIDALIA ONION SALAD

My grandfather, a produce vendor in New York, taught us to enjoy fresh fruits and vegetables at the height of their flavor. I still shop with this in mind.

Dairy/Pareve/Passover   *Serves 6 to 8*

1 cup water	1 cup mayonnaise
1 cup sugar	1 cup dairy or pareve sour
1 cup white vinegar	cream
4 medium Vidalia onions,	1 teaspoon whole celery
thinly sliced	seeds, or more, to taste

Whisk together water, sugar and vinegar. Pour over onions. Cover, marinate overnight. In a medium bowl, combine mayonnaise, sour cream and celery seeds. When ready to serve, drain onions, coat with mayonnaise mixture.

In 1931, a farmer in Toombs County, Georgia, discovered his onions were sweet, not the fashion of the times. Yet, in the 1940s, a farmers' market was built in Vidalia to promote the onions. That gave the crop its name. Today, Vidalia onions are a trademarked product grown in 20 Georgia counties and loved throughout the country.

Vidalia onions are the sweet choice for any occasion. Passover seder, Vidalia, Georgia, 1947.

AVOCADO AND HEARTS OF PALM SALAD

Pareve/Passover   *Serves 6*

VEGETABLES

6	ripe small avocados, peeled, pitted, cubed
1	(14-ounce) can hearts of palm, drained, cubed
1	large red onion, thinly sliced into rings
	Several sprigs parsley, chopped

VINAIGRETTE DRESSING

¼	cup white wine vinegar
½	cup olive oil
2	sprigs fresh parsley, finely chopped
1	sprig fresh basil, finely chopped
2	tablespoons chopped white onion
¼	cup orange juice
1	tablespoon dried thyme
2	green onions, finely chopped
2	garlic cloves, minced
1	teaspoon salt
1	teaspoon pepper

SALAD

9	cups crisp lettuce or watercress
	Tomato slices
	Lime wedges

In large bowl, combine avocados, hearts of palm, red onion and parsley. Toss carefully to avoid mashing avocados. Cover and refrigerate.

In medium bowl, vigorously whisk together dressing ingredients until oil and vinegar are well blended. Add dressing to vegetables, toss lightly. Serve vegetables on bed of crisp lettuce or trimmed watercress. Garnish with tomato slices and lime wedges.

BROCCOLI AND ZUCCHINI SALAD

Two green vegetables create a healthy and delicious salad.

Pareve/Passover   *Serves 4*

1   bunch broccoli, finely chopped
1   small zucchini, finely diced
1   small red onion, finely diced
1   cup dark raisins
⅓   cup lemon juice
⅓   cup sugar

½   cup vegetable oil
½   teaspoon salt
1   cup unsalted, shelled sunflower seeds
2   tablespoons poppy seeds, optional

Combine first 4 ingredients. In small bowl whisk together lemon juice, sugar, oil and salt, pour over salad. Toss with sunflower seeds and poppy seeds.

Blass & Cohen Groceries & Meats, Atlanta, Georgia, c.1950.

Old-Fashioned Pickled Green Tomatoes

My Mama used to make pickled tomatoes in crocks she kept in the "fruit cellar". As a child, my friends and I thought the greatest after-school treat was to go down to the cellar and scoop out a crisp pickled tomato.

Pareve/Passover   *Yields 2 quarts*

12	small or medium green tomatoes	16	cups hot water
8	garlic cloves, divided	¾	cup pickling salt
4	hot peppers or pinch of dried pepper flakes, divided	½	cup white vinegar
		½	teaspoon dill weed or sprigs of fresh dill, if available, divided

Wash tomatoes well. Pack into two 1-quart jars. If tomatoes are too large, cut in halves or quarters. Combine garlic with peppers or pepper flakes. Add ½ to each jar. Mix water, salt and vinegar. Pour over tomatoes. Sprinkle with dill. Tightly close jars and put in warm, dark place at room temperature 5 to 7 days. Tomatoes will lose their bright green color. Refrigerate for longer storage.

Tofu Salad Dressing

Pareve   *Yields 3 cups*

1½	cups olive oil	½	teaspoon dried basil
½	cup cider vinegar	¼	cup minced onion
¼	cup soy sauce	1	pound silken tofu
1	clove garlic		

Process all ingredients well, refrigerate. Serve with greens and other ingredients on hand, such as avocados, dried cranberries, pine nuts, cashews and Mandarin oranges.

Soups FROM MY CHILDHOOD

SOUPS

Chicken Mushroom and Barley Soup

Meat   *Serves 10 to 12*

1   (3-pound) stewing hen,
    cleaned
3   carrots, peeled, thinly sliced
3   medium onions, thinly
    sliced
½   cup dried lima beans, rinsed
½   cup barley
½   cup dried navy beans, rinsed
1   medium sweet potato,
    peeled

1   medium parsnip, peeled
1   pound mushrooms,
    quartered
3   medium bunches fresh dill
    or 2 tablespoons dried
    dill weed
    Salt
½   teaspoon pepper

Place hen in large pot of boiling water, reduce heat. Simmer 30 minutes, skim foam as it forms. Add vegetables and all remaining ingredients, bring to boil. Reduce heat to strong simmer. Cover, cook 2½ hours, stirring frequently. Remove hen from pot, discard skin and bones. Cut meat into bite size pieces, set aside. Remove and purée sweet potato and parsnip. Return sweet potato, parsnip and chicken to soup, refrigerate overnight. Reheat and serve the next day.

After an exhilarating day outdoors, enjoy a hearty bowl of soup.
Arbeiter Ring (Workmen's Circle) at Black Rock Mountain State Park,
Mountain City, Georgia, 1933.

SOUTHWEST CHICKEN CHILI

This chili freezes well.

2	pounds chicken breasts	¼	teaspoon salt
1	small whole onion	1	(15.25-ounce) can white kernel corn, drained
1	stalk celery, halved		
1	tablespoon oil	1	(15-ounce) can great Northern beans, drained
2	medium onions, chopped		
2	garlic cloves, finely chopped	1	(15.25-ounce) can butter beans, drained
3	cups chicken stock		
2	tablespoons chopped fresh cilantro or ½ teaspoon ground coriander	1	(16-ounce) can navy beans, drained
		1	teaspoon chipotle chili pepper and 1 can chopped green chilies, optional
2	tablespoons lime juice		
1	teaspoon ground cumin		
½	teaspoon dried oregano	¼	cup water
¼	teaspoon red pepper sauce	2	tablespoons flour

Place chicken breasts, whole onion and celery in large pot, cover with water and bring to boil. Reduce heat, cover and simmer 30 minutes or until cooked. Strain and discard vegetables. Remove chicken, cool. Remove skin and bones, discard. Chop or shred cooked chicken meat. Heat oil in 4-quart pot over medium heat, sauté chopped onions and garlic until tender. Add to chicken with all remaining ingredients except water and flour. Cover, heat to boiling. Reduce heat, uncover and simmer 20 minutes. To thicken, slowly whisk water into flour until smooth, stir into chili. Add chicken. Slowly stir chili until well blended, simmer until thickened. Top as desired.

Be creative with optional toppings. Try chopped green onions, diced tomatoes, chopped fresh cilantro, sliced avocado, pareve sour cream or crushed tortilla chips.

Sautéed Chicken Soup with Knaidel Cubes

There is nothing more comforting than chicken soup. Kids love it, doctors recommend it, and Jewish mothers everywhere dispense it for almost every ailment.

Meat / Passover   *Serves 6 to 8*

Chicken Stock

1	(4-pound) whole fryer, roaster or stewing chicken	2-3	stalks celery with leaves, cut in chunks
1	large onion, unpeeled, halved	1	parsnip, unpeeled, cut in chunks
2	carrots, unpeeled, cut in chunks		Salt and pepper

Vegetables and Noodles

2	carrots, peeled, sliced	2	cups cooked noodles, any type
2	celery stalks, sliced		

Knaidel Cubes

4	large eggs, beaten	1	teaspoon salt
½	cup water		Dash of pepper
¼	cup melted vegetable shortening		Dash of garlic powder
		1	cup matzah meal

Remove fat from inside chicken. Place fat in large soup pot, cook on medium heat until fat is rendered, discard remaining pieces. Add whole chicken to pot, brown on all sides in hot fat, 10 to 15 minutes. Remove chicken, set aside. In same pot, sauté vegetables until brown. Return chicken to pot, add water to cover. Cover, simmer 1½ to 2 hours, until stock is golden and chicken pulls apart easily. Remove chicken, cool. Discard skin and bones, refrigerate. Strain and discard vegetables. Season soup with salt and pepper, refrigerate overnight. Next day, skim off fat, heat soup and adjust seasonings. In large saucepan, heat 3-inches water to boiling. Add carrots and celery, boil 8 minutes until just tender. Return chicken to soup pot with freshly cooked carrots, celery, cooked noodles, knaidel cubes or matzah balls.

For knaidel cubes, in large bowl, combine eggs with water, shortening, salt, pepper and garlic powder, mix well. Add matzah meal, combine just until incorporated. Spoon batter into lightly greased flexible plastic ice cube trays. Level off excess with knife, freeze. Remove cubes from tray into plastic bag, store up to 30 days. To cook, drop frozen knaidels into boiling, salted water. Boil gently 25 minutes.

When I was a newlywed, this is how my mama said to make chicken soup. "Just put a chicken in the pot and cover it with water." "How much water?" I asked. "That depends on the size of the pot and the size of the chicken. You learn as you go along, my dear."

MATZAH BALLS

Pareve/Passover   *Yields 12*

2-3	tablespoons grated onion	¼	teaspoon pepper
1-2	tablespoons grated celery	4	large eggs
2	teaspoons vegetable oil	¼	cup vegetable oil
1⅛	cups matzah meal	¼	cup seltzer water
1	teaspoon salt		

The Great Matzah Ball Debate

As Jewish holidays approach, the ongoing debate over matzah balls heats up. Which is better, the 'floater' or the 'sinker'? Some believe fluffy and light is the way to go, while others think a matzah ball has no credibility unless it rivals the consistency of a golf ball. Some cooks claim secret ingredients make floaters, while others say it is experience and a gentle touch. Fluffy matzah balls should be served immediately. Hard matzah balls make great leftovers. The debate continues...

Sauté onion and celery in 2 teaspoons oil. In mixing bowl, combine matzah meal, salt and pepper. In separate bowl, combine eggs, oil and seltzer water. Stir into matzah mixture. Add sautéed vegetables, stir. Cover tightly, refrigerate 30 minutes. Bring large pot of salted water to boil, reduce to simmer. With damp hands, make balls about 1-inch in diameter, drop into water. Cover, cook 40 to 45 minutes or until light and fluffy. Remove from liquid with slotted spoon. Use immediately or freeze.

To freeze, lay wax paper on cookie sheet. Place single layer of matzah balls on wax paper. When frozen, transfer to plastic bags, store up to 30 days. Bring to room temperature before adding to soup.

To serve as side dish, slice matzah balls into halves or quarters, sauté in 2 tablespoons butter or pareve margarine with ½ cup sliced onions.

It's a "matzah ball brigade." Sisterhood of Temple Beth Israel, Macon, Georgia, c.1955

Nana's Vegetable Beef Soup

Sharing this recipe is one way of remembering my grandmother
who was so dear to me. This is old-fashioned comfort food.

Meat   *Serves 20*

3	pounds beef short ribs		1	(10-ounce) frozen lima beans
5	beef marrow bones		2	stalks celery, diced
2	ears fresh corn, kernels removed		1	(28-ounce) can diced tomatoes, drained
½	pound fresh peas or 1 (10-ounce) package frozen peas		1	parsnip, peeled, diced
			1	turnip, peeled, diced
2	sweet potatoes, peeled, diced			Salt and pepper
2	white potatoes, peeled, diced		1	tablespoon sugar
½	pound fresh string beans, trimmed, snapped in half		4	ounces dried mushrooms
			8	ounces farfel
2	onions, diced		1	(10-ounce) frozen mixed vegetables

Vegetable soups are best when made 1 day ahead. The flavors blend and the beans become very soft. When reheating, add small amount of water or stock, as needed.

In soup pot, cover short ribs and bones with water. Bring to boil, lower heat and simmer 45 minutes. Stir in remaining ingredients, except farfel and mixed vegetables. Cover, simmer 2 to 3 hours, adding water as needed. Stir occasionally. Add farfel and frozen mixed vegetables, cook additional 30 minutes.

This soup freezes well.

Nana will love this recipe.
Hadassah, Atlanta Chapter, Southside Sewing Circle,
c.1950.

Soups

DADDY'S BRUNSWICK STEW

*My daddy would stay up all night making enough of his famous
Brunswick stew to serve 100 people for our family's annual summer get-together.*

Meat   *Serves 20*

Vegetable oil
½ green pepper, seeded,
    cleaned, diced
½ stalk celery, scraped, diced
2½ pounds onions, diced
2 large garlic cloves, minced
2½ pounds ground beef chuck
1 (2½-pound) chicken
   Salt, pepper, garlic powder,
   basil, thyme, oregano,
   optional
2½ pounds veal stew meat
½ cup apple cider vinegar

2 (28-ounce) cans puréed
   tomatoes
1 (16-ounce) can lima beans
2 (12-ounce) cans corn
1 (12-ounce) bottle chili sauce
5 ounces Worcestershire sauce
1-3 teaspoons hot pepper sauce
   Juice of 3 lemons
1 tablespoon salt
1½ teaspoons thyme
1½ teaspoons allspice
1 tablespoon chili powder
1½ teaspoons sugar
½ teaspoon sage

Heat oil in skillet, sauté green pepper and celery. Add onions and garlic, sauté until limp, set aside. Brown beef, drain off excess fat. In large pot, place chicken, beef, sautéed vegetables and seasonings of choice. Cover with water, cook 2 to 3 hours, until very tender. In another large pot, cover veal with water. Cook 2 to 3 hours, until very tender. Remove chicken and veal from pots. Reserve both stocks. Cool, shred chicken and veal. Place meats back into chicken stock. Add vinegar, tomatoes, lima beans and corn. Combine chili sauce, Worcestershire sauce, hot pepper sauce and lemon juice, add to stock pot. Stir in spices, simmer 3 hours or longer, stirring often. Thin with reserved veal stock as needed.

*Let the butcher help choose the tastiest meats
for this stew.
Max Siegel's Kosher Market, Atlanta, Georgia, c.1940.*

Super Supper Soup

*Serve this hearty soup with crusty French bread, a nice Burgundy
and a crisp green salad. Top off this meal with Honey Crunch Pecan Pie (page 245).*

Meat   *Serves 15 to 20*

Soup

1-2	pounds boneless beef stew meat, such as flanken	1	pound zucchini
2-3	pounds beef bones	1	(16-ounce) can white corn, drained
2	tablespoons vegetable oil	1	(23-ounce) can crushed tomatoes
2	leeks, white part only, chopped	1	(10-ounce) package frozen okra
3	pounds onions, chopped	1	(16-ounce) can or frozen lima beans or chickpeas, drained
2	(14-ounce) cans beef stock		
3	(14-ounce) cans vegetable stock		Salt and pepper
½	cup barley		Basil, thyme, marjoram and parsley, as desired
2	stalks celery	½	cup red wine
2	pounds carrots, peeled	1	pound mushrooms
2	pounds white potatoes, peeled		
1	pound yellow squash		

Optional Ingredients

Hot sauce   Red pepper flakes
Worcestershire sauce

Cut meat into bite size pieces, brown with bones in oil in soup pot. Add leeks and onions, sauté lightly with meat. Add both stocks and barley with enough water to cover bones and meat. Simmer 1 hour. Cut next 5 ingredients into bite size pieces. Add to pot, simmer 15 minutes. Stir in corn, tomatoes, okra, lima beans, seasonings, red wine, mushrooms and optional ingredients. Simmer until vegetables are soft. Remove bones before serving.

Browning soup bones intensifies the flavor of soup or stock. Preheat oven to 400°. Place soup bones in a large shallow greased roasting pan. Bake, uncovered, about 30 minutes or until the bones are well browned, turning occasionally. Drain off fat. Place browned bones in the soup. Add 1 cup of water to the roasting pan. Scrape browned bits, blend with water and add to soup.

SPLIT PEA SOUP

Split pea soup warms body and soul.

1 ounce dried mushrooms, soaked overnight in water to cover	2 medium onions, chopped
	2 garlic cloves, minced
3 pounds beef short ribs	1 (14-ounce) can diced tomatoes
1 beef bone	Pepper
16 cups water	4 cups split peas, soaked overnight in water to cover
1 tablespoon plus 1 teaspoon salt	
4 carrots, peeled, sliced	1 cup barley
4 stalks celery, sliced	

For homemade croutons, cut day-old bread into ½-inch cubes. Toss with enough vegetable oil or olive oil to coat lightly. Sauté on all sides until golden, about 5 to 10 minutes. Transfer to paper towels, sprinkle with garlic salt or other seasonings of choice. Cool completely. Make up to 1 day in advance. Store in airtight container at room temperature.

Remove dried mushrooms from soaking liquid. Strain liquid to remove grit. Reserve clear liquid. Brown short ribs in roasting pan in oven or on top of stove. Place meat and bone in large stock pot. Cover with water, add salt and bring to boil. Reduce heat, skimming stock as necessary and simmer 1 hour or until meat is tender. Remove and reserve meat. Discard bones. Add carrots, celery, onions, garlic, tomatoes, dried mushrooms, reserved mushroom liquid, pepper and split peas. Simmer 1½ hours or until peas are tender. Return meat to pot, cook an additional hour. Stir in barley 30 minutes before serving soup. Adjust seasonings.

This recipe will serve a large family.
Family gathering, Atlanta, Georgia, c.1915

SPINACH AND WHITE BEAN SOUP

To sneak healthy greens and lean protein into the family diet, look no further.
This soup is healthy and hearty. Serve with Tuscan Bread Salad (page 59).

Meat   *Serves 10*

2	pounds dried white beans, navy or cannellini	2	teaspoons dried rosemary
2	tablespoons olive oil	1	bay leaf
2	tablespoons pareve margarine	1½	teaspoons pepper
4	medium onions, chopped	1½	pounds kosher smoked sausage, optional
4	garlic cloves, finely chopped	15	carrots, peeled, sliced
10	cups chicken stock	1½	pounds fresh spinach, chopped
6	cups water	1	teaspoon or more of salt

Cover beans in water, soak, refrigerated 8 hours. Drain. Heat oil and margarine in soup pot. Sauté onions until tender, but not brown. Add garlic, sauté 1 minute. Add stock, beans, 4 cups water, rosemary, bay leaf and pepper. Simmer on low heat until beans are tender, about 1 hour. Slice sausage into ¼-inch slices. In skillet, brown slices while stirring over medium heat. Drain well. Stir carrots, spinach, salt and 2 or more cups of water into soup. Bring to gentle boil, cook for 10 minutes. Add sausage, simmer 15 minutes more. Discard bay leaf, adjust seasonings.

When I got married, Mama used to say, 'put a little of this and a little of that.' I said, 'Mama, I can't cook like that!' 'Then start off with a teaspoon, taste it, and if you need more, add more.'

FRANKLY DIVINE LENTIL SOUP

Warm and satisfying all year round, but especially on a cold winter night.

Meat   *Serves 8 to 10*

2	cups lentils		Generous pinch of thyme
1	quart water		Generous pinch of marjoram
2	onions, diced	2	white potatoes, peeled, diced
2	tablespoons pareve margarine	1	tablespoon tarragon vinegar
			Salt and pepper
4-6	cups beef stock or bouillon		Dash of hot pepper sauce
1½	cups red wine, divided	1	teaspoon chopped parsley
1	large carrot, peeled, sliced	4	kosher frankfurters, sliced
1	bay leaf	1	diced tomato
2	stalks celery, diced		Pareve sour cream
¼	teaspoon cumin		

Rinse lentils, picking out stones. Cover with water and soak overnight. In large stock pot, sauté onions in margarine until golden brown. Add lentils with soaking water, beef stock, 1 cup red wine, carrot, bay leaf, celery, cumin, thyme and marjoram. Cover, simmer 45 minutes. Add potatoes and remaining wine. Simmer 45 minutes more. Remove bay leaf. Purée soup in batches in food processor or blender, return to pot. Stir in vinegar, salt, pepper, hot pepper sauce, parsley and frankfurters. Stir, reheat, allow to stand 10 minutes before serving. Garnish with diced tomato and dollop of pareve sour cream.

Kitchen of The Jewish Home, Atlanta, Georgia, 1957.

Velvety Artichoke Soup

Here is a creamy soup that borders on bliss. Follow with
Sandy Springs Sautéed Snapper (page 100) and
Lemon Sunshine Ice Box Cake (page 235).

Dairy/Meat/Pareve   **Serves 4**

½   cup finely chopped shallots
3   bay leaves
    Pinch of thyme
    Cayenne pepper
4   tablespoons butter or pareve
    margarine
2   tablespoons flour
1   (14-ounce) can vegetable or
    chicken stock

1   (14-ounce) can artichoke
    hearts, drained, ¼-inch
    diced
3   sprigs parsley, finely
    chopped
1½ cups light cream or pareve
    soy milk
    Salt
    Dash of nutmeg

In soup pot, sauté shallots, bay leaves, thyme and cayenne pepper in butter or margarine. Stir in flour until well blended. Add stock, simmer 15 minutes. Add artichoke hearts and parsley. Simmer another 10 minutes. Remove from heat, discard bay leaves. Blend in cream or milk. Season with salt and nutmeg.

No fresh parsley? An equal amount of chopped celery leaves can be substituted for fresh parsley in hearty soups.

Spring Green Asparagus Soup

This lovely asparagus soup celebrates spring, the season of new beginnings.

Dairy/Pareve   **Serves 6 to 8**

2   pounds asparagus
3   tablespoons olive oil
1   large onion, chopped
4   cups vegetable stock or
    pareve chicken soup

2-3 cups milk or pareve soy
     milk
½   pound kosher faux crabmeat
    Salt and pepper
    Sherry
    Croutons

Snap off tough ends of asparagus and discard. Cut spears into ½-inch pieces. Heat oil in skillet, sauté asparagus with onion. Transfer to medium pot with stock or soup. Cover, gently simmer 20 minutes. Purée in batches in processor or blender, return to pot. Add milk, simmer 5 minutes. Stir in crabmeat, season with salt, pepper and sherry. Simmer 5 minutes. Garnish with croutons.

Baked Winter Squash Soup

Dairy / Meat / Pareve / Passover   *Serves 12*

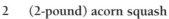

2	(2-pound) acorn squash	10	cups vegetable or chicken stock, divided
2	(2-pound) butternut squash	¾	teaspoon ground mace
1	stick unsalted butter or pareve margarine, divided	¾	teaspoon ground ginger
8	teaspoons firmly packed dark brown sugar, divided		Pinch of cayenne pepper
			Salt
			Crème fraîche or pareve sour cream
3	carrots, peeled, halved		Snipped fresh chives
1	large onion, thinly sliced		

Preheat oven to 350°. Cut squash in ½ lengthwise. Scoop out and discard seeds. Put 1 tablespoon butter or margarine and 1 teaspoon sugar in cavity of each half. Place squash, cut side up, in shallow roasting pan. Layer carrots and onion slices around squash. Pour in 2 cups stock. Cover tightly, bake 2 hours. Remove from oven, allow vegetables to cool slightly. Scoop squash pulp from skins. Place pulp in soup pot with carrots, onions and cooking liquid. Stir in remaining 8 cups stock, mace, ginger, cayenne and salt. Stir well, bring to boil. Reduce heat, simmer, uncovered, 10 minutes.

In blender or food processor, purée soup in batches. Return to pot, adjust seasonings and heat thoroughly. Garnish each serving with dollop of crème fraîche or pareve sour cream plus sprinkling of chives.

I watched the pots on the stove while my mama worked as a milliner in the other room. I still remember her warning, "Don't let it burn, dear."

Coach and Six Black Bean Soup

From its opening in the early 1960s, The Coach and Six Restaurant was known as an oasis on Peachtree Street and a gathering place. The fragrant breads and the best black bean soup in town kept diners returning for more.

Meat   *Serves 8 to 10*

Soup

4 cups dried black beans	2 green peppers, seeded, diced
3 quarts cold water	½ cup pareve margarine
3 quarts chicken stock	3 tablespoons flour
3 onions, minced	Salt and pepper
4 stalks celery, minced	1 cup sweet red wine
2 medium carrots, peeled, diced	

Toppings

Hot sauce	Parsley
Minced hard-cooked eggs	Chopped green onions
Lime slices	Kosher imitation bacon bits

Soak beans overnight in cold water. Drain, place in large pot. Cover with chicken stock, bring to boil. Reduce temperature to simmer. Cover, cook until tender, 2½ hours. Sauté onions, celery, carrots and peppers in margarine in large skillet until lightly browned and soft. Sprinkle with flour, stir 2 minutes. Season with salt and pepper. Drain beans when soft, reserving cooking liquid. Combine beans and vegetable mixture. Purée in batches in blender or processor. Transfer to pot with reserved cooking liquid. Bring to simmer, stir in red wine and hot sauce. Top as desired.

Beverlee Shere, Coach and Six Restaurant, Atlanta, Georgia

Coach and Six Restaurant, 1987.

Harvest Pumpkin Soup

This is a great autumn menu item that can be served hot or cold for Sukkot and/or Thanksgiving. Try serving this in small, scooped-out pumpkins instead of soup bowls.

Dairy/Meat/Pareve　　　　　　　　　　　　　　*Serves 8*

4 tablespoons butter or pareve margarine	3 (32-ounce) cans vegetable or chicken stock
2 medium onions, diced	1 teaspoon salt
4 stalks celery, diced	¼ teaspoon white pepper
2 large carrots, peeled, sliced	1 generous tablespoon curry powder, optional
4 tablespoons flour	Sprigs of fresh dill or parsley
1 (16-ounce) can puréed pumpkin	

Melt butter or margarine in large soup pot. Sauté onions until golden brown. Add celery and carrots, cooking about 1 minute, blend in flour. Stir pumpkin into pot, gradually add stock and seasonings. Bring to boil, cover and simmer 30 minutes. Add curry powder. Purée soup in blender, 1 or 2 cups at a time. Garnish with dill or parsley sprigs.

Pumpkin soup takes the chill out of a cool autumn night in the sukkah.
Celebrating Sukkot, The Temple, Atlanta, Georgia, c.1905.

CREAMY SWEET POTATO SOUP

Call them sweet potatoes or call them yams,
everyone will come calling when this soup is served.

Dairy/Pareve/Passover   *Serves 8*

SOUP

1	large onion, chopped	1	large sweet potato, peeled, thinly sliced
2	large leeks, white and light green parts, washed, thinly sliced	1	medium white potato, peeled, thinly sliced
2	garlic cloves, minced	¾	cup dry white wine
3	carrots, peeled, coarsely chopped	5	cups vegetable or chicken stock
1	bay leaf		Salt and pepper
3	tablespoons butter or olive oil		

TOPPING

½	cup pecan halves		Salt
2	tablespoons butter or pareve margarine		Dairy or pareve sour cream

In soup pot, sauté onion, leeks, garlic, carrots and bay leaf in butter or olive oil for 5 minutes, or until vegetables begin to soften. Do not brown. Stir in all potatoes, on low heat, sauté 2 minutes. Add wine. Bring to boil, simmer to reduce by half. Add stock. Simmer 20 to 40 minutes, until vegetables and potatoes are soft. Discard bay leaf. Purée mixture in batches in blender or food processor. Return to pot. If necessary, thin with water, up to 1½ cups, to desired consistency. Season with salt and pepper.

For topping, sauté pecan halves in sizzling butter or margarine. Salt lightly, drain on paper towels. When cool, break pecans into pieces. Garnish with pecans and dollop of sour cream.

In our family, on Yom Kippur in the 1940s, breaking the fast took all night. After the fish, everybody got up, took a walk, read the paper or played with the kids. Then we all came back to the table for soup. We took another break before the main course. This was the way our family did it in those days.

ROASTED TOMATO SOUP

Roasting the tomatoes intensifies the flavor in this wonderful soup.

Meat / Pareve   *Serves 2*

1½ pounds large tomatoes, such as Beefsteak, halved
3   large garlic cloves, unpeeled
1   medium onion, halved crosswise, unpeeled
1   tablespoon plus 1 teaspoon olive oil, divided
     Salt and pepper
2   cups chicken or vegetable stock, divided
¼   cup tomato juice
1   teaspoon tomato paste
¼   teaspoon Worcestershire sauce
1   tablespoon firmly packed brown sugar
1   bay leaf
1   tablespoon chopped fresh basil
½   cup cooked fresh corn kernels

Preheat oven to 400°. In medium bowl, combine tomatoes, garlic, onion and 1 tablespoon olive oil. Season with salt and pepper. Spoon onto lightly greased baking sheet, roast until vegetables soften and caramelize, about 30 minutes. Remove from oven, cool. Discard peels and seeds from garlic and tomatoes. Remove and discard peel and ends from onion. Place roasted vegetables in food processor with ½ the chicken stock and remaining olive oil. Pulse in processor to desired thickness, making tomato purée.

In large heavy pot over medium heat, simmer tomato purée with remaining chicken stock, tomato juice, tomato paste, Worcestershire sauce, brown sugar and bay leaf and/or basil 10 minutes. Discard bay leaf. Season with salt and pepper. Garnish with corn.

Roasting is so flavorful.
Tau Epsilon Pi, University of Georgia, Athens, Georgia, 1947.

SLOW ROASTED VIDALIA ONION SOUP

*Chef Michael Tuohy, indulges Atlantans with seasonally influenced,
ingredient focused cuisine at Woodfire Grill. Tuohy is a pioneering force behind
Georgia's Organic Growers. He incorporates the freshest offerings from small local farms.
This recipe showcases the Georgia grown sweet Vidalia onions.*

Dairy/ Meat / Pareve/ Passover   *Serves 12*

6	medium Vidalia onions	1	cup heavy cream or pareve soy milk
¼	cup canola or grape seed oil	2	tablespoons finely chopped fresh thyme
2	leeks, white part only, chopped		Kosher salt and white pepper
2	stalks celery, chopped	1	bunch fresh chives, chopped
2	quarts low sodium vegetable or chicken stock		
1	cup sweet sherry		

Preheat oven to 300°. Wrap each onion separately in foil. In shallow pan roast until onions are tender, soft when lightly squeezed, about 1½ to 2 hours. Heat oil in large pot, sauté leeks and celery until softened, but not browned. Remove onions from foil. Cut into quarters, add to pot with chicken stock and sherry. Simmer 45 minutes. Stir in cream or milk and thyme, remove from heat. In batches, purée mixture in blender or processor until smooth. Season with salt and pepper. Garnish with chives.

Chef Michael Tuohy, Woodfire Grill, Atlanta, Georgia

During World War II, Fannie Smith, a Jewish resident of Vidalia, Georgia, won a national good citizenship award given to immigrants by the Daughters of the American Revolution. She won the award because she distributed apples to soldiers on troop trains during stopovers in Vidalia. She collected their parting messages to loved ones, contacted families and gave assurances of the soldiers' well being. One of those soldiers was Buddy Hackett.

VEGETARIAN MUSHROOM BARLEY SOUP

This is a great soup for Shabbat lunch. It can be made overnight in a crockpot.

Dairy/Pareve   *Serves 12*

1	pound mushrooms, sliced	1	(14-ounce) can crushed tomatoes
2	medium onions, chopped		
3	garlic cloves, chopped	2	large carrots, peeled, grated
2	stalks celery, chopped	2-4	sprigs fresh dill
4	tablespoons butter or pareve margarine	½	teaspoon pepper
		1-2	teaspoons salt
4	quarts water	1	teaspoon sugar
6	vegetable bouillon cubes	2	tablespoons butter or pareve margarine, melted
1	cup barley, rinsed well		
		2	tablespoons flour

In large skillet, sauté mushrooms, onions, garlic and celery in 4 tablespoons butter or margarine. Bring water to boil in large soup pot. Add sautéed vegetables, bouillon cubes, barley, tomatoes, carrots, dill, pepper, salt and sugar. Cover, simmer 1½ hours. Make paste with 2 tablespoons butter or margarine and flour. Slowly stir into hot soup, simmer 45 minutes.

If using crockpot, cook vegetables 6 hours on low setting. Add butter flour paste, cook on low 1 more hour.

To thicken soups, use flour for hot soups and cornstarch for cold soups. To prevent lumps, remove pot from heat when adding thickener. An immersion blender will emulsify the thickening liquid, removing lumps from soups or gravies.

CHILLED BORSCHT BISQUE

Hot borscht in the old country and cold borscht in the new.

Dairy/Pareve/Passover   *Serves 4 to 6*

2   cups mashed potatoes, about 4 large potatoes
¼   teaspoon onion powder
¾   teaspoon salt
¾   cup dairy or pareve sour cream

1   (1-quart) jar prepared beet borscht, strain if using a food processor
    Green onions, chopped
    Cucumber, peeled, diced

Combine potatoes, onion powder, salt and sour cream. Gradually stir into borscht. Blend all ingredients on high, in batches, in blender or processor. Process for 30 seconds. If using blender, add beet liquid also. Chill, garnish with green onion and cucumber.

Farband Labor Zionist Order celebrates Israel Independence Day, Atlanta, Georgia, 1956.

TOMATO OR TROPICAL GAZPACHO

*A treasure from the famous Souper Jenny. Her soups draw
crowds all year long. This gazpacho recipe is a great gift to all.*

Pareve/Passover   *Serves 8 to 10*

TOMATO GAZPACHO

1 red, yellow and green bell pepper, seeded, cut in small chunks	3 yellow tomatoes, cut in chunks
3-4 seedless cucumbers, unpeeled	1 jalapeño pepper, seeded
1 Vidalia onion, cut in chunks	1 bunch cilantro, coarsely chopped
1 garlic clove	Sea salt and pepper
3 red tomatoes, cut in chunks	1 (46-ounce) can vegetable juice, or more

TROPICAL GAZPACHO

1 large mango, peeled, pitted	1 pineapple, peeled, cut in chunks, with juices
1 (8-ounce) can Mandarin oranges, with juice	Fresh ginger

For preparation of Tomato Gazpacho, combine all ingredients, except
vegetable juice, in large bowl. Cover ingredients with vegetable juice by
2-inches, mix. Purée, in batches, in processor. Refrigerate until ready to
serve.

For Tropical Gazpacho variation, combine tropical ingredients with all
Tomato Gazpacho ingredients, except vegetable juice. Cover ingredients
with vegetable juice by 2-inches, mix. Purée, in batches, in processor.
Refrigerate until ready to serve.

Jenny Levison, Souper Jenny Restaurant, Atlanta, Georgia

SUMMER STRAWBERRY SOUP

*This refreshing low-calorie soup makes an excellent first course
for a warm weather dinner, followed by Grilled Gingered Fish Steaks (page 110)
and Chocolate Mocha Roulade (page 217).*

Dairy/Passover   *Serves 4 to 6*

2	pints strawberries, hulled	⅛	teaspoon ground cardamom
½	cup cold water	2	cups plain yogurt
½	cup orange juice		Fresh mint leaves
½	cup sugar		

In food processor, purée strawberries with water. In small pan, combine orange juice, sugar and cardamom. Stir over medium heat until sugar dissolves. Remove from heat, blend in yogurt and add to puréed strawberries until well combined. Chill thoroughly. Garnish with fresh mint.

*Enjoying the sunshine on Washington Street,
Atlanta, Georgia, c.1939.*

BUCKHEAD BLUEBERRY BISQUE

*Starting in late June, luscious fresh blueberries arrive at
road-side produce stands. This beautiful bisque is not to be missed.*

Dairy / Pareve   *Serves 3*

1½ cups fresh blueberries
½   cup water
¼   cup sugar
1   tablespoon lemon juice
    Dash of ground cinnamon
    Dash of ground cloves

1   tablespoon dry red wine
⅓   cup dairy or pareve sour
    cream
    Dairy or pareve sour cream
    Mint sprigs

In blender, purée berries and water. Pour into medium saucepan. Stir in sugar, lemon juice, cinnamon and cloves. Bring to boil, stirring to dissolve sugar. Reduce heat, cover and simmer 5 minutes. Pour into medium bowl, refrigerate until cool. Stir in wine and ⅓ cup sour cream until blended. Refrigerate covered until cool. Ladle soup into bowls. Using pastry tube, pipe sour cream in spiral pattern on top of each bowl of soup. Gently swirl sour cream into designs using a toothpick. Garnish with mint sprigs.

Excerpt from a letter sent from a child at sleep-away camp in Maine: "I don't know why you spend all this money to send me way up here to camp. All we do is pick blueberries."

Catch OF THE DAY

Fish

Traditional Gefilte Fish

Gefilte fish is the traditional first course of the Passover seder in Ashkenazi homes. Store-bought just does not compare with these delicate rich fish dumplings. It is not difficult and the rewards are great.

Pareve/Passover   *Serves 15 to 30*

Fish Stock

2-3	fish heads, skin and bones, rinsed	1-2	garlic cloves
2	large onions, quartered	2	tablespoons salt
3	stalks celery, cut in thirds	½	teaspoon white pepper
5	carrots, peeled, cut in thirds	½	teaspoon sugar

Gefilte Fish Balls

2	medium onions, cut in small chunks	2	tablespoons salt
1	garlic clove	½	teaspoon white pepper
3½	pounds fish fillets, skinned, cut in chunks	¼	teaspoon sugar
2	large eggs, beaten	½-¾	cup ice water
1	tablespoon matzah meal		Lettuce
			Carrot slices
			Horseradish (page 98)

Combine stock ingredients in 2-quart stock pot. Cover with cold water, bring to boil. Lower heat, simmer for 30 minutes. Strain stock into clean bowl, discarding solids. Return stock to pot, bring to boil before adding fish balls.

Place onions and garlic in food processor, pulse quickly to finely chop, taking care not to over process. Place in very large bowl. In processor, coarsely chop fish, 2 cups at a time, being careful not to purée. Put chopped fish in with onions and garlic. Stir in eggs, matzah meal, salt, pepper and sugar. Gradually beat in ice water until mixture is light and easy to handle. Wet hands, form fish mixture, ⅓ cup at a time, into balls. Gently lower into stock pot with large spoon. Cover pot, simmer 2 to 3 hours. Remove from heat, allow fish balls to cool in stock. Remove fish balls with slotted spoon. Place in large plastic or glass containers, refrigerate. Strain stock. Place stock in saucepan, heat. Add carrots, cook until tender, cool slightly. Pour over fish balls and refrigerate. Serve cold gefilte fish on bed of lettuce. Garnish with carrot slices and horseradish. Fish will keep 5 to 6 days. Do not freeze.

Preorder the fish for this recipe, requesting that it be filleted and that the heads, skin and bones be reserved.

Historically, local fish were used to make gefilte fish, thus there was a variety of tastes from place to place. Whitefish and pike are traditional choices for Jews coming from Eastern Europe where those fish were readily available.

RAINBOW GEFILTE FISH

A delicious and colorful twist on traditional gefilte fish.

Dairy/Pareve/Passover   *Serves 8*

1	(10½-ounce) package frozen chopped spinach	Juice of 1 lime, divided
3	(22-ounce) loaves frozen plain gefilte fish, defrosted	¼ cup finely diced red bell pepper
1	(22-ounce) loaf frozen salmon gefilte fish, defrosted	3 ounces dairy or pareve cream cheese, softened
1	tablespoon minced fresh dill	¼ cup finely chopped chives
		Grape tomatoes
		Thinly sliced cucumbers
		Horseradish (see below)

Preheat oven to 350°. Spray 9-inch springform pan with nonstick spray. Thaw spinach, drain and squeeze out water. Place each loaf of gefilte fish in separate bowl. In bowl #1, combine plain fish with well drained spinach. In bowl #2, combine plain fish with dill and juice of ½ lime. In bowl #3, combine salmon fish with red bell pepper. In bowl #4, combine plain fish with cream cheese, chives and remaining juice.

In the bottom of prepared pan, place mixture from bowl #1, smooth evenly with spatula. Repeat with contents of bowls #2, #3 and top with contents of bowl #4. Cover tightly. Bake 1 hour or until center is firm. Cool, refrigerate up to 2 days. Remove sides from pan, place on serving platter. Garnish with grape tomatoes and cucumbers. Serve with horseradish.

OUR BEST CHRAIN, HORSERADISH

"My zaide would always grate the horseradish for my bubbe. I'll never forget the picture. He would be crying and laughing simultaneously as he grated on his old-fashioned grater."

Pareve/Passover   *Serves 24*

1	(8-ounce) can beets	3 tablespoons white vinegar
1	cup peeled, grated horseradish root	2 teaspoons sugar
		¼ teaspoon salt

Drain beets, reserving ½ cup beet juice. Dice beets, add to grated horseradish in food processor. Pulse just until beets have same texture as horseradish. Heat reserved ½ cup beet juice, mix in small bowl with vinegar, sugar and salt. Add to horseradish mixture. Place in glass jar, refrigerate up to 30 days.

ORANGE GLAZED GROUPER

Dairy / Pareve   *Serves 6*

GROUPER

Juice of 1 small lemon
Juice of 1 small orange
6   (5-ounce) grouper fillets

Salt and pepper
1   tablespoons butter or pareve
     margarine

GLAZE

1   cup orange marmalade
¼   cup orange juice

2½   tablespoons orange liqueur

GARNISH

3   green onions, thinly sliced   3   orange slices, halved

In small bowl, whisk juices together. Season fish with salt and pepper. Melt 1 tablespoon butter or margarine in large skillet over medium high heat. Transfer fish to skillet. Spoon fruit juices over fish. Sauté 3 to 5 minutes per side or until nearly cooked.

Preheat broiler. In small saucepan, combine orange marmalade, juice and liqueur, heat until warm. Grease glass baking dish. Spoon ½ glaze into pan, follow with fish and remaining glaze. Broil fish 2 to 5 minutes until lightly browned. Garnish with green onions and orange slices.

It doesn't take a professional chef to prepare this gourmet dish!
ZEP Chemical Sales Force meeting, Atlanta, Georgia, 1951.

Fish

BAKED HALIBUT IN TOMATO SAUCE

Halibut isn't the only fish that likes tomato sauce, red snapper likes to swim in it too.

Pareve / Passover   *Serves 4*

3	carrots, peeled, sliced ¼-inch thick	1	(24-ounce) can crushed tomatoes
1	green pepper, 1-inch strips	4	(2-inch thick) halibut steaks
1	celery stalk, thinly sliced		Salt, pepper and garlic salt
1	large onion, quartered, thinly sliced	½	teaspoon dried dill

Preheat oven to 350°. Place vegetables in glass baking dish large enough to hold fish. Place fish on top of vegetables. Season with salt, pepper, garlic salt and dill. Cover, bake 25 to 30 minutes. Serve fish with vegetables.

Don't rub your belly when the little fish is still in the pond.

~Yiddish proverb

SANDY SPRINGS SAUTÉED SNAPPER

Pair with Cornucopia Salad (page 55) and Potato Kugelettes (page 154) for a colorful and complete meal.

Dairy / Pareve   *Serves 4*

2	tablespoons pine nuts	1	tablespoon butter or pareve margarine
2	teaspoons olive oil	1	medium shallot, minced
1¼	pounds snapper fillets	2	tablespoons drained capers
2	tablespoons flour	2	tablespoons golden raisins
⅛	teaspoon salt	1	tablespoon lemon juice
	Pepper		

Lightly toast pine nuts in small skillet until golden, set aside. Heat olive oil in large nonstick skillet over medium heat. Dust fillets with flour. Sauté 10 minutes per inch of thickness, turning half way through cooking time. Season with salt and pepper. Remove from pan, keep warm. Add butter or margarine to pan. Sauté shallot 1 minute. Stir in capers, raisins and lemon juice until hot. Pour sauce over fish. Sprinkle with pine nuts.

Tel Aviv Tilapia

This palate-pleasing dish is guaranteed to bring smiles all around.

Dairy   *Serves 2*

Parmesan Flour

¼ cup flour	1½ cups grated Parmesan cheese

Fish

2 (5-6 ounce) tilapia fillets	Juice of 1 lemon
1 large egg, slightly beaten	2 tablespoons white wine
1 tablespoon olive oil	¼ cup vegetable stock
1 teaspoon chopped fresh garlic	Salt and pepper
3 teaspoons drained capers	1 tablespoon butter

Combine flour and Parmesan cheese in shallow pan, set aside. Coat fish in flour mixture, shake off excess. Dip fish into beaten egg then press into flour mixture second time. Add olive oil to nonstick skillet, heat until fairly hot. Place fish in skillet, brown on both sides. Remove from pan, keep warm. Add remaining ingredients, except butter to pan. Simmer, reduce by half. Remove from heat. Add butter, stirring to incorporate. Place fish on plates, spoon sauce over fillets.

Tilapia was a popular food item throughout ancient Israel. It still is a favorite throughout the Middle East and Mediterranean. Tilapia can be found in the Sea of Galilee, the Jordan River and the Mediterranean Sea.

Atlantans arriving in Israel, c.1970.

PECAN TILAPIA WITH MANGO SALSA

The Mango Salsa is delicious. It can also be served with roast chicken, BBQ beef or fajitas.

Dairy / Pareve / Passover   *Serves 4*

MANGO SALSA

1	jalapeño pepper			Salt and pepper
2	ripe mangoes, peeled, pitted			Juice of 2 limes
1	small red onion, minced		1	teaspoon fish seasoning or
2	minced garlic cloves			green hot sauce, optional

TILAPIA

1	cup chopped pecans	4	tilapia fillets
4	tablespoons butter or pareve margarine		

*W**hen preparing hot peppers, wear disposable, not rubber, gloves to protect hands. Remove gloves by pulling them off inside out, then throw them away.*

Remove veins and seeds from jalapeño, finely mince. Combine all salsa ingredients, adding as much jalapeño as desired. Refrigerate in sealed container.

Fishing on vacation off the eastern coast, 1938.

Preheat oven to 400°. Place chopped pecans on flat plate. Press fish onto nuts, coating each side. Melt butter or margarine in a large ovenproof skillet. Sauté fish in hot butter, 2 to 3 minutes on each side. Place skillet in oven, bake 10 minutes or until fish is done, flaky and white throughout. Serve with Mango Salsa.

Refrigerated mango chunks are fine to use in place of fresh mangoes. Substitute pineapple, peach, apple, papaya, cantaloupe, strawberries or almost any fruit for mango.

TILAPIA SANTORINI

This tilapia dish is prepared in the Greek islands.
Enjoy this fish with a good bottle of white wine and crusty bread.

Dairy / Passover   *Serves 4*

4	tilapia fillets	3-4	tablespoons olive oil
2	tablespoons Greek Seasoning	10	ounces fresh spinach
	Salt and pepper	1	(4-ounce) jar sun-dried tomatoes, drained, chopped
	Minced garlic		
	Fresh dill	4	ounces feta cheese

Place fish on plate, season both sides with Greek Seasoning, salt, pepper, garlic and dill. Heat olive oil in large skillet. Brown fish lightly on both sides. Lay spinach on top of fish. Cover skillet, simmer for 3 minutes. Remove from heat. Sprinkle with sun-dried tomatoes and feta cheese. Cover, cook another 5 minutes.

Greek Seasoning

This pareve herbal blend enhances the flavors of salads, poultry, fish and meats.

2	teaspoons sea salt	1	teaspoon dried lemon zest or peel
1	teaspoon cracked black pepper	1	teaspoon dried thyme
2	teaspoons onion powder	1	teaspoon fennel seeds
2	teaspoons dried parsley	½	teaspoon crushed marjoram leaves
1	teaspoon dried oregano		
1	teaspoon dried basil	½	teaspoon dried spearmint
1	teaspoon dried rosemary		

In a coffee bean grinder, grind all ingredients and store, up to 6 months, in airtight container.

Fish dishes are usually light-flavored, so the way in which it is prepared should determine the choice of wine. Try a light white for simply prepared fish, or a white Burgundy for richer dishes.

Parmesan Crusted Sea Bass

Deliciously moist with subtle flavors.

Dairy / Passover   *Serves 4*

½ cup grated Parmesan cheese
⅓ cup butter, softened
2   tablespoons mayonnaise
2   green onions, thinly sliced

2   tablespoons rinsed, drained capers
4   (5-ounce) sea bass fillets
    Juice of 1 lemon
    Pepper

Preheat broiler. In small bowl, combine cheese, butter, mayonnaise, green onions and capers. Place sea bass on lightly greased broiler pan. Drizzle with lemon juice and sprinkle with pepper. Broil 10 minutes, remove from oven. Sprinkle with cheese mixture. Press into fish. Broil again until topping is lightly browned and bubbly, about 3 minutes.

Almost all the rules of matching wine with food are made to be broken. However, the general principle of red wine with red meat and white wine with white meat or fish works quite well. The exceptions are those of taste. Although roast chicken is a white meat, it goes very well with fruity red wines, as does salmon and fresh tuna. The bottom line, drink whatever suits the palate.

Pacific Rim Sea Bass

Complement this Asian fusion dish with Cool Sesame Asparagus (page 145).

Dairy / Pareve   *Serves 2 to 3*

1   pound sea bass fillets
¼ cup minced ginger
2   garlic cloves, minced or
    more if desired
3   tablespoons chopped parsley
    or cilantro

½ cup minced green onions
½ cup olive oil
¼ pound butter or pareve
    margarine
½ teaspoon soy sauce

Preheat oven to 450°. Lightly grease 13x9-inch glass dish. Place fish in dish. Cover, cook for 20 minutes. Layer ginger, garlic, parsley or cilantro and green onions in order over fish. Heat olive oil with butter or margarine in small saucepan. Bring to just below a boil. Pour over fish. Allow to rest 5 minutes. Place fish on serving platter and drizzle with soy sauce.

Any firm fish, such as halibut, tuna or haddock may be used for this recipe.

FISH EN PAPILLOTE

Engage guests by inviting them to prepare their own entrée.

Dairy/Pareve   *Serves 8*

4	small onions, thinly sliced, caramelized
4	ears corn, kernels removed
1	tablespoon vegetable oil
	Fresh rosemary and thyme
1	pound very thin green beans, trimmed
2	large sweet potatoes, peeled, sliced, cut julienne
2	avocados, peeled, pitted, ½-inch cubed
2	yellow squash, sliced, cut julienne
2	zucchini, sliced, cut julienne

16	roasted garlic cloves
	Minced cilantro, optional
8	tablespoons cream, white wine, sherry or fish stock
8	halibut, cod, grouper or snapper fillets
2	sprigs thyme, finely chopped
16	lime or lemon slices, skin and pith removed
	Salt and pepper
8	tablespoons butter or pareve margarine

Preheat oven to 500°. Caramelize onions. Sauté corn in hot oil with rosemary and thyme, using a lid to contain popping corn. Corn is done when slightly brown. Remove to drain on paper towels.

Cut eight 24x12-inch pieces of parchment or lightly greased foil, fold in ½ lengthwise. Place ⅛ of each prepared ingredient in center part of each square, beginning with vegetables, liquid, and then, fish. Top each fillet with thyme, citrus slices, salt, pepper and butter or margarine. Fold into airtight pouches with space for steam. Lightly mist parchment paper with nonstick spray. Place all pouches on baking sheet. Bake approximately 10 minutes or until sauce is bubbling. Transfer to plates. Cut an "X" in the top of pouches to allow steam to escape, open very carefully.

Fishing off the coast of Florida, c.1958.

Caramelizing onions gives any dish a rich, velvety taste and deep brown color. The key is to cook the onions slowly. Heat equal amounts of olive oil and butter or pareve margarine in a heavy skillet. Add sliced onions. Sauté while stirring for 5 minutes. Add a dash of sugar and a dash of salt, then reduce heat to low. Cook, stirring frequently, about 15 minutes or until onions are golden brown.

Baked Ginger Honey Salmon

Serve this flavorful fish with Apple Walnut Tzimmes Surprise (page 159).
This honey-flavored entrée is a good choice for Rosh Hashanah.

Pareve   *Serves 4*

3	tablespoons lemon juice	1	tablespoon minced fresh cilantro
1	tablespoon honey		
1	tablespoon finely grated fresh ginger	1	(22-ounce) salmon fillet
		⅛	teaspoon salt
1	teaspoon soy sauce	⅛	teaspoon pepper

Preheat oven to 450°. In small bowl, combine lemon juice, honey, ginger, soy sauce and cilantro. Place salmon in shallow baking pan. Brush with ½ honey mixture, season with salt and pepper. Bake fish 10 minutes per inch of thickness. Halfway through baking, brush with remaining honey mixture.

Gingered Salmon Supreme

This recipe is made in advance. The tomato flowers
add vibrant color, providing a showy dish for company.

Dairy/Pareve   *Serves 12*

12	salmon fillets	2	bunches green onions, trimmed, cut on diagonal, divided
	Milk or pareve soy milk, to cover		
2	(3-inch) pieces fresh ginger, peeled	¼	cup sugar
		1½	cups lite soy sauce
	Olive oil		Cherry tomato flowers

Preheat oven to 350°. Using glass dish, soak salmon fillets in enough milk to cover, marinate 25 minutes. Cover dish, place in oven. Poach 30 to 40 minutes, until just cooked, but not dry. Drain, cool 20 minutes. Gently separate salmon from skin. Remove bones and white milky film. Refrigerate 2 hours.

To make ginger sauce, finely chop ginger in processor, sauté in olive oil 2 minutes. Add 1 bunch cut green onions, sugar and soy sauce. Sauté until crisp tender. Remove from heat, cool. Pour ½ ginger sauce over salmon. Reserve remaining ginger sauce in airtight container, refrigerate. Marinate overnight. Before serving, pour ¼ cup reserved ginger sauce on large platter. Place serving size salmon pieces on platter. Drizzle with remaining sauce. Sprinkle second bunch of green onions over and around fish. Serve at room temperature. Garnish with cherry tomato flowers.

Cherry Tomato Flower

*P*lace tomato, stem side up, on cutting board. Slice tomato down the center, but do not cut completely through. Rotate ¼ turn, slice tomato again, creating quarters, being careful not to cut completely through. There will be 4 sections resembling petals of a flower. With a sharp knife, carefully scrape away the membrane and seeds. Allow the petals to fall open. Place a small drop of coarse mustard in the center point. Cover and refrigerate until ready to serve.

WINE-POACHED SALMON WITH ORANGE SALSA

A good fruity salsa is the perfect mate for a luscious poached salmon.

Pareve/Passover   *Serves 6*

MANDARIN ORANGE SALSA

2	(11-ounce) can Mandarin oranges, ½ cup juice reserved	12	small grape tomatoes, halved
3	tablespoons finely chopped basil	1	tablespoon olive oil
		¼	cup red wine
1	cup finely diced red onion	1	teaspoon salt
½	cup finely diced celery	½	teaspoon finely ground black pepper

SALMON

2	cups orange juice	6	(6-ounce) skinless, boneless salmon fillets
1	tablespoon grated orange zest		Fresh dill
1	cup white wine		Lemon slices

In medium bowl, combine all salsa ingredients and mix well. Refrigerate at least 4 hours.

In deep saucepan, bring orange juice, orange zest and wine to slow boil. Reduce to simmer, lower fillets into liquid, adding liquid, if necessary, to keep fillets covered. Gently simmer for 15 minutes. Remove pan from heat, allow fish to rest for 10 minutes. Remove fish to serving platter. Garnish with fresh dill and lemon slices. Serve with Mandarin Orange Salsa.

There is a very important "rule of thumb" for cooking with any wine: don't cook with any wine you wouldn't drink.

SALMON WITH ONIONS AND CAPERS

Pareve/Passover   *Serves 4*

2	teaspoons olive oil, divided	1	medium onion, sliced
4	(6-ounce) skinless salmon fillets	¼	cup drained capers
½	teaspoon salt	2	tablespoons balsamic vinegar
⅛	teaspoon pepper	1	teaspoon sugar

Preheat oven to 350°. In nonstick 12-inch skillet, heat 1 teaspoon oil. Over medium high heat, sauté fillets, rounded side down for 2 minutes until lightly browned. Turn, sauté 2 more minutes. Transfer salmon to 13x9-inch glass baking dish. Sprinkle with salt and pepper. In same skillet, add remaining oil. Sauté onion over medium heat 5 minutes or until tender. Stir in capers, vinegar and sugar. Stir while simmering 2 minutes. Spoon onion-caper mixture over salmon. Cover dish with foil. Bake 15 minutes.

*M*ake an exception to the white wine with fish rule. Try Pinot Noir with salmon or, if white is preferred, consider Pinot Gris.

Capers make this salmon dish pop.
Joy Seekers Club, Atlanta, Georgia, c.1910.

SALMON CROQUETTES

An old family favorite, this was served
on Thursdays, which was our dairy meal night.

Dairy   *Serves 2*

1   (14.75-ounce) can Alaskan   8   butter flavored cheese
    Red Sockeye Salmon   crackers, crumbled
1   medium onion, grated   Canola oil
2   large eggs, beaten

Drain salmon. Remove skin and large bones. Crumble evenly. Add onion,
eggs and cracker crumbs. Combine, form into 2 patties. Sauté in small
amount of canola oil until browned on both sides. Drain on double layer
of paper towels. Serve hot or at room temperature.

These can be baked on greased baking sheet at 350°, 8 to 10 minutes per side or
until lightly browned.

SIMPLY GOOD SALMON LOAF

Quick and simple, a great dish to take to friends.

Dairy / Pareve   *Serves 4 to 6*

1   (14.75 ounce) can salmon   1   teaspoon lemon juice
½   cup breadcrumbs   1   (2.8-ounce) can fried onion
2   large eggs, separated   rings, divided
8   ounces dairy or pareve sour
      cream

Preheat oven to 350°. Grease 9x5x3-inch loaf pan. Drain, saving liquid,
bone and flake salmon. Soak breadcrumbs in reserved liquid. Beat egg
whites until stiff, set aside. Beat egg yolks, mix with salmon, sour cream,
lemon juice, ⅔ can onion rings and soaked breadcrumbs. Fold in beaten
egg whites. Pour into prepared pan. Top with remaining onion rings. Bake
uncovered 25 minutes.

To double this recipe, use 13x9-inch glass dish. This recipe freezes well.

GRILLED GINGERED FISH STEAKS

*Preparing dinner doesn't get much easier than
beautifully grilled fish with ginger, onion and sesame.*

Pareve   *Serves 4*

4	(¾-inch) thick fish steaks or fillets, halibut, salmon or tuna	½	teaspoon finely chopped fresh ginger
¼	cup lite soy sauce	1	tablespoon sesame seeds, toasted
3	tablespoons minced onion	1	tablespoon sugar

Rinse fish, pat dry. Place in a single layer in shallow pan. Place remaining ingredients in blender. Blend on low speed 30 seconds, scraping down sides of blender once. Pour sauce over fish, turning to coat both sides. Marinate 30 minutes, turning occasionally. Preheat grill to medium heat and treat with nonstick grill spray. Remove fish from marinade. Place on grill 4-inches from coals. Cook 5 minutes on each side or until fish flakes easily.

Fish can be grilled three ways; with each use nonstick grill spray. For the first method, place fish in a fish grilling basket, available at cooking supply stores. For the second method, place fish on a rimless baking sheet, turning with a spatula. For the third method, place fish directly on the grill, using disposable grill grates, if available, for easy clean up.

Atlantans on a fishing vacation, c.1940.

Tuna Steaks Provençal

Tuna is a hearty fish with a wonderful texture and body. Serve with Wild Rice Crunch (page 165), Rosemary Focaccia Bread (page 198) and a glass of Pinot Noir.

Pareve/Passover   *Serves 4 to 6*

4	tablespoons olive oil, divided
1	medium onion, finely chopped
3	minced garlic cloves
2	fresh hot peppers, seeded, finely chopped
2	pounds (2-inch thick) tuna steaks
3	tablespoons sun-dried tomato paste

1	cup dry white wine or dry vermouth
3-4	medium tomatoes, peeled, seeded, chopped
	Salt and pepper
15-20	fresh basil leaves
3	tablespoons red wine vinegar
12	black oil cured olives
4	anchovy fillets, cut in (1-inch pieces), optional

In shallow 12-inch nonstick sauté pan, heat 3 tablespoons olive oil over medium heat. Add onions, sauté until golden, about 8 minutes. Add garlic and chopped peppers. Sauté while stirring for 2 minutes. Remove vegetables from pan, set aside. Add remaining tablespoon of oil, sear tuna quickly on both sides over high heat. Reduce heat, return onions and peppers to pan. Dissolve tomato paste in wine or vermouth, add to pan. Stir in tomatoes, salt and pepper. Reduce heat, simmer 7 to 10 minutes, until done. Tear basil leaves into small pieces, stir into pan with vinegar, olives, and anchovy pieces. Stir while cooking 1 additional minute. Serve immediately or at room temperature.

Olive oil is a healthy alternative to butter or margarine.

1 teaspoon butter or margarine =
¾ teaspoon olive oil

1 tablespoon butter or margarine =
2¼ teaspoons olive oil

¼ cup butter or margarine =
3 tablespoons olive oil

1 cup butter or margarine =
¾ cup olive oil

Fish

VERSATILE FISH STEW

*This is simple to prepare and, oh, so good. Add favorite
vegetables to the stew and serve over rice for a hearty meal.*

Pareve/Passover   *Serves 4 to 6*

6 tablespoons olive oil	1⅓ cups cold water
1 cup chopped onion	⅔ cup dry white wine
2-3 large garlic cloves, minced	2 pounds tilapia or other
⅔ cup chopped fresh parsley	mild white fish, cut
⅔ cup chopped fresh cilantro	into 2-inch pieces
1 cup diced tomato, fresh or	Salt and pepper
canned	

Heat olive oil in large pot over medium high heat. Sauté onion and garlic
4 minutes. Stir in parsley and cilantro, cook 2 minutes. Add tomato, cook
another 2 minutes. Add water, wine and fish. Simmer until fish is cooked
through, about 10 minutes. Season with salt and pepper.

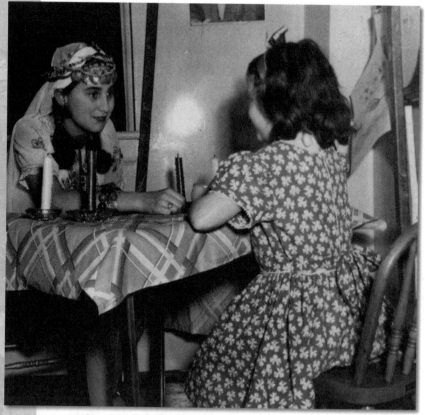

*Amaze friends with this outstanding fish stew!
Fortune telling at the Purim carnival at The Temple,
Atlanta, Georgia, c.1946.*

Kosher "Crab" Cakes

Enjoy this kosher version of the full-bodied taste of Maryland's Eastern Shore.
Perfect for a luncheon with Cartersville Crispy Two-Week Slaw (page 57).

Pareve　　　　　　　　　　　　　　　*Serves 5 to 6*

1 pound kosher faux crabmeat	1 tablespoon chopped parsley
2 tablespoons mayonnaise	1 teaspoon fish seasoning
1 tablespoon Dijon mustard	Juice of ½ lemon
3 egg whites	1 cup breadcrumbs
½ red bell pepper, minced	Mango Salsa (page
¼ cup minced green onions	136), pareve creamy
1 tablespoon Worcestershire	horseradish or tartar
sauce	sauce, optional
Dash of hot sauce	Lemon wedges

Preheat oven to 400°. Spray rimmed baking sheet with nonstick spray. With paper towels, pat crabmeat well to absorb moisture. Combine all ingredients, except breadcrumbs, salsa and lemon, mix well. Fold in breadcrumbs until well distributed. Shape into cakes. Place on prepared baking sheet. Bake 10 minutes or until brown. Serve with Mango Salsa, horseradish or tartar sauce. Garnish with lemon wedges.

Kosher imitation crab, shrimp or lobster meat is created from kosher fish, usually Alaskan pollack. The fish is boned, rinsed and mixed with seasonings and sugar.

PARSLEY MUSTARD BUTTER

Dairy/Pareve/Passover   *Yields 1 cup*

½ cup minced parsley
½ cup unsalted butter or
   pareve margarine,
   softened

1 tablespoon minced shallots
   or green onions
1 tablespoon Dijon or stone
   ground mustard

Combine all ingredients and blend well. Keep refrigerated.

LIME CHIVE BUTTER

Dairy/Pareve/Passover   *Yields ⅓ cup*

Juice of 1 lime
¼ cup plus 2 tablespoons
   unsalted butter or pareve
   margarine

1 tablespoon minced chives
1 teaspoon minced fresh dill
   or ½ teaspoon dried dill
   weed

Combine all ingredients and blend well. Keep refrigerated.

These butters are simple and lend great flavor to grilled or sautéed fish. Make them the night before or minutes before serving.

LEMON WINE BUTTER

Dairy/Pareve   *Yields 1 cup*

1 cup butter or pareve
   margarine
  Juice of ½ lemon
1 teaspoon chopped parsley

½ teaspoon Worcestershire
   sauce
1 ounce white wine
  Dash of white pepper

Stir all ingredients over low heat until blended. Keep warm until fish is ready to serve.

FROM THE *Farm*

MEAT & POULTRY

BEER-BASTED BRISKET

Serves 6 to 8

8   stalks celery
2   large onions, sliced
1   (4-5 pound) brisket,
       trimmed, first cut
    Salt and pepper

    Garlic powder
1   (12-ounce) bottle chili sauce
1   cup water, or more
12 ounces beer

Preheat oven to 325°. Spread celery and onions on bottom of pan just large enough to hold brisket. Season both sides of brisket with salt, pepper and garlic powder. Place brisket on top of vegetables, fat side up. Pour chili sauce over brisket. Fill chili bottle with water, cover and shake, pour around brisket. Place foil very lightly over meat. Bake 3 hours. Pour beer around brisket, cover tightly, bake additional 1½ hours. Cut against the grain before serving.

Beer, the secret ingredient!
Joy Seekers Club, Atlanta, Georgia, 1912.

*S*peaking of pans... Did you hear the story about the newlywed who asked her mother why her brisket recipe required the ends be removed before cooking? Mom replied, "Because that's the way my mother did it." When the bride called her grandmother with the question, Nana replied, "I never had a pot that was big enough for the whole brisket!"

NEVER-FAIL BRISKET

During World War II, soldiers from Fort Mac
always came to our house for Shabbat and holiday dinners.

Meat   *Serves 12*

1 (4-5 pound) brisket, trimmed, first cut	1 tablespoon Worcestershire sauce
¼ cup canola oil	1 (1-ounce) package dry onion soup mix
½ cup ketchup	1½ cups water
2 garlic cloves, crushed	5 pounds small red new potatoes, peeled around the center as decoration
2 tablespoons browning sauce, such as Kitchen Bouquet	

Preheat oven to 350°. Place brisket in roasting pan, fat side up. Whisk together oil, ketchup, garlic, browning sauce and Worcestershire sauce. Pour over meat. Sprinkle top with dry onion soup mix. Cover tightly, bake 30 minutes. Add water, baste and cover. Continue cooking 40 to 45 minutes per pound. One hour before meat is done, add red potatoes. Refrigerate brisket overnight. Remove fat, slice against the grain. Reheat covered, 45 minutes at 350°.

Atlanta WAC (Women's Army Corps) at
Fort McPherson, Atlanta, Georgia, c.1943.

YELLOW JACKET BRISKET

Georgia Tech fans are loyal to their team, the Yellow Jackets.
What better tribute to the team than this colorful dish.

Meat / Passover   *Serves 8 to 10*

1	(4-5 pound) brisket, trimmed, first cut	1	(8-ounce) can tomato sauce
	Yellow mustard	1	cup water
	Salt and pepper	3	carrots, peeled, chopped
½	teaspoon garlic powder	3	stalks celery, chopped
1	(12-ounce) jar peach preserves	1	large onion, chopped

Preheat oven to 400°. Rub both sides of brisket with mustard, place in roasting pan. Roast in oven 15 minutes per side. Reduce oven to 350°. Season brisket with salt, pepper and garlic powder. Spread with peach preserves. Combine tomato sauce and water. Pour over brisket. Place carrots, celery and onion around and over brisket. Cover, bake 3 hours or until tender.

For easy spreading, microwave preserves on full power 30 seconds.

Phi Epsilon Pi at Georgia Institute of Technology, Atlanta, Georgia, 1919.

The secret to easy slicing of cooked meats lies in resting the meat. Cover with aluminum foil, allow to rest 10 minutes for flank steak, 20 minutes for brisket, corned beef or pot roast. Also allow poultry to rest before carving, 10 minutes for Cornish hens, 20 minutes for whole chickens and duck, and 30 minutes for a whole turkey.

SPINACH-STUFFED BRISKET

This stuffed brisket is perfect for Passover or any special occasion.

STOCK

2¼ cups chicken stock	⅓ cup balsamic vinegar
¾ cup dry red wine	

SPINACH STUFFING

3 tablespoons olive oil	1 (10-ounce) package frozen chopped spinach, thawed, squeezed dry
2 cups chopped onions	
4 garlic cloves, finely chopped	2 matzahs, finely crumbled
1 tablespoon chopped fresh thyme	Salt and pepper
	1 large egg, lightly beaten

BRISKET

1 (4-5 pound) brisket, trimmed, first cut	3 celery stalks, sliced
Salt and pepper	5 garlic cloves
2 pounds onions, thinly sliced	1 tablespoon chopped fresh thyme
3 large carrots, peeled, cut into 1-inch pieces	1 bay leaf
	Salt and pepper

Simmer chicken stock over medium heat. Reduce to 1½ cups. Add wine and vinegar. Remove from heat, set aside. Heat olive oil in large skillet over medium heat. Sauté onions, garlic and thyme until onions soften, about 5 minutes. Remove from heat, cool 15 minutes. Stir in spinach and matzah. Season with salt and pepper. Stir in egg.

CONTINUED ON NEXT PAGE

Coca Cola®, a symbol of American culture available in almost every nation in the world, is served at the most strictly kosher events. On the market since 1886, Coca Cola® was certified kosher for daily use as well as Kosher for Passover in 1935, through the efforts of Rabbi Tobias Geffen, an Orthodox rabbi who served Atlanta's Congregation Shearith Israel from 1910 until his death in 1970 at the age of 99.

Seder in Eastman, Georgia, c.1946.

Preheat oven to 350°. Cut a deep pocket in 1 side of brisket, leaving ¾-inch border of meat uncut on remaining 3 sides. Fill pocket with stuffing. Skewer or sew pocket closed. Sprinkle salt and pepper over entire brisket. Arrange ½ the onions in bottom of large roasting pan. Place brisket on onions, fat side up. Top with remaining onions and pour ¼ cup chicken stock into pan.

Bake uncovered until meat and onions begin to brown, about 1 hour. Add carrots, celery, garlic, thyme and bay leaf. Pour remaining chicken stock over brisket, cover tightly. Reduce temperature to 300°, cook until tender, about 2½ hours. Remove from oven, uncover. Allow brisket to stand for 30 minutes. Remove fat from brisket. Thinly slice brisket against grain. Arrange meat and vegetables on platter. Skim fat from pan juices, adjust seasonings with salt and pepper. Serve with pan juices.

When preparing to serve for an occasion other than Passover, add 1 tablespoon of Worcestershire sauce with wine and vinegar to stock.

BRISKET WITH TZIMMES

Guests will make a tzimmes, a fuss, about this brisket.

Meat / Passover   *Serves 8 to 10*

2	pounds beef brisket, trimmed		¾	cup pitted prunes
			1	pound carrots, peeled, cut into 2-inch chunks
3	medium sweet potatoes, peeled, cut into 2-inch chunks		½	cup firmly packed brown sugar
3	medium white potatoes, peeled, cut into 2-inch chunks		3	tablespoons sugar
			1	tablespoon salt
1	large onion, thinly sliced		2	cups hot water

Preheat oven to 350°. Cut meat into portion size pieces. Arrange meat on the bottom of heavy roasting pan. Add potatoes, onion, prunes and carrots. Dissolve sugars and salt in water. Pour over meat and vegetables. Cover, bake 1½ hours or until meat is tender.

Tzimmes is a sweet casserole, usually including fruit, meat and vegetables. It is cooked very slowly. It's sweet flavor, makes it a wonderful dish for Rosh Hashanah and many other Jewish holidays.

Meat & Poultry

Rabbi's Savory Cholent

Rabbi Yossi New, a brilliant spiritual leader, is the founding rabbi of Congregation Beth Tefillah and introduced Chabad to Georgia, where there are now eight Chabad Centers.

Meat　　　　　　　　　　　　　　　　　　　　*Serves 10 to 12*

½	cup kidney beans		Paprika
½	cup baby lima beans	½	(1-ounce) package instant onion soup
½	cup pinto beans		
1	cup barley	¼	cup honey
1½	pounds flank steak, cut into cubes	2	onions, coarsely chopped
		¼	cup ketchup
5	potatoes, peeled, cut into cubes	2	onions, finely chopped
		1	roll pareve or meat kishka
	Salt and pepper		

In large pot, cover all beans with water, soak 1 hour, drain well. Place beans, barley, flank steak and potatoes in 7-quart crock pot. Sprinkle with salt, pepper and paprika. Add onion soup mix and honey. Cover generously with water, stir to mix flavors. Add coarsely chopped onions and ketchup, stir lightly. Sprinkle with finely chopped onions. Remove plastic wrap from kishka, wrap well in aluminum foil and place on top. Add more water if needed to cover kishka. Cook on lowest setting overnight.

To cut recipe in half, use ½ of all ingredients and prepare in 4-quart crock pot.

The secret to juicy cholent is lots of water. "On Friday afternoon, turn the crock pot on, pray a lot and your cholent will be delicious."

Mama made big pots of cholent. The children took it to the baker on Friday afternoon to cook in his oven. How the cholent came out depended on where he placed it in the oven. It was sometimes thick, sometimes soupy. The children went back to pick it up on Saturday afternoon.

MOUTHWATERING BEEF RIBS

My mama said it, so it must be true. "How one is raised, it sticks."
These tangy, slightly sticky ribs hit the spot.

Meat   *Serves 8 to 10*

¼	cup chopped onions	2	tablespoons firmly packed brown sugar
2	teaspoons vegetable oil	1	cup chili sauce
½	cup water	½	teaspoon salt
2	tablespoons white vinegar	¼	teaspoon paprika
1	tablespoon Worcestershire sauce	4-6	pounds beef ribs
¼	cup lemon juice		

Preheat oven to 450°. Sauté onions in oil in medium saucepan. Add water, white vinegar, Worcestershire sauce, lemon juice, brown sugar, chili sauce, salt and paprika. Simmer 20 minutes. Place ribs in roasting pan, cover tightly bake 15 minutes. Reduce heat to 350°. Remove cover, pour sauce over ribs. Bake 1 hour, basting frequently.

Grill ribs 7 to 10 minutes on each side, basting often with sauce.

MILLEDGEVILLE SHORT RIBS

This gourmet version of a southern classic combines the love
of barbeque with an insatiable sweet tooth. Serve with Speaking of
Cornbread (page 201) and a large pitcher of Mango Nectar Iced Tea (page 192).

Meat   *Serves 6 to 8*

4	pounds short ribs	1	cup beef bouillon
2-3	onions, sliced	¼	cup currant or strawberry jam
2	teaspoons salt	1	teaspoon tarragon vinegar
1	tablespoon Worcestershire sauce	1	(20-ounce) bottle ketchup
	Dash of hot sauce		

Preheat oven to 425°. Sear short ribs over high heat in ovenproof skillet until brown. Remove ribs from skillet. Cover bottom of skillet with onions, top with ribs. Whisk remaining ingredients in mixing bowl. Pour over ribs, cover tightly. Bake until browned and very tender, 2 to 3 hours.

Searing meat is done in a hot skillet. Cook over high or medium high heat, turning to brown on all sides. This technique quickly browns meat capturing juices to be released during a slow cooking process.

"Have It Your Way" London Broil

Three marinades give this steak a new taste each time it is served.

Marinade 1

½   cup dark corn syrup
¼   cup soy sauce
2   tablespoons vinegar
2   tablespoons grated fresh ginger
2   garlic cloves, minced
3   green onions, finely chopped

Marinade 2

1   cup ketchup
1½   cups water
1   garlic clove, minced
2   tablespoons mustard
2   tablespoons Worcestershire sauce
3   tablespoons vegetable oil
1   teaspoon seasoned salt
¼   teaspoon pepper
1   teaspoon onion powder

Marinade 3

3   garlic cloves, finely minced
½   teaspoon dried thyme
½   teaspoon cayenne pepper
¼   cup soy sauce
2   tablespoons Worcestershire sauce
1   tablespoon vegetable oil
3   tablespoons lime juice
1   teaspoon salt
½   teaspoon pepper

Steak

1   (3-pound) London broil or flank steak

Whisk chosen marinade ingredients in medium bowl. Place meat in sealed plastic bag with marinade. Refrigerate several hours or overnight. Turn meat twice. Grill or broil in oven 7 minutes per side or until desired doneness, basting frequently with sauce. To serve, cut thin slices of meat on the diagonal against the grain.

To marinate meat or fish, place item and marinade in a sealable plastic bag. Seal, refrigerate and turn occasionally. Best of all, no clean up.

BARBECUED FLANK STEAK

My daddy used to cut flank steak or London broil by placing meat on a
cutting board, with an inverted saucer under the meat. He sliced it against the grain.

Meat **Serves 8 to 10**

1	cup ketchup	3	tablespoons vegetable oil
1½	cups water	1	teaspoon seasoned salt
1	garlic clove, minced	¼	teaspoon pepper
2	tablespoons prepared yellow mustard	1	teaspoon onion powder
2	tablespoons Worcestershire sauce	2	(3-pound) flank steaks

In medium bowl, whisk all ingredients, except steaks. Pour over meat, cover, marinate several hours or overnight. Grill steaks, basting frequently with marinade. Slice thinly on the diagonal against the grain.

The smoky, spicy and often sweet sauces in barbeque do not usually pair well with wine, hence the recommendation of cold beer or freshly brewed iced tea. If choosing a wine with barbeque, select a simple, fruity Zinfandel, a Petit Syrah or Beaujolais.

Congregation Shearith Israel picnic, Atlanta, Georgia, c.1950.

MACADAMIA STEAK WITH FRUIT SALSA

Before moving to Atlanta, Chef Boucher reigned at the
Hyatt Regency in Kauai. He is well-known for his Hawaiian flair.

Meat   *Serves 2*

STEAK

1	(12-ounce) boneless rib eye steak

Salt and pepper
Olive oil

MACADAMIA NUT CRUST

½ cup finely chopped macadamia nuts

2 tablespoons chopped parsley

1 cup panko, Japanese breadcrumbs

3 tablespoons pareve margarine, melted

1 tablespoon Dijon mustard

2 tablespoons white wine

TROPICAL FRUIT SALSA

½ cup diced fresh mango

½ cup diced fresh pineapple

1 teaspoon grated fresh ginger

2 tablespoons sugar

½ tablespoon finely chopped mint

½ cup diced fresh papaya

1 tablespoon lime juice

Hawaiian performance by the women of
The Progressive Club,
Atlanta, Georgia, 1960.

Preheat oven to 325°. Season steak with salt and pepper. In large sauté pan, heat olive oil almost to smoking point. Sear meat on both sides, 1 to 2 minutes, until golden brown. Remove from pan, set aside 4 to 5 minutes.

Combine nut crust ingredients in medium bowl. Gently pat crust on meat. Bake in oven until desired doneness is achieved, about 30 minutes for medium.

CONTINUED ON NEXT PAGE

In saucepan bring mango, pineapple, ginger and sugar to a slow simmer for 3 to 4 minutes. Add mint and papaya. Remove from heat, stir in lime juice. Set aside, keep warm. To serve, slice meat, arrange on serving platter and top with Tropical Fruit Salsa.

David Boucher, Executive Chef, and Rafael Camarillo, Executive Sous Chef,
Hyatt Regency, Atlanta, Georgia

HOLIDAY STUFFED VEAL BREAST

L'Dor v'Dor... from generation to generation, passed down from my
mother to me, to my son and to my grandson. This recipe is a specialty of the house.

Meat / Passover   *Serves 8 to 10*

POTATO KUGEL STUFFING

5	pounds russet or Idaho potatoes, peeled	10	ounces schmaltz, chicken fat, melted, divided
1½	pounds onions, grated		Kosher salt and pepper
4-5	large eggs, beaten		Matzah meal

VEAL

1	whole breast of veal, with pocket cut	3	cups finely chopped onions
3	cups finely chopped celery	3-4	garlic cloves, finely chopped
			Salt and pepper

Preheat oven to 350°. Finely grate potatoes into large bowl. Drain thoroughly, reserving liquid. When starch settles, carefully pour off water and reserve starch. Stir potato starch and onions into potatoes. Beat in eggs and 8 ounces chicken fat. Season with salt and pepper. Stir in enough matzah meal to thicken mixture. Fill veal breast pocket with potato mixture. Secure opening with skewers.

In large shallow roasting pan, make bed of celery, onions and garlic. Place veal breast, bone side down, on top of vegetables. Rub top with remaining chicken fat. Season generously with salt and pepper. Cover tightly. Roast 3 hours. Uncover, continue roasting 1½ hours, allowing veal to brown. Baste 2 to 3 times, adding boiling water as needed. Let meat rest 15 to 30 minutes. Slice against the grain.

When preparing a smaller portion, purchase ½ veal breast, buying the leaner,
pointed end. Divide all other ingredients in half.

In 1788, Mordechai Sheftall, a second-generation Savannah Jew, devised his own methods for keeping kosher in a place where there were neither rabbis nor kosher food. He carried a butchering knife with him on his business travels so that he might slaughter livestock according to the laws of kashruth.

VALDOSTA VEAL CUTLETS

A lightly dressed pasta and Brussels Sprouts with
Pecans (page 147) will turn this classic dish into an elegant dinner.

Meat   *Serves 4*

1	pound boneless veal cutlets, ¼-inch thick	½	cup dry vermouth, marsala or white wine
¼	cup flour	½	teaspoon salt
4	tablespoons pareve margarine	2	tablespoons water
			Pepper
12	cherry tomatoes	1	tablespoon chopped parsley
½	pound mushrooms, sliced	4	parsley sprigs

Pound veal to ⅛-inch thickness. Cut veal into 3x2-inch pieces. Coat each piece lightly with flour. In 10-inch pan melt margarine over medium heat, gently sauté cherry tomatoes, remove. Quickly sauté veal in same skillet with remaining margarine, a few pieces at a time, until lightly browned on both sides. Add more margarine if necessary. Remove veal from pan. Add mushrooms, wine, salt, water and pepper to same skillet, bring to a boil. Reduce heat to low, cover, simmer until mushrooms are tender. Return veal to skillet to warm. Stir in chopped parsley. Arrange meat on platter with cherry tomatoes. Garnish with parsley sprigs.

Deglazing produces either a sauce or a base for soup or sauce. After browning meat, poultry or fish, remove item from pan and set aside. Discard excess fat from pan. Over a low to medium heat, add wine or stock a little at a time, stirring and scraping the bottom to loosen the flavorful browned bits. Before serving as a sauce, adjust seasonings and add pareve margarine.

ORANGE-GLAZED LAMB CHOPS

Delicious with Waycross Corn (page 149) and Pomegranate Pilaf (page 166).

LAMB CHOPS

2	garlic cloves, minced	2	teaspoons salt
1	tablespoon paprika	½	teaspoon pepper
1	tablespoon ground rosemary	8	lamb chops

ORANGE BASTING SAUCE

¼	cup pareve margarine	¼	cup dry red wine
1	(6-ounce) can frozen orange juice concentrate, thawed		

GARNISH

Mint jelly, optional

Combine garlic, paprika, rosemary, salt and pepper. Rub on chops. Combine sauce ingredients in small saucepan. Heat and stir until well blended. Lamb chops may be grilled, broiled or baked in preheated 350° oven. Baste several times with sauce. Serve with mint jelly, if desired.

Dining at The Standard Club, Atlanta, Georgia, c.1919.

Hazelnut Cherry Rack of Lamb

The hazelnut crust and cherries elevate this dish to gourmet status.

Lamb

2   (8-rib) lamb racks
3-4 tablespoons Dijon mustard
⅓   cup breadcrumbs
⅓   cup finely chopped
      hazelnuts

¼   cup finely chopped fresh
      parsley
1   teaspoon chopped fresh
      thyme
½   teaspoon pepper
¼   teaspoon salt

Cherry Wine Sauce

⅔   cup dry red wine
⅓   cup beef stock
3   tablespoons honey
½   teaspoon thyme
¼   teaspoon salt
¼   teaspoon dry mustard

2   teaspoons cornstarch
2   tablespoons balsamic
      vinegar
1   (16½-ounce) can pitted dark
      cherries, drained

Preheat oven to 400°. Place lamb racks in large roasting pan, fat side up. Spread mustard over lamb. Combine breadcrumbs, hazelnuts, parsley, thyme, pepper and salt. Press into lamb. Place in oven, roast 10 minutes. Cover exposed bones with foil to prevent browning. Reduce heat to 375°. Roast 30 minutes or until meat thermometer reaches 150° for medium rare. Allow lamb to rest 15 minutes before carving.

For sauce, combine first 6 ingredients in saucepan, boil 5 minutes. Blend cornstarch and vinegar. Stir into sauce. Boil 1 minute, stir in cherries. Serve warm over lamb chops.

Lamb Chops with Shallot Wine Sauce

Simple and scrumptious.

Serves 2

Lamb Chops

½ cup red currant jelly   1   rack of lamb, French cut
½ cup Dijon mustard

Shallot Wine Sauce

½ cup minced shallots   2   tablespoons crushed fresh
½ cup pareve margarine   rosemary
1 cup dry white wine

Combine jelly and mustard in small saucepan. Simmer 5 minutes, stirring to melt jelly. Allow to cool completely. Separate lamb chops from rack, leaving eye fat intact. Place lamb chops in sealable plastic bag, cover with sauce, seal tightly and marinate overnight in refrigerator. For medium rare, grill chops over hickory coals for 2 to 2½ minutes per side, basting with sauce. If using a gas grill, cook on medium high heat 2 minutes per side for medium rare.

Sauté shallots in margarine. Stir in white wine and rosemary. Simmer until sauce is slightly reduced, 5 to 10 minutes. Serve with the lamb.

A grilling tip from professional chefs — remove meats from refrigerator 30 to 60 minutes prior to grilling for even cooking.

Rosemary Grilled Lamb Chops

Meat   *Serves 4*

¼ cup Dijon mustard   1   tablespoon firmly packed
½ cup soy sauce   brown sugar
4 garlic cloves, minced   1   teaspoon honey
¼ cup chopped fresh rosemary   8   lamb chops

In medium bowl, whisk mustard, soy sauce, garlic, rosemary, brown sugar and honey. Place lamb chops in a large baking dish. Cover with sauce, turning to coat. Cover, refrigerate overnight. Before grilling, allow lamb to reach room temperature. Preheat grill to medium heat. Grill chops about 7 minutes on each side for medium, adjusting time for desired doneness.

SWEET AND SOUR STUFFED CABBAGE

This is an updated version of a classic Eastern European dish.

Meat   *Yields 10 to 12 rolls*

1	large cabbage, cored		Dash hot sauce
1	pound ground chuck	1	(16-ounce) can sauerkraut, drained
1	large egg, beaten		
	Salt and pepper	1	(14-ounce) bottle ketchup
1	(16-ounce) can tomatoes, diced, with liquid, divided	¼	cup vinegar
		¼	cup sugar

Preheat oven to 350°. Bring large pot of water to boil. Boil cabbage 5 minutes or until soft. Drain well. Separate leaves. Mix ground chuck, egg, salt, pepper, 3 tablespoons tomatoes and dash of hot sauce. Place cabbage leaves rib side down. Fill wide end of each leaf with heaping tablespoon of meat mixture. Fold cabbage envelope style, encasing beef mixture. Roll tightly, secure with wooden toothpicks. In large shallow roasting pan, make bed of remaining tomatoes and sauerkraut. Place cabbage rolls in roasting pan, seam side down. Whisk together ketchup, vinegar and sugar. Pour over stuffed cabbage rolls. Cover, bake 2½ to 3 hours, basting occasionally with sauce.

This dish freezes well and can be reheated in a microwave oven.

Instead of boiling, freeze a head of cabbage overnight. When thawed, the leaves will be soft and ready to roll.

Unstuffed Cabbage

All the taste of Stuffed Cabbage with less work in much less time.

Meat   *Serves 3 to 4*

Meatballs

1	pound ground beef	1	tablespoon soy sauce
¼	cup uncooked rice	2	tablespoons grated onion
1	tablespoon Worcestershire sauce		Salt and pepper

Sauce

¼	cup grated onion	2	tablespoons lemon juice
2	tablespoons vegetable oil	4	pareve crumbled gingersnaps
1	(15-ounce) can tomato sauce	¼	cup firmly packed brown sugar
1	cup canned petite diced tomatoes, with liquid		Salt and pepper

Cabbage

½   small head of cabbage, chopped

Combine meatball ingredients, form into small or medium meatballs. Preheat oven to 350°. Sauté onion in oil, stir in remaining sauce ingredients. Layer ⅓ of cabbage in bottom of 2-quart greased casserole. Top with layer of meatballs followed by ⅓ of the sauce. Repeat layers ending with sauce. Cover, bake 1 hour. Remove cover, bake an additional 30 minutes.

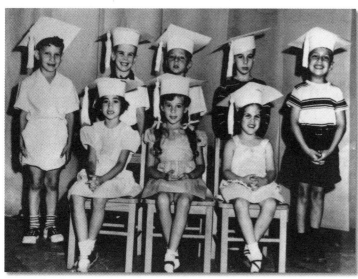

No need to be a genius to prepare this cabbage recipe. Congregation Children of Israel kindergarten graduation, Augusta, Georgia, c.1950s.

Macon Meatballs

Bring out the chafing dish for a party or serve meatballs over noodles for a casual supper.

Meat　　　　　　　　　　　　　　　　　　　　　*Serves 4 to 6*

Meatballs

2	slices pareve bread		Salt and pepper
1	pound ground beef		

Sauce

½	cup chili sauce	1	(16-ounce) can sauerkraut, optional
½	cup ketchup		
1	tablespoon fresh lemon juice	1	(16-ounce) can whole berry cranberry sauce, optional
¼	cup firmly packed dark brown sugar		

Preheat oven to 350°. Soak bread in water, squeeze out excess liquid. Season meat with salt and pepper, combine with bread. Form into 1½ to 2-inch meatballs. Place in roasting pan, bake uncovered 20 minutes. Remove meatballs, place in serving casserole.

Mix sauce ingredients, pour over meatballs. Cover, bake 30 minutes. Remove cover, bake another 10 minutes.

Sweet 'n Spicy Corned Beef

This innovative twist on a traditional dish will delight your palate.

Meat　　　　　　　　　　　　　　　　　　　　　*Serves 8 to 10*

Corned Beef

1	(3-4 pound) corned beef brisket	2	stalks celery, diced
		2	garlic cloves, minced
1	onion, diced	1	bay leaf

Sauce

½	cup firmly packed brown sugar	1	teaspoon Dijon mustard
		1	teaspoon white horseradish
3	tablespoons orange juice	1	teaspoon soy sauce
2	teaspoons red wine vinegar		

In large heavy pot, cover corned beef with water. Add onion, celery, garlic and bay leaf. Partially cover pot, simmer 2½ to 3 hours. Drain, reserving ¼ of stock. Place corned beef in roasting pan. Preheat oven to 325°. In medium saucepan, combine sauce ingredients with reserved stock. Bring to boil, pour over corned beef. Bake 15 minutes. Remove, slice against the grain. Serve with sauce.

Sweet and Sour Tongue

Tongue

1 (3-pound) fresh, pickled or smoked tongue

Sauce

1	(12-ounce) can apricot juice	4	tablespoons vinegar
12	pareve crumbled gingersnaps	½	cup sugar
		½	cup white raisins

Don't open a shop unless you know how to smile.

~Yiddish proverb

In large pot, boil tongue, covered, 3 to 3½ hours. Drain, peel, cool and thinly slice. Lay out slices in large pot or roasting pan. In a saucepan, combine sauce ingredients, adjusting vinegar and sugar, as desired, simmer 15 minutes, stirring constantly. Pour over tongue, simmer 15 minutes.

Corned beef, pastrami or tongue, all are treats when served at the local deli or prepared at home.
Snack 'N Shop Delicatessen, Atlanta, Georgia, 1951.

SOUTHERN FRIED CHICKEN

A southern cookbook would not be complete without
a recipe for fried chicken. Here is the best recipe in Atlanta.

Meat   *Yields 20 pieces*

1	cup pareve buttermilk substitute		Salt
20	plump chicken pieces, combination of breasts, thighs, legs and wings	2	cups flour
			Vegetable oil

Whisk pareve buttermilk substitute mixture, let stand 6 minutes. Pour mixture over chicken in sealable plastic bag, seal tightly. Refrigerate 3 hours or overnight. Remove each piece of chicken, drain and season with salt. Dip marinated chicken into flour, coating each piece lightly. Shake off excess.

Fill deep skillet with enough vegetable oil to nearly cover chicken. Heat oil to 375° or until drops of water sizzle when dropped carefully into oil. Using tongs, place chicken in hot oil. Pan fry until golden brown, turning once. Drain before serving.

Buttermilk Substitute

1 tablespoon apple cider vinegar or lemon juice

Pareve rice or soy milk

Combine vinegar or juice with enough milk to equal 1 cup. Allow to stand 4 to 6 minutes before adding to a recipe.

When frying, heating oil to the exact temperature is critical to ensure proper cooking. Thus, a frying thermometer is an excellent tool in the kitchen.

Lots of oil is required for the best Southern Fried Chicken.
Chanukah performance at Ahavath Achim Congregation,
Atlanta, Georgia, 1950.

HONEYED APPLE CHICKEN

The scent of cinnamon adds fall holiday flair to this flavorful chicken dish.

Meat   *Serves 2 to 4*

3	Granny Smith apples, peeled, cored, cut into wedges	1	pound skinless, boneless, chicken breasts or tenders
2	tablespoons vegetable oil	2	tablespoons olive oil
2	tablespoons honey	1	cup chicken stock
¼	cup flour	1	cup apple juice
	Dash of salt and pepper	1	cup cranberry juice
		1	cinnamon stick

In large skillet, sauté apple slices in heated vegetable oil 2 minutes on medium high heat. Drizzle with honey. Sauté apples until tender. Transfer apples to bowl, set aside. Combine flour, salt and pepper. Coat chicken with flour mixture. Heat olive oil in same skillet. Add floured chicken in small batches, sauté until lightly browned on all sides, adding more olive oil if necessary. Set browned chicken aside. Combine chicken stock and juices in medium bowl. Whisk in remaining flour from chicken coating. Pour stock mixture into hot skillet, stirring continuously to prevent lumps. Add cinnamon stick, bring to boil. Stir until it begins to thicken. Add chicken and apples. Stir, simmering 10 minutes for tenders or 20 minutes for breasts. Sauce should be thick and chicken cooked through.

"We used to pick our Shabbos chicken from the cages sitting on the street in front of the kosher butcher shop."

GRILLED CHICKEN WITH FRUIT SALSA

CHICKEN MARINADE

¾ cup dry white wine	1 teaspoon dried basil or 1 tablespoon minced fresh basil
¼ cup orange juice	Salt
2 tablespoons lemon juice	4 boneless chicken breasts
1 tablespoon vegetable oil	
Pepper	

PEACH OR MANGO SALSA

3 peaches or 1 large mango, peeled, diced	1 tablespoon minced fresh cilantro
3 tablespoons minced onion	1 tablespoon vegetable oil
1½ tablespoons white wine vinegar	

CRANBERRY PEAR SALSA

12 ounces fresh cranberries	1 tablespoon minced orange zest
1½ cups coarsely chopped pears	1 tablespoon canola oil
¼ cup honey	Pinch of salt
½ cup sugar	
1 Serrano chili, stemmed, seeded and minced, optional	

Combine marinade ingredients and chicken in large sealable freezer bag. Seal, turn to coat. Refrigerate 4 hours or overnight. Remove chicken from marinade. Grill over indirect heat 5 minutes on each side or until cooked through. Transfer chicken to serving plates. Top chicken with salsa of choice or serve with all three on the side.

To prepare Peach Salsa or Mango Salsa, combine recipe ingredients, cover and refrigerate 2 hours or more.

To prepare Cranberry Pear Salsa, pulse cranberries in food processor until coarse. Combine all ingredients, cover and refrigerate 2 hours or more.

Indirect grilling is used to cook larger cuts of meats, whole chickens and turkeys. For charcoal grills, place the coals around the edges of the grate, putting a drip pan in the center. Place the food to be grilled over the drip pan. When using a gas grill, turn the center burner off. With any type grill, the lid should be down, raised only when basting or turning food.

WHOLE ROASTED LEMON CHICKEN WITH VEGETABLES

The talented Annette Marcus has catered innumerable Atlanta simchas with her marvelous kosher food. Now try her famous Lemon Chicken at home.

Meat / Passover   *Serves 6 to 8*

2	(3-pound) chicken fryers	2	medium onions, sliced ⅓-inch thick
2	large lemons	4	stalks celery, sliced ¾-inch thick
1	teaspoon salt		
1	teaspoon pepper	4	carrots, peeled, sliced ¾-inch thick
1	tablespoon oregano		
4	garlic cloves, minced	½	cup lemon juice
½	cup olive oil, divided	½	cup chicken stock

Preheat oven to 550°. Clean chickens and discard fat. Pat dry inside and out. Pierce lemons all over with fork. Place 1 whole lemon in the cavity of each chicken. In small bowl, blend salt, pepper, oregano, garlic and ¼ cup olive oil into paste. Rub paste over both chickens. Distribute onions, celery and carrots in bottom of large roasting pan. Place chickens, breast side up, on top of vegetables. Stir together lemon juice, chicken stock and remaining ¼ cup olive oil. Pour over chickens. Bake uncovered 20 minutes. Turn chickens over to breast side down, roast 20 minutes, basting vegetables twice. Reduce heat to 450°, return chickens to breast side up. Roast 20 minutes, basting twice. Remove pan from oven, place chickens on cutting board, let rest 10 minutes. Remove lemons from cavities. Cut chickens into quarters. Arrange chicken and vegetables on serving platter. Cut lemons in half, put in cheesecloth and squeeze juice over all.

Annette Marcus Catering, Atlanta, Georgia

Red wines including Cabernet Sauvignon, Merlot, Pinot Noir, Beaujolais and fruity Zinfandel match well with roast chicken, as do whites such as Chardonnay, Pinot Blanc and Riesling. With other chicken dishes, consider the sauces and preparation. Light sautés or sauces may pair best with whites, while tomato-based sauces and entrées might match best with dry reds.

BEER CAN CHICKEN

Chicken with a sense of humor.

Serves 2 to 4

1	(4-pound) whole chicken	1	teaspoon pepper
2	tablespoons vegetable oil	3	tablespoons Wonderful Rub
2	tablespoons salt	1	(12-ounce) can beer

Discard neck and giblets from chicken. Rinse chicken inside and out, pat dry. Brush chicken lightly with oil. Rub inside and out with salt, pepper and rub. Open beer can, drink or discard 6 ounces. Place beer can on solid surface. Holding a chicken leg in each hand, fit bird cavity over beer can. Transfer to center grate of grill and balance bird on beer can and legs, like a tripod. Grill over medium high, indirect heat with lid down. Grill 1¼ hours or until internal temperature registers 165° in breast area and 180° in thigh or until thigh juice runs clear when pierced with sharp knife. Remove from grill, allow chicken to rest 15 minutes. Remove can, carve chicken.

A Wonderful Rub

¼ cup pepper

3 tablespoons firmly packed brown sugar

2 tablespoons paprika

2 tablespoons cumin

2 tablespoons kosher salt

Combine all ingredients.

HERB-GRILLED CHICKEN BREASTS

A tangy combination of vinegar, lemon and lime assures a memorable dinner.

Meat / Passover   *Serves 4 to 6*

3	garlic cloves, crushed		Juice of ½ large lemon
1½	teaspoons salt		Juice of ½ large lime
½	cup firmly packed brown sugar	⅓	cup vegetable oil
			Pepper
3	tablespoons whole grain mustard	6	boneless chicken breasts
¼	cup cider vinegar		Minced fresh herbs and lemon or lime slices

Combine garlic, salt, sugar, mustard, cider vinegar, lemon and lime juices.

Whisk in oil and pepper. Put chicken in sealed plastic bag with marinade. Refrigerate overnight. Turn several times while refrigerated. Remove from refrigerator, bring to room temperature. Remove chicken from marinade, pat dry. Preheat grill to medium heat. Grill chicken 4 minutes on each side or until done. Garnish with minced herbs and lemon or lime slices.

DIJON CHICKEN KABOBS

Supper on a stick is fun for kids of all ages.

Meat   *Serves 4 to 6*

2   whole skinless, boneless, chicken breasts
2   large garlic cloves, minced
2   tablespoons Dijon mustard
2   tablespoons soy sauce
2   tablespoons honey
    Salt and pepper
    Fresh or dried herbs

¼   cup white wine vinegar
⅓   cup olive oil
3   bell peppers, any color, seeded, cut into 2-inch squares
½   pound whole mushrooms, cleaned
    Wooden skewers, 6 inches

Cut chicken into 1½-inch cubes, set aside. Whisk together garlic, mustard, soy sauce, honey, salt, pepper, herbs, vinegar and olive oil. Marinate chicken in ½ the marinade, peppers and mushrooms in the other ½ at room temperature 1 hour, or up to 4 hours in refrigerator. Soak skewers in water for 30 minutes. Remove chicken and vegetables from marinade. Thread chicken, pepper squares and mushrooms onto skewers. Place skewers in single layer on baking sheet. Broil or grill until chicken is lightly browned, turning until cooked on all sides.

Basil, oregano, rosemary and many other herbs work well with this recipe.

Clean mushrooms, when ready to use to avoid browning. Trim tough stems with a knife. Use a soft vegetable brush, damp cloth or knife to clean the tops. Use water sparingly to avoid sogginess. Dry carefully before using in a recipe.

Dijon Chicken Kabobs, great for tailgating!
Temple Israel Sunday school picnic,
Valdosta, Georgia, c.1957.

CHICKEN WITH SPANISH RICE

1	(4-pound) frying chicken, cut up	1	(12-ounce) can vegetable juice
1¼	teaspoons salt	¾	cup water
½	teaspoon pepper	1	cup sliced mushrooms
½	teaspoon paprika	½	teaspoon dried marjoram
¼	cup olive oil	⅓	cup halved, pitted black or green olives
1	garlic clove, minced		
1	medium onion, chopped	1	(10-ounce) package frozen artichoke hearts, thawed
1	cup uncooked long grain rice	1	tomato, cut in wedges
		1	(4-ounce) jar sliced pimientos

Preheat oven to 375°. Season chicken with salt, pepper and paprika. In large skillet, brown chicken slowly in olive oil. Remove chicken from pan. In same skillet, sauté garlic and onion. Add rice, stirring to brown slowly. Stir in vegetable juice, water, mushrooms, marjoram and olives. Spoon mixture into 3-quart casserole or 13x9-inch dish, top with chicken pieces. Cover dish tightly, bake 1 hour. Uncover, place artichokes, tomato wedges and pimientos on top. Cover, bake an additional 20 to 25 minutes.

Prepare this recipe, kick up your heels and flamenco!
Spanish ball night at The Standard Club, Atlanta, Georgia, 1925.

ZESTY MEDITERRANEAN CHICKEN

The orange marmalade and ginger form a glaze over the chicken.
The apricots and figs add fruity flavors to the juices.

Meat / Passover   *Serves 6 to 8*

2	(2½-pound) chickens, cut into eighths	½	cup orange juice
1½	cups orange marmalade	¼	cup red wine vinegar
	Salt and pepper	¼	cup firmly packed brown sugar
2	large garlic cloves, finely minced	1	cup pitted black olives
½	teaspoon dried thyme	1½	cups dried apricots
1	teaspoon ground cumin	1	cup small dried figs
1	teaspoon ground ginger	1	cup large pecan pieces
			Grated zest of 1 orange

Preheat oven to 375°. Remove excess fat from chicken. Rinse and pat dry. Place chicken skin side up in shallow roasting pan. Spread marmalade over chicken. Season with salt, pepper, garlic, thyme, cumin and ginger. Pour orange juice and vinegar into pan. Bake 20 minutes uncovered. Remove from oven. In bowl, sprinkle sugar over olives, apricots and figs. Pour over chicken. Bake an additional 35 to 40 minutes until chicken is golden brown and juices run clear when leg meat is pierced with knife. With fork and slotted spoon, transfer chicken, olives and dried fruit to large serving platter. Skim fat from pan juices. Drizzle chicken with some spoonfuls of pan juices. Garnish with pecans and orange zest. Serve remaining pan juices in gravy boat.

Zest refers to the colored part of an orange, lemon or lime. Avoid the white under layer, the pith, which is quite bitter.

CHICKEN BLINTZES
WITH HOT CRANBERRY SAUCE

*It is easy to master these simple crêpes and to
turn leftover chicken or turkey into a delicious new meal.*

Meat / Passover   *Serves 4 to 8*

BLINTZ BATTER

3   large eggs
¼   cup water
½   teaspoon salt

1   (10.5-ounce) can condensed clear chicken broth
⅔   cup Passover cake meal

BLINTZ FILLING

2½ cups diced cooked chicken
2   large eggs, beaten
1   medium onion, diced

1   tablespoon chicken fat or pareve margarine
½   teaspoon salt
    Dash of pepper

CRANBERRY SAUCE

1   (16-ounce) can jellied cranberry sauce
2   tablespoons water

Chicken fat or pareve margarine

Combine eggs, water, salt and chicken broth. Gradually add Passover cake meal, stirring constantly to prevent lumps. Pour 3 tablespoons batter in hot, lightly greased nonstick skillet or crêpe pan. Rotate until batter fills the bottom to form 6-inch circle. Fry over moderate heat until edges pull away from pan. Flip crêpe onto clean cloth, with cooked side up. Repeat until all batter is used.

Combine filling ingredients in bowl. In small saucepan, break up cranberry sauce with fork and add water. Stir over low heat until well blended.

Assemble blintzes by placing 1 heaping tablespoon filling in center of each crêpe. Fold in side edges and roll tightly. Fry until golden in small amount chicken fat or pareve margarine. Serve with hot Cranberry Sauce.

CRISPY DUCK A L'ORANGE

Simple, yet elegant. Serve with a green salad, Colorful Roasted Veggies (page 161), Barley Almond Casserole (page 163) and a nice Pinot Noir.

Meat   *Serves 2 to 4*

DUCK

1	(4-pound) duck	½	cup frozen orange juice
1	teaspoon salt		concentrate, thawed
½	teaspoon pepper		Slices of orange

ORANGE CURRANT SAUCE

1	(10-ounce) jar red currant jelly	1	tablespoon white vinegar
1	cup canned brown gravy	1	tablespoon fresh lemon juice
½	cup frozen orange juice concentrate, thawed	2	tablespoons orange liqueur
½	cup chicken stock	1	orange
		1	cup water

Preheat oven to 325°. Season duck with salt and pepper. Pierce skin in several places. Place duck breast side up on rack in a roasting pan. Roast 2 hours, basting with orange juice 3 to 4 times. Remove fat from pan drippings, reserve for sauce. Cut duck in half or quarters. Arrange on serving platter. Garnish with twisted orange slices.

In saucepan, melt jelly over medium heat, stirring often. Add drippings, gravy, orange juice, chicken stock, vinegar, lemon juice and liqueur. Bring to boil. Reduce heat to low and simmer 10 minutes, stirring occasionally. Remove zest from orange in ribbons, avoiding white membrane. Cut orange zest into thin strips. In small saucepan, bring zest and water to boil. Reduce heat to low, simmer 3 minutes. Drain well. Stir orange zest into sauce. Serve sauce with duck.

Oranges, a special treat for the children of the Hebrew Orphans' Home, Atlanta, Georgia, c.1890.

For the past several years, a team of Atlanta's rabbis have expended much elbow grease in all night sessions to make grills and ovens kosher in several snack bars at Turner Field, home of the Atlanta Braves. They make these preparations for Kosher Day at the ballpark, a benefit for the local Jewish day schools.

GRILLED DUCK BREAST

Marinated duck lends itself particularly well to grilling. The smoky fragrance that permeates the duck enhances its flavor. This is a nice alternative to chicken.

Meat / Passover   *Serves 2 to 4*

4   (4-ounce) skinless, boneless duck breasts

MARINADE

¼   cup olive oil

2   tablespoons balsamic
     vinegar

2   tablespoons honey

1   tablespoon freshly cracked
     peppercorns
    Salt

Trim excess fat and membrane from duck breasts. Whisk together marinade ingredients in small bowl. Cover all sides of duck with marinade, place in 3-quart glass baking dish. Cover and refrigerate overnight. Spray grill with nonstick spray before heating. Preheat grill. Grill 4 to 5 minutes on each side, depending on thickness of duck breast. Slice thinly against the grain.

THE *Good Earth's* GIFTS

Vegetables & Side Dishes

Springtime Asparagus Parmesan

Dairy   *Serves 4*

1   pound fresh asparagus
1   tablespoon olive oil

2   ounces shredded Parmesan
    cheese

Preheat oven to 400°. Snap off tough ends from asparagus, discard. Arrange spears in 13x9-inch baking dish. Drizzle with olive oil, toss to coat. Bake 12 to 15 minutes or until tender. Remove from oven, top with cheese. Return to oven, bake until cheese melts, about 5 minutes.

Both thin and fat asparagus spears are tender; proper trimming is the key. Gently bend a spear until it breaks. The natural breaking point will separate the spear from the tough end.

Cool Sesame Asparagus

A sweet and saucy taste of the Far East.

Pareve   *Serves 4*

1   pound fresh asparagus
1   tablespoon unhulled sesame
    seeds
1   tablespoon white vinegar

1   tablespoon seasoned rice
    vinegar
1   tablespoon soy sauce
1   tablespoon honey
1   teaspoon sesame oil

Snap off tough ends of asparagus, discard. Blanch spears and pat dry. Toast sesame seeds in a nonstick skillet over medium heat, 2 to 3 minutes, stirring constantly. Whisk vinegars, soy sauce, honey and sesame oil in bowl. Add asparagus, toss to coat. Refrigerate 3 hours, tossing occasionally.

To blanch vegetables, cook in boiling water just until tender and vibrant green, then plunge into a bowl of ice water to halt cooking. Drain cooled vegetables on paper towels. Refrigerate in airtight container.

Broccoli Gratin
with Mustard Streusel

Dairy   *Serves 8 to 10*

Mustard Streusel

4	tablespoons butter	2½	cups homemade breadcrumbs
⅓	cup minced onion		Salt and pepper
2	garlic cloves, minced	1	cup grated Parmesan cheese, divided
½	teaspoon dry mustard		
4	tablespoons Dijon mustard, divided		

Broccoli

3	pounds broccoli florets	½	cup whipping cream

For streusel, melt butter in large skillet over medium heat. Sauté onion and garlic 4 minutes. Stir in dry mustard, 2 tablespoons Dijon mustard and breadcrumbs. Sauté until crisp and golden, about 8 minutes. Season with salt and pepper. When cool mix in ¾ cup Parmesan cheese. In boiling water, cook broccoli about 3 minutes until crisp tender. Drain well, cool on paper towels.

Preheat oven to 350°. Butter 13x9-inch baking dish. In large bowl, whisk whipping cream, remaining 2 tablespoons mustard and ¼ cup cheese. Add broccoli, toss to coat evenly. Arrange broccoli in prepared dish. Sprinkle with streusel. Bake 30 minutes.

Save all types of leftover bagels, rolls, crackers and sandwich bread. Give them a whirl in a food processor and store in small bags in the freezer. Use the crumbs to make stuffing or casserole toppings.

BRUSSELS SPROUTS WITH PECANS

Georgia pecans make these Brussels sprouts the perfect side dish.

Dairy/Meat/Pareve/Passover   *Serves 6*

½   cup chopped onion
3   chopped garlic cloves
1   tablespoon butter or pareve margarine
5   cups thinly sliced, trimmed Brussels sprouts, about 1 pound

⅓   cup pareve chicken powder dissolved according to directions or chicken stock
1   tablespoon firmly packed brown sugar
¼   teaspoon salt
¼   teaspoon pepper
2   tablespoons chopped pecans, lightly toasted

In large skillet over medium high heat, sauté onion and garlic in butter or margarine 3 minutes or until softened. Stir in Brussels sprouts, sauté 2 minutes. Add stock and brown sugar. Simmer 5 minutes or until liquid almost evaporates, stirring frequently. Season with salt and pepper. Sprinkle with pecans.

Brussels sprouts are a variety of cabbage developed in Belgium in 1785. Belgians claim that Brussels sprouts eaten at the beginning of a meal prevent intoxication.

To prepare Brussels sprouts, remove outer leaves and trim a thin slice from the stem. Cut lengthwise for paddle-shaped pieces held together by the stem or crosswise for slaw.

Solomon Myers's Pecan Plant, Valdosta, Georgia, c.1920.

Vegetables & Side Dishes

GINGER ORANGE ROASTED CARROTS

Orange marmalade is the twist that makes these carrots shout.

Pareve/Passover   *Serves 8*

2	pounds baby carrots	2	tablespoons orange
2	tablespoons olive oil		marmalade
½	teaspoon salt	1	tablespoon water
2	tablespoons sugar	½	teaspoon grated fresh ginger

Preheat oven to 450°. Toss carrots with olive oil and salt. Place in single layer in large roasting pan. In small saucepan over medium heat, combine sugar, marmalade, water and ginger. Simmer, stirring until smooth. Remove from heat. Place carrots in oven, roast 10 minutes. Toss with warm orange mixture. Continue roasting 10 to 12 minutes or until brown and tender.

COBB COUNTY CORN FRITTERS

Dairy/Pareve   *Serves 15 to 18*

1	(16-ounce) can yellow corn, kernels with liquid	1½	teaspoons salt
1½	cups flour	½	cup milk or pareve soy milk
1	teaspoon baking powder		Vegetable oil
2	large eggs, beaten		Butter or pareve margarine
			Maple syrup

In medium bowl, whisk together corn, flour, baking powder, eggs, salt and milk. Fill large skillet halfway with oil, heat to medium high. Drop mixture by ⅛ cup spoonfuls into skillet. Deep fry until puffy, golden brown and crisp. Drain on paper towels. Serve immediately with butter or margarine and maple syrup.

COUNTRY CORN PUDDING

No southern picnic dinner would be complete without this tasty treasure.

Dairy   *Serves 8 to 10*

1	(16-ounce) can creamed corn	16	ounces sour cream
1	(15-ounce) can kernel corn, drained	2	large eggs, beaten
3	ears fresh corn, kernels removed	1	(8.5-ounce) package corn muffin mix
1	stick melted butter or pareve margarine	¼	cup shredded Swiss cheese

Preheat oven to 350°. Combine all ingredients. Spoon into 13x9-inch baking dish, bake until brown, about 45 minutes.

A delicious option is to sprinkle ½ cup firmly packed brown sugar on top before baking. To prepare in individual servings, bake in muffin pans, coated with nonstick spray. Pour mixture into each cup until almost full. Bake 15 to 18 minutes.

WAYCROSS CORN

Nothing says summer like fresh sweet corn. Its marriage with flavorful skinny green beans results in a colorful, fresh side dish.

Dairy / Pareve   *Serves 6*

¼	cup finely chopped shallots or green onions	3	cups fresh uncooked corn kernels, about 6 ears
2	tablespoons unsalted butter or olive oil	1	teaspoon salt
¼	pound haricots vert or other green beans, trimmed, cut into ¼-inch pieces	1	tablespoon finely grated fresh lime zest
		1	tablespoon fresh lime juice

In large skillet, sauté shallots or green onions in butter or olive oil until softened, 3 to 4 minutes. Add beans, corn and salt. Cook over moderate heat, stirring until vegetables are tender, about 6 more minutes. Remove from heat. Stir in lime zest and lime juice.

The National Council of Jewish Women was established at Atlanta's Cotton States and International Exposition in 1895 by German-Jewish women members of The Temple. They sponsored southern cooking classes for new immigrants who had arrived during the mid-1890s through the 1920s. Council members believed that learning to speak English was not enough; learning to "cook southern" was as equally an important ingredient for becoming Americanized.

Vegetables &
Side Dishes

DIJON GREEN BEANS WITH ALMONDS

Green beans all dressed up and ready to party!

Pareve   *Serves 6 to 8*

2	pounds fresh green beans	1	tablespoon red wine vinegar
1	tablespoon Dijon mustard	¼	cup olive oil
1	tablespoon minced shallots	6	ounces sliced almonds,
1	teaspoon minced garlic		toasted
2	tablespoons chopped parsley		

Steam green beans until crunchy, about 7 minutes. While cooking, make sauce. If making in advance, plunge green beans into ice water, drain.

Mix together mustard, shallots, garlic, parsley and red wine vinegar in medium bowl. Gradually pour olive oil into sauce mixture, whisking briskly. Heat large skillet. Add green beans, cover with sauce. Sprinkle with almonds, toss and heat thoroughly.

Jewish National Fund dinner, Atlanta, Georgia, 1925.

Hazelnut Portobello Mushrooms

These versatile mushrooms can be served as a side dish or an entrée.

Pareve/Passover   **Serves 12**

Mushrooms

12 medium Portobello   Olive oil
    mushrooms, stems and   Kosher salt
    veins removed   Pepper

Hazelnut Topping

2   cups coarsely chopped   2   tablespoons finely grated
    hazelnuts, toasted   lemon zest
2   garlic cloves, finely chopped   Kosher salt and pepper
¼   cup finely chopped parsley

Brush mushrooms on both sides with olive oil. Season with salt and pepper. Grill over medium heat 5 to 6 minutes on each side. Combine topping ingredients in medium bowl. Sprinkle evenly over warm mushroom caps.

Easy Potato Latkes

This recipe is a time-saver with an impressive result.

Dairy/Pareve/Passover   **Serves 8 to 10**

2   (16-ounce) bags shredded   3   large onions, finely
    hash brown potatoes   chopped, well drained
6   large eggs, beaten   Salt and pepper
½   cup matzah meal or   Vegetable oil
    flour   Warm applesauce
                                 Dairy or pareve sour cream

In food processor, pulse potatoes, ½ bag at a time, 3 to 5 times until chopped. In large bowl, mix potatoes with eggs, matzah meal or flour, onions, salt and pepper. Heat skillet with oil 1-inch deep. Drop ¼ cup latke mixture into skillet, brown well on both sides. Drain on paper towels. Serve with applesauce and sour cream or freeze.

To peel an onion, slice it in half lengthwise, through the root. Cut some off the top of each half, pull away the papery skin and tough outer layer.

MINI CHEESE LATKES

This recipe will light your night!

Dairy   *Serves 10 to 12*

4	large potatoes, peeled	1 teaspoon lemon juice
2	large eggs, beaten	1 cup grated Swiss cheese
1	teaspoon salt	Vegetable oil
1	tablespoon flour	Sour cream
2	tablespoons grated onion	Applesauce
½	teaspoon baking powder	

Cut potatoes in small pieces. Place first 7 ingredients in processor, blend. Allow mixture to rest in bowl 15 minutes. Spoon liquid off top. Fold in Swiss cheese, mix well. Heat skillet with oil 1-inch deep. Drop mixture by teaspoonfuls into hot skillet, brown well on both sides. Drain on paper towels. Serve with sour cream and applesauce or freeze.

To freeze cooled latkes, place on wax paper lined cookie sheets, up to 2 layers per pan. Cover top layer with wax paper. Fully cover cookie sheets with heavy duty foil. To serve, place single layer of frozen latkes on cookie sheet, bake 10 minutes at 400° or until hot, turning once.

Lighting the chanukiah, Thomson, Georgia, 1948.

SWEET POTATO LATKES

Dairy/Pareve/Passover   *Serves 8 to 10*

1½   pounds sweet potatoes,
     peeled, about 2-3 potatoes
½   pound onions, halved, about
     2-3 onions
1-2   tablespoons minced fresh
     ginger
2   large eggs

⅓   cup matzah meal
1   tablespoon sugar
     Salt and pepper
     Vegetable oil
     Applesauce
     Dairy or pareve sour cream

Cut potatoes into chunks. Pulse potatoes with onions in food processor. Put cheesecloth or clean dish towel into bowl, pour in potato onion mixture and squeeze to remove moisture. Return mixture to processor with ginger, eggs, matzah meal and sugar. In cast iron skillet, heat ¼-inch of oil, testing readiness by dropping in a potato shred until it sizzles. Using ¼ cup measure, scoop sweet potato mixture, place into hot oil and spread with fork to ½-inch thickness. Tuck in edges to prevent burning. Flip over to brown on both sides. Drain latkes on paper towels. Keep warm in 250° oven while frying remaining latkes. Serve with sour cream and applesauce or freeze.

If frozen, warm latkes on cookie sheet without defrosting at 400°, 10 minutes or until crisp.

Cook slowly as the sugar in sweet potatoes will cause latkes to brown more rapidly than those made with white potatoes.

*New World Club Chanukah performance,
Atlanta, Georgia, 1949.*

POTATO KUGELETTES

Good things come in small packages.

Meat / Passover   *Serves 4 to 6*

	Matzah meal, for dusting	2	large eggs, beaten
1	cup white potatoes, peeled, finely grated, well drained	1	teaspoon kosher salt
			Pepper
½	cup grated onion	2	tablespoons rendered chicken fat or pareve fat

Preheat oven to 375°. Coat 24 miniature muffin cups with nonstick spray, dust with matzah meal. Combine all ingredients except fat. Place 2 tablespoons mixture in each cup, baste tops with fat. Bake 15 to 20 minutes until cooked through and golden.

To keep mashed potatoes moist, top them with a thin layer of milk or cream, dairy or pareve and cover. They will keep up to 4 hours. Stir in the milk, whip and reheat.

POTATO CAULIFLOWER SMASH

Make the pareve version, as this is fabulous with grilled steak or lamb chops.

Dairy / Pareve / Passover   *Serves 6 to 8*

1	(2-pound) head cauliflower	2	tablespoons unsalted butter or pareve margarine, melted
3	pounds Yukon Gold potatoes, peeled, quartered	½	cup warm milk or pareve soy milk
	Salt		White pepper
1	shallot, finely chopped		Juice of 1 lemon

Core and cut cauliflower into 1½-inch florets. Put potatoes and cauliflower into large pot with enough water to cover by 2 inches. Season with salt. Cover, bring to boil. Simmer 30 minutes or until very soft. Drain vegetables, transfer to large bowl and mash. Sauté shallot in butter or margarine, add to warm milk and combine with potato mixture. Mash until well blended. Season with salt, white pepper and lemon juice. Serve hot.

POTATO TURNIP SMASH

Follow above recipe substituting 2 large turnips for cauliflower, omitting lemon juice. Sprinkle top with freshly ground Parmesan cheese for dairy preparation. Bake 15 minutes at 350°.

SPINACH MUSHROOM TIMBALES

Delicate and delicious with a silky custard consistency.

Dairy/Passover   *Serves 10*

3	(10- ounce) packages frozen chopped spinach	1	pound mushrooms, chopped
	Butter	⅓	cup grated Parmesan cheese
	Grated Parmesan cheese	4	large eggs, beaten
2	tablespoons butter	1½	cups heavy cream
1	medium onion, chopped		Nutmeg
			Salt and pepper

Preheat oven to 350°. Defrost spinach and squeeze dry. Cut rounds of wax paper to fit in bottom of ten 5-inch ramekins or molds. Butter each mold, sprinkle lightly with Parmesan cheese, set aside. Melt 2 tablespoons of butter in skillet, sauté onion until limp. Add mushrooms and additional butter, if necessary. Sauté 2 to 3 minutes longer. Remove from heat. Transfer to mixing bowl, stir in remaining ingredients. Spoon into prepared molds. Sprinkle additional cheese over tops. Place ramekins in roasting pan filled with 1-inch of water. Bake 25 minutes or until set. Loosen edges of each mold with a knife. Invert onto platter. Remove wax paper before serving.

The Don't Worry Club, Atlanta, Georgia, c.1950.

GLAZED ACORN SQUASH
WITH ORANGE BUTTER

Orange provides a burst of flavor to make this squash irresistible.

Dairy / Meat / Pareve   *Serves 6 to 8*

ORANGE BUTTER OR MARGARINE

½ stick unsalted butter
   or pareve margarine,
   softened
2 teaspoons orange liqueur

2 teaspoons freshly grated
   orange zest
1 tablespoon minced green
   onions, green part only
   Salt and pepper

GLAZED SQUASH

2 large acorn squash, seeded,
   cut into ½-inch thick
   slices
½ cup orange liqueur
¾ cup vegetable or chicken
   stock

¼ cup fresh orange juice
2 tablespoons firmly packed
   light brown sugar
   Salt and pepper

Combine orange butter ingredients in bowl. Roll mixture into cylinder shape in wax paper. Chill 2 hours or until firm.

A country outing,
Macon, Georgia, 1927.

Preheat oven to 400°. In shallow baking dish, arrange squash in single layer. Combine remaining ingredients in saucepan, bring to boil, immediately pour over squash. Cover tightly, bake 15 minutes or until tender. Remove dish from oven and drain liquid into skillet. Turn off oven. Put squash back into oven to keep warm. Boil cooking liquid until syrupy. Pour over squash. Slice orange liqueur butter or margarine ⅛-inch thick. Alternate butter with squash on serving plate.

SQUASH MEDLEY BAKE

So-o-o-o-o southern...it melts in the mouth

Dairy   *Serves 8 to 10*

2	pounds yellow squash	3	large eggs
2	pounds zucchini squash	2	tablespoons sugar
2	large onions, divided	1	teaspoon salt
6	ounces butter, or more, divided	1	teaspoon pepper
1½	cups butter flavored crackers	4-5	ears fresh corn, kernels removed
		¼	cup cheese cracker crumbs

Preheat oven to 350°. In processor, grate squash and onions, reserving about ¼ onion. Sauté grated squash and onions in 6 ounces butter until thoroughly cooked. While vegetables cook, crush butter flavored crackers with reserved onion in processor, using metal blade. Blend in eggs, sugar, salt and pepper. In medium skillet, sauté corn in 4 tablespoons butter. Combine all ingredients except cheese cracker crumbs. Spoon into greased 2-quart casserole, top with cheese cracker crumbs. Bake 45 minutes.

For easy removal of seeds in squash or cucumbers, roll the vegetable in palms with medium pressure to soften the insides which loosens the seeds. Cut vegetable in half lengthwise, scoop out the seeds with a spoon.

CRANBERRY COCONUT SWEET POTATOES

A side dish that is sweet enough to be a dessert.

Dairy/Pareve   *Serves 6 to 8*

3	pounds unpeeled sweet potatoes	2	tablespoons firmly packed brown sugar
1/3	cup maple syrup	1/4	cup sweetened coconut flakes
1/3	cup dried cranberries	1/4	teaspoon ground ginger
3	tablespoons butter or pareve margarine	1/2	cup roughly chopped pecans

In medium pot, cover sweet potatoes with water, bring to boil. Cook over medium heat 20 minutes until fork tender. Drain, set aside to cool. In small saucepan, stir together remaining ingredients except pecans. Cook over low heat 5 minutes.

Preheat oven to 350°. Lightly coat large casserole dish with nonstick spray. Peel then cut sweet potatoes into large chunks and place in prepared casserole. Top with cranberry mixture, sprinkle with chopped pecans. Bake 7 to 8 minutes or until pecans are lightly toasted.

SAVANNAH SWEET POTATO SOUFFLÉ

Dairy/Pareve/Passover   *Serves 10*

4	pounds sweet potatoes, cooked, peeled	1	teaspoon freshly grated lemon zest
1/2	cup butter or pareve margarine, melted	1/2	teaspoon ground ginger
6	large eggs, separated	1/2	teaspoon salt
3/4	cup sugar		Kosher miniature marshmallows
1/2	cup milk or pareve soy milk		

Preheat oven to 325°. Mash potatoes, beat on low speed of electric mixer until smooth. Add melted butter or margarine and egg yolks, beat very well on medium high speed. Mix in sugar, milk, lemon zest, ginger and salt. In separate bowl, beat egg whites until stiff but not dry, fold into potato mixture. Place in buttered 2-quart soufflé dish or casserole, bake 1 hour. Top with marshmallows for final 15 minutes of baking.

APPLE WALNUT TZIMMES SURPRISE

Dairy/Pareve/Passover   *Serves 10 to 12*

4 sweet potatoes	½ cup dried whole apricots
4 tablespoons butter or pareve margarine, divided	Juice of 1 lemon
	Brown sugar
2 pounds carrots, peeled, thinly sliced	3 bananas, cut in ½-inch slices
4 apples, peeled, sliced	Sugar, to dip
1-1½ cups walnuts	Orange zest

Preheat oven to 450°. Bake sweet potatoes 1 hour, or until soft. Cool, peel and cut into bite size chunks. In a large skillet, melt 2 tablespoons butter or margarine. Sauté carrots, apples, walnuts and apricots for 5 minutes. Add lemon juice and enough brown sugar to sweeten. Reduce oven temperature to 350°. Dip bananas in sugar. In a fresh skillet, cook bananas in remaining 2 tablespoons butter or margarine at medium to high temperature, to caramelize bananas. Toss with sweet potatoes, carrots, apples, walnuts and apricots. Place in greased casserole. Sprinkle with zest. Bake until hot, about 15 minutes.

P. Lazarus & Son, Quitman, Georgia, c.1910.

Vegetables &
Side Dishes

ASHKENAZI CHAROSET

Making charoset with Mom or Grandma is, for many, an early Passover memory.
Preparing a family recipe together is the way to hand it down to children and grandchildren.

Pareve/Passover   *Yields 2¾ cups*

2	cups peeled, finely chopped Red Delicious apples	2	tablespoons honey
1	cup peeled, finely chopped Golden Delicious apples	1	teaspoon cinnamon
¾	cup chopped walnuts	3	tablespoons red Passover wine

Combine all ingredients, mix well and refrigerate.

SEPHARDIC CHAROSET

Fruit, nuts and spices are ground into "mortar" using Mediterranean fruits.

Pareve/Passover   *Yields 3 cups*

1	cup chopped dates	½	cup chopped walnuts
1	cup chopped dried apricots	1	teaspoon cinnamon
1	cup peeled, chopped apple	3	tablespoons honey
½	cup golden raisins	3	tablespoons blackberry wine

Place ingredients in food processor. Process, leaving mixture coarse, adding more wine, if necessary.

COLORFUL ROASTED VEGGIES

Pareve/Passover   *Serves 6*

1   large eggplant, cut into large chunks

3   Yukon Gold potatoes, peeled, cut into large chunks

4   carrots, peeled, cut into large chunks

1   green pepper, cored, seeded, sliced

1   red pepper, cored, seeded, sliced

1   yellow pepper, cored, seeded, sliced

1   medium yellow onion, cut into wedges

1   pint cherry tomatoes

1   cup prepared vinaigrette dressing

1-2 tablespoons olive oil

In large bowl, combine vegetables. Toss with vinaigrette dressing. Pour into plastic bag. Refrigerate 4 hours. Preheat oven to 400°. Coat roasting pan with olive oil, preheat in oven. Drain vegetables, reserving vinaigrette. Roast 30 to 40 minutes, stirring and basting with vinaigrette every 15 minutes. Serve hot or cold.

Stuff pita bread with leftover roasted veggies for a flavor-packed sandwich the next day.

The local produce stand will have all the assorted vegetables needed for this recipe.
Raymond Saul's stall at the Farmers' Market, Atlanta, Georgia, c. 1925.

*Vegetables &
Side Dishes*

THE RABBI'S VEGETARIAN CHOLENT

Rabbi Hillel Norry, of Congregation Shearith Israel, teaches vegetarian cooking in Atlanta. This is his healthy, yet delicious, spin on the traditional Shabbat dish.

Pareve   *Serves 4 to 6*

4 medium Yukon Gold potatoes, peeled, quartered	½ cup uncooked basmati rice or barley
4 medium carrots, peeled, cut into chunks	1½ cups barbecue sauce
2 (8-ounce) packages of seitan or wheat gluten	2 bay leaves Pepper
8 ounces small mushrooms, stemmed, halved	6 cups or more, vegetable stock
1 medium onion, quartered	1 tablespoon kudzu powder or cornstarch dissolved in small amount warm stock or water
½ cup dried apricots	4 eggs, eggshells washed well

Preheat oven to 400°. In large Dutch oven, combine all ingredients, except kudzu or cornstarch and eggs. Make sure there is enough liquid to cover all solid ingredients, stir well. Add kudzu or cornstarch, stir well. Gently nestle whole eggs into mixture. Bake on center rack 2 hours, or until rice is cooked, vegetables tender and sauce is thickened. Eggs will be hard-cooked. Remove eggs, serve on the side.

*K*udzu is available in most health food stores in the macrobiotic section. It is available in small packets as white, starchy chunks that dissolve into powder when you crush them. It is an excellent thickener that can be used in place of cornstarch or flour in all kinds of recipes.

Cooking for the Minyanaires Club at Ahavath Achim Congregation, Atlanta, Georgia, c.1965.

HONEYED WINTER TURNIPS

Turn up the flavor on this often overlooked vegetable.

Dairy/Pareve/Passover   *Serves 6*

6	medium turnips, peeled, diced	¼	cup honey
1	tablespoon butter or pareve margarine	¼	cup water
		¼	teaspoon salt

Preheat oven to 350°. In double boiler, steam turnips until tender. Place in 11x7-inch buttered baking dish. Combine remaining ingredients in small saucepan. Heat, stir until butter melts. Pour over turnips. Bake 1 hour or until turnips are brown and glazed.

BARLEY ALMOND CASSEROLE

Rediscover the taste and texture of this ancient grain.

Meat/Pareve   *Serves 6 to 8*

6	tablespoons pareve margarine or butter, divided	¼	cup chopped green onions, green part only
⅓	cup slivered almonds		Salt and pepper
1	medium onion, chopped	2	(14-ounce) cans chicken, beef stock or 28-ounces pareve chicken powder reconstituted
1	cup medium barley, rinsed, drained		
¾	cup minced parsley, divided		

Preheat oven to 350°. Melt 2 tablespoons margarine or butter in large skillet. Sauté almonds, remove with slotted spoon, set aside. Add remaining margarine or butter, onion and barley. Stir until lightly browned. Stir in ½ cup parsley, green onions and almonds. Season with salt and pepper. Boil stock, stir into mixture. Pour into greased 2-quart casserole, sprinkle with remaining parsley. Bake uncovered 1 hour.

A table is not blessed if it has fed no scholars.

~Yiddish proverb

Vegetables & Side Dishes

SOUTHWEST VEGETARIAN CASSEROLE

Fill tortillas instead of baking in a casserole for taco night.

Dairy   *Serves 3 to 4*

1	(16-ounce) can vegetarian spicy refried beans	4	tablespoons olive oil
1	(16-ounce) can crushed tomatoes	2	cups cooked white or brown rice
1	pound vegetarian ground beef	8	ounces Cheddar cheese

Preheat oven to 325°. Combine beans and tomatoes in saucepan. Heat on low flame until bubbly, stirring often. In skillet, sauté beef in olive oil until thoroughly heated. In casserole, layer beef, beans, rice and cheese until all ingredients are used, ending with cheese. Bake uncovered 10 minutes or until cheese is melted.

Vacationing in Mexico, c.1950.

Wild Rice Crunch

An exotic taste and a beautiful complement to any entrée.

Dairy / Pareve   *Serves 4*

1	(6-ounce) box long grain and wild rice	3	tablespoons butter or pareve margarine
1	cup chopped onion	2	(8-ounce) cans sliced water chestnuts, drained
1	cup chopped celery	½	cup dried cranberries
5	ounces mushrooms, sliced	⅓	cup sliced almonds, toasted

Preheat oven to 350°. Prepare rice as directed on box. In skillet, lightly sauté onions, celery and mushrooms in butter or margarine, fold into cooked rice. Stir in water chestnuts and dried cranberries. Pour mixture into greased 2-quart baking dish. Sprinkle with almonds. Bake 20 minutes.

Porcini Risotto

There are few side dishes that equal the taste and texture of this creamy risotto.

Dairy / Meat / Pareve   *Serves 6 to 8*

¾	ounce dried porcini mushrooms	2	cups Arborio rice
1	cup hot water	¾	cup dry white wine
5½	cups vegetable or chicken stock	1	tablespoon finely chopped fresh sage, or 1 teaspoon dried sage
2	tablespoons unsalted butter or pareve margarine	1½	cups grated Parmesan cheese, optional
2	tablespoons olive oil		Salt and pepper
2	yellow onions, chopped		

In small bowl, soak mushrooms in hot water 30 minutes to soften. Drain, reserving liquid. Chop mushrooms, set aside. In pot, bring stock to simmer. In large saucepan, melt butter or margarine with olive oil. Sauté onions until brown. Add rice, stirring until white spots appear in center of grains, about 1 minute. Add wine, stir until absorbed, about 2 minutes. Add mushrooms, chopped sage, reserved mushroom liquid and 1 ladleful of stock. Reduce heat to simmer, stirring constantly, until liquid is absorbed. Slowly add remaining stock, stirring constantly, until rice is tender, slightly firm in center. Cook 20 to 25 minutes until mixture is creamy. Add Parmesan cheese or softened margarine, season with salt and pepper. Stir to mix well.

Wild rice is not actually rice. It is a long grain marsh grass.

In 1861, in the midst of the Civil War, President Abraham Lincoln ordered the blockade of southern ports in an attempt to strangle the Confederacy. David Mayer, Atlanta's most influential Jewish citizen in the 19th century, served as Georgia Governor Joseph Brown's antebellum commissary officer. Mayer donated rice to the food starved city of Atlanta, "...to relieve in some small part, at least, the sorrows of our poor sufferers."

Vegetables & Side Dishes

POMEGRANATE PILAF

A delicious play on tart and sweet, especially good with chicken.

Dairy / Meat / Pareve   *Serves 4*

3	tablespoons unsalted butter or pareve margarine	½	cup chopped dried apricots
1	small red onion, diced	½	cup chopped almonds
1	cup jasmine rice	½	cup pomegranate seeds
1½	cups vegetable or chicken stock	1	tablespoon chopped fresh thyme leaves
			Salt and pepper

Melt butter or margarine in medium pot. Sauté onion 3 to 5 minutes. Stir in rice. Sauté 1 minute, stirring to coat. Add vegetable or chicken stock, bring to boil. Reduce heat to low, cover. Cook 15 to 20 minutes until rice absorbs all liquid. Remove from heat. Fluff rice. Stir in apricots, almonds, pomegranate seeds and thyme. Season with salt and pepper. Serve immediately.

The significance and symbolism of the pomegranate in Judaism is especially important for the New Year. Jewish tradition says that there are 613 seeds in a pomegranate which represent the 613 mitzvot of the Torah. During Rosh Hashanah we wish for our good deeds to be as numerous as the seeds of the pomegranate.

GRILLED PINEAPPLE PILAF

A wonderful twist on the famous San Francisco treat.

Dairy / Meat / Pareve   *Serves 6 to 8*

2	tablespoons butter or pareve margarine	2	cups chicken or vegetable stock
⅓	cup vermicelli noodles, broken into pieces	½	fresh pineapple, cored
1	cup white rice	½	cup chopped green onions
			Salt and pepper

Melt butter or margarine in medium saucepan over medium heat. Add vermicelli and rice. Sauté stirring frequently, until vermicelli is golden and rice is opaque. Add chicken or vegetable stock, bring to boil. Reduce heat. Simmer covered, 20 minutes or until liquid is absorbed. Slice pineapple into 1-inch thick slices. Grill over medium hot coals 8 to 10 minutes, turning once. Remove from grill and dice. Add to rice with green onions, salt and pepper. Serve hot, room temperature or cold.

FROM THE
LAND OF *Honey*

Milk & Honey

Brunch, Dairy & Pasta

ARTICHOKE AND PARMESAN STRUDEL

An outstanding savory strudel.

Dairy　　　　　　　　　　　　　*Yields 10 slices*

2	(9-ounce) cans artichoke hearts, drained	¾	teaspoon dried tarragon
1½	cups cottage cheese		Dash of pepper
1½	cups grated Parmesan cheese	1	(1-pound) package phyllo dough
3	eggs		Vegetable oil or butter
½	cup minced green onions	½	cup bread crumbs

Preheat oven to 350°. Mash artichokes with fork. Blend in cheeses, eggs, onions, tarragon and pepper. Mix well. With pastry brush, oil or butter 1 sheet of phyllo dough. Sprinkle with bread crumbs. Add another sheet, repeating for total of 3 layers.

Mound filling 1-inch high along edge of prepared dough layers. Roll up, tucking in ends. Oil outside of roll. Cut on a diagonal into 1-inch segments without cutting all the way through. Bake 25 to 30 minutes. Serve warm or at room temperature.

This can be made ahead and frozen before baking. Bake without thawing, using the same time and temperature directions as above.

Phyllo dough can be tricky, so it helps to know the basics. Defrost dough exactly according to directions or the sheets may stick together. Always use butter or oil between sheets. Keep sheets covered with a damp towel until ready to use.

MINIATURE BROCCOLI QUICHES

Quiche is a classic open faced tart that is perfect for brunch or a light supper.

Dairy   *Serves 8 to 12*

CRUST

3	ounces cream cheese	1	cup flour
½	cup butter		

FILLING

5	ounces frozen chopped broccoli	½	cup half-and-half
		3	large eggs, beaten
1	cup finely shredded Swiss cheese	1	teaspoon salt
			Dash of hot pepper sauce

Beat cream cheese, butter and flour until smooth. Form into ball. Wrap in wax paper, refrigerate. Defrost broccoli, drain well and finely chop.

Preheat oven to 400°. When dough is chilled, shape into 1-inch balls. Press balls against bottom and sides of ungreased miniature muffin cups. Into each muffin cup spoon 1 teaspoon broccoli and 1 teaspoon cheese. In small bowl, whisk half-and-half, eggs, salt and hot pepper sauce. Spoon 1½ teaspoons mixture into each cup on top of broccoli and cheese. Bake 25 minutes. Cool slightly. Invert onto wire rack, cool completely. Serve or freeze.

If frozen, thaw, then heat on a baking sheet at 350°, 5 to 10 minutes.

EASY FISH QUICHE

4	large eggs, beaten	2	cups flaked cooked fish, any variety, or kosher faux crabmeat
1	cup mayonnaise		
4	tablespoons flour		
1	cup milk	2	cups diced Swiss cheese
		1	cup chopped green onion
		2	(9-inch) pie shells

Preheat oven to 350°. Beat together eggs, mayonnaise, flour and milk until well blended. Stir in fish or crabmeat, cheese and green onion. Spread mixture into 2 pie shells. Bake 40 minutes or until knife inserted in center comes out clean.

Allow quiches, cheese pies and tarts to set for 15 minutes before slicing.

Something's fishy!
Two girls enjoying a "smoke" and Leslie's Illustrated Magazine, Macon, Georgia, 1910.

CRUSTLESS THREE CHEESE QUICHE

Use leftover vegetables in this very simple and impressive dish.

Dairy   *Serves 8*

½ pound mushrooms, thinly sliced
½ cup finely chopped onions
3 tablespoons butter or margarine
4 large eggs
1 cup sour cream
¾ cup small curd cottage cheese
½ cup grated Parmesan cheese
¼ cup flour

¼ teaspoon salt
Dash pepper
⅛ teaspoon hot sauce
2 cups shredded Monterey Jack cheese
1 cup diced fresh or cooked vegetables, such as broccoli, spinach or tomatoes
Butter or margarine

Preheat oven to 350°. In medium skillet, sauté mushrooms and onions in butter or margarine until soft. Remove from skillet, drain well and transfer to large bowl. In food processor, blend next 8 ingredients. Pour over mushrooms, mix well. Fold in Monterey Jack cheese and vegetables. Pour into 9-inch deep dish pie plate. Dot with butter, loosely cover with foil. Bake 45 minutes or until knife inserted in center comes out clean. Let stand 5 minutes. Cut into wedges to serve.

CHEESE TOMATO HERB PIE

The flavor of perfectly ripe summer tomatoes is highlighted in this delicious creation.

Dairy   *Serves 6*

1	(9-inch) deep dish pie shell		Salt and pepper
3	medium tomatoes, peeled, seeded, drained, sliced	¾	cup grated sharp Cheddar cheese
1	teaspoon Italian herb seasoning or 1 tablespoon fresh minced basil	⅓	cup mayonnaise

Preheat oven to 425°. Bake pie shell 5 minutes. Reduce heat to 400°. Cover bottom of pie shell with tomato slices. Sprinkle with Italian herb seasoning or basil, salt and pepper. Combine Cheddar cheese with mayonnaise spread mixture on top of tomatoes. Bake 30 to 35 minutes.

Tomatoes are best kept at room temperature.

In rural Georgia, much like in other states, small, family farms formed the backbone of America's agricultural production. Across the country, the development of huge conglomerates, the mechanization of agribusiness and increased urban sprawl have altered the rural landscape, decreasing the number of these family farms.

Family farm, Martinez, Georgia, c.1902.

CHEESE BLINTZES

"I used to make these blintzes with my mama.
Now my daughter comes to make blintzes with me."

CRÊPES

2	large eggs	1	cup water
¼	teaspoon salt		Vegetable oil
¾	cup flour		

FILLING

8	ounces cream cheese, softened	1	(8-ounce) package farmer cheese

TOPPINGS, OPTIONAL

Sour cream

Blueberries or other fresh berries

Beat eggs well. Add salt and flour. Slowly add water until it reaches the consistency of thin batter. Heat small skillet. When hot, brush with vegetable oil to coat pan. Pour thin layer of batter into pan. Cook on 1 side until crêpe easily slides out of pan onto tea towel. Repeat until all batter is used.

In medium bowl, mix cheeses. When crêpes are cool, place 1 tablespoon cheese mixture in middle of each crêpe. Fold in ends of crêpe and roll up around cheese mixture. Place seam side down on baking sheet. When ready to serve, melt butter in skillet. Sauté blintzes on both sides until lightly browned. Serve hot with sour cream and blueberries or Fruit Compote.

Fruit Compote for Blintzes and Waffles

4½ cups fresh or defrosted frozen berries, peaches or canned cherries

2 teaspoons cornstarch

¾ cup sugar

½ teaspoon lemon peel

Combine all ingredients in medium saucepan. Bring to boil over medium heat. Cook 3 minutes, stirring constantly. Serve warm.

MOM'S BLINTZ CASSEROLE

Perfect for a large celebration or a special family brunch.
Make ahead for ease on day of entertaining.

Dairy   *Serves 6 to 8*

BATTER

½	cup sugar	¼	cup milk
2	large eggs	1	teaspoon vanilla
1	cup flour		Pinch of salt
3	teaspoons baking powder		

FILLING

2	pounds farmer cheese or		Pinch of salt
	1 pound cream cheese and		Juice of 1 large lemon
	1 pound cottage cheese	2	tablespoons sour cream
2	large eggs	8	ounces butter, melted
¼	cup sugar		

Combine batter ingredients in large bowl, stir until mixed well. Preheat oven to 300°. Combine filling ingredients in food processor or blender until smooth. Pour ½ of batter into buttered 2-quart oblong casserole. Spoon filling evenly on top of batter. Top with remaining batter. Bake 1½ hours.

Serve with blueberry or cherry compote and sour cream.

Birthday party, Atlanta, Georgia, c.1949

Need the juice of just ½ lemon but don't want to clean the juicer? Make a few cuts into a lemon half, wrap it in a paper coffee filter and squeeze the juice into a bowl.

To have zest available when needed for a recipe, save lemon, lime or orange peels when only juice is needed in a recipe. Freeze the peels in a plastic bag. It is easy to grate while the peel is frozen.

Brunch, Dairy & Pasta

FRENCH TOAST SOUFFLÉ

Easy for a crowd!

Dairy   *Serves 6 to 8*

7 large eggs, lightly beaten	½ cup sugar
2½ cups half-and-half	¼ teaspoon salt
1 teaspoon vanilla	10 (1-inch) thick slices challah
1½ teaspoons ground cinnamon	4-8 tablespoons butter or
¼ teaspoon nutmeg, optional	margarine
½ teaspoon grated orange zest, optional	Confectioners' sugar

Beat eggs with next 7 ingredients. Soak each challah slice in mixture 1 minute turning once. Melt 1 tablespoon butter or margarine in large skillet. Drain bread slightly, brown in skillet about 1 minute on each side, adding more butter, 1 tablespoon at a time, as needed. Pour ½ of egg mixture in 13x9-inch dish. Layer challah slices in pan. Pour remaining egg mixture over bread. Cover, refrigerate overnight.

Preheat oven to 350°. Bake uncovered 40 to 50 minutes or until set in the center. Dust with confectioners' sugar. Serve with warm maple syrup.

Birthday party, Atlanta, Georgia, 1925.

STRAWBERRY STUFFED FRENCH TOAST

Strawberry preserves are a wonderful filling for French toast.
Challah, rich in eggs, is the best bread to use. Try
Czernowitzer Challah (page 193) as homemade is the best of the best!

Dairy / Pareve   *Serves 4 to 6*

6	ounces dairy or pareve cream cheese, softened	1¼	teaspoons vanilla
⅓	cup strawberry preserves	½	teaspoon ground cinnamon
10	(1-inch) thick slices challah	½	teaspoon nutmeg
6	large eggs	3	tablespoons unsalted butter or pareve margarine, divided
1¼	cups milk or pareve soy milk		Maple syrup

Preheat oven to 300°. Place baking sheet in oven. Blend cream cheese and preserves in small bowl, set aside. Cut through top crust of each bread slice making 2-inch deep pocket. Spoon 1 generous tablespoon cheese mixture into each bread pocket. Whisk eggs, milk, vanilla, cinnamon and nutmeg in medium bowl. Pour into pie plate. Dip bread slices in egg mixture, coating both sides. Melt 1 tablespoon butter or margarine in large nonstick skillet over medium heat. Place bread in skillet, cook until golden brown, about 2 minutes per side, add butter or margarine to pan as needed. Reduce heat to 150°. Transfer French toast to preheated baking sheet, keeping warm in oven until ready to serve. Serve with maple syrup.

This is superb with sliced bananas or fresh sliced strawberries.

Pancakes, waffles and French toast can be dressed up by serving with melted pats of flavored butter on top. These delightful flavor boosters can be found in the Bread chapter (page 213 and 214).

Southern Belle Belgian Waffles

Dairy/Pareve   *Serves 4*

2	cups flour	2	cups milk or pareve soy milk
2	teaspoons baking powder	3	large eggs, separated
2	tablespoons confectioners' sugar	2	teaspoons vanilla
1	tablespoon vegetable oil		Pinch of salt
			Maple syrup

Combine all ingredients except egg whites and maple syrup, blend well. Beat egg whites until soft peaks form. Gently fold into batter, being careful not to over mix. Using ladle, pour mixture into hot, greased waffle iron and bake 2 minutes or until done. Repeat with remaining batter. Serve with maple syrup.

To dress these waffles up, serve with berries, whipped cream, butter, fruit syrup or toasted pecans.

Cinnamon Butter Pancakes

Cinnamon butter can be refrigerated for up to 1 month.
It is wonderful on scones, muffins and bread, as well as these pancakes.

Dairy   *Yields 16 pancakes*

Cinnamon Butter

4	ounces unsalted butter or margarine	$\frac{1}{8}$	teaspoon vanilla
2	tablespoons maple syrup	$\frac{1}{4}$	teaspoon cinnamon
		$\frac{1}{8}$	teaspoon salt

Pancakes

6	eggs, separated	1	cup milk
3	tablespoons sugar	$\frac{1}{2}$	teaspoon salt
$\frac{3}{4}$	cup small curd cottage cheese	$\frac{1}{4}$	teaspoon vanilla
$\frac{1}{4}$	cup sour cream		Butter or margarine
1	cup unsifted flour		Blueberry syrup

Beat cinnamon butter ingredients until smooth, set aside. Beat egg yolks with sugar until thick and light yellow. Add cottage cheese and sour cream, beat until smooth. Sift in flour. Blend in milk, salt and vanilla. Beat egg whites until soft peaks form. Fold into cheese mixture. Let stand 5 minutes. Melt butter or margarine in skillet, pour $\frac{1}{4}$ cup batter at a time, cooking until bubbly. Flip and cook until lightly browned. Serve with cinnamon butter and hot blueberry syrup.

SPINACH CHEESE FRITTERS

A splendid spin on spinach.

Dairy   *Serves 10*

3	large eggs, beaten
2	(10-ounce) packages frozen chopped spinach, thawed, drained
¼	cup cottage cheese
3	tablespoons breadcrumbs

2	tablespoons grated Parmesan cheese
1	tablespoon flour
1	teaspoon salt
2	tablespoons vegetable oil
3	tablespoons unsalted butter

In large bowl, beat eggs. Blend in spinach, cottage cheese, breadcrumbs, Parmesan cheese, flour and salt. Stir well. Refrigerate 20 minutes. In large skillet or griddle, over medium high heat, melt oil and butter. Place heaping spoonfuls of batter in skillet, pat into pancake shape. Fry until brown on each side. Add additional oil as needed for frying.

CLASSIC CHEESE STRATA

A strata is a savory bread pudding. This one makes an excellent brunch or dinner dish.

Dairy   *Serves 10*

14	slices dense white bread Vegetable oil
1	pound grated Cheddar cheese, divided
3	cups milk, divided

12	large eggs, divided Salt and pepper
1	stick unsalted butter, melted, divided

Preheat oven to 325°. Remove crusts from bread. Cut slices into triangles, divide into 4 stacks. Grease 3-quart casserole with oil. Arrange ½ the bread triangles in casserole. Sprinkle with ½ the cheese and/or any variation. In blender or processor, blend milk, eggs, salt and pepper. Pour ½ mixture evenly over cheese. Drizzle with ½ the melted butter. Repeat the process ending with butter. Bake 1 hour 15 minutes until firm in middle.

Variations: fresh sliced tomatoes, sautéed onions, peppers, spinach, Parmesan or Gruyère cheeses.

JALAPEÑO GRITS SOUFFLÉ

Grits are as southern as it gets!

Dairy   *Serves 8 to 10*

3 cups water	¾ cup diced roasted poblano peppers, seeded or 2 jalapeño peppers, seeded, minced
1 cup half-and-half or cream	
2 teaspoons salt	
1 cup stone ground white grits	
5 large eggs, separated	¼ cup diced roasted red bell peppers, seeded
1½ cups grated white or yellow sharp Cheddar cheese	
4 ounces goat cheese	4 tablespoons unsalted butter
1 tablespoon minced garlic	Salt and pepper
	½ cup chopped cilantro

Preheat oven to 375°. Butter 2-quart casserole or soufflé dish. In 3-quart saucepan, bring water, cream and salt to boil. Stir in grits, reduce heat to medium. Cover, cook, stirring often, until thick, smooth and creamy. Beat egg yolks. Slowly add 1 to 2 soup spoonfuls of hot grits into yolks. Mix yolks into hot grits. Stir in cheeses, garlic, peppers and butter. Season with salt and pepper. Remove from heat, cool to room temperature. An hour before serving, in stainless steel bowl, beat egg whites until stiff peaks form. Gently fold egg whites and cilantro into grits, spoon into prepared dish. Cover, bake 30 to 40 minutes until grits are set. If surface browns too quickly, cover with foil.

To roast peppers, broil 5 minutes, turning often, until peppers are blistered and blackened. Place in plastic or paper bag. Seal, let stand 1 minute to loosen skin. Remove skin, cut peppers in half and remove seeds.

Entertaining troops during World War II, Atlanta, Georgia, 1943.

Salmon and Egg Brunch Casserole

*Canoe, a top Atlanta restaurant, is famous for its
stellar Sunday brunch. This is one of the most popular dishes.*

Dairy   *Serves 10 to 12*

4	cups cubed French bread	4	cups milk
¼	cup unsalted butter, melted	4	teaspoons Dijon mustard
3	cups sliced mushrooms	1	teaspoon salt
4	cups grated Cheddar cheese	½	teaspoon pepper
6	ounces Nova salmon, diced	½	teaspoon paprika
5	green onions, chopped	¼	teaspoon cayenne pepper
8	large eggs, beaten		

Place bread cubes in 13x9-inch glass dish, drizzle with butter. Layer mushrooms, cheese, Nova and green onions over bread. In large bowl whisk remaining ingredients, pour evenly into dish, cover. Refrigerate overnight. Preheat oven to 325°. Bake 1 hour until firm.

Executive Chef Gary Mennie, Canoe Restaurant, Atlanta, Georgia

*When the
stomach is empty,
so is the brain.*

~Yiddish proverb

*Brunch, Dairy
& Pasta*

EGG BLOSSOM SOUFFLÉ

*A favorite at Southern simchas for decades, this beautiful dish
looks best fresh from the oven as the eggs blossom up through the tomato slices.*

Dairy   *Serves 8*

½	cup flour	4	ounces margarine, melted
1	teaspoon baking powder	½	green pepper, diced
1	teaspoon salt	1	onion, grated
	Pepper	½	pound mushrooms, sliced
12	eggs, well beaten	1	large tomato, thinly sliced
1	pint cottage cheese		Parsley flakes
1	pound Cheddar cheese, grated		

Preheat oven to 350°. Grease 13x9-inch baking dish. Mix together flour, baking powder, salt and pepper. Blend with beaten eggs. Whisk in all other ingredients except tomato and parsley. Pour into baking dish. Lay tomato slices on top, pushing slightly into mixture, but not covering tomato completely with mixture. Sprinkle with parsley flakes. Bake 40 to 45 minutes. Allow to set 15 minutes before serving.

This can be made up to 2 days ahead, refrigerate. Reheat at 350°.

The secret to a good omelet is the pan. A high quality, heavy nonstick pan works perfectly.

POTATO ONION OMELET

An omelet that kids and grownups alike will adore.

Dairy/Pareve   *Serves 2*

3	large eggs	¾	cup canned potato sticks
1	tablespoon cream or pareve soy milk	¼	cup canned fried onion rings
2	tablespoons unsalted butter or pareve margarine	2	tomatoes, sliced

Beat eggs with cream or milk, set aside. Melt butter or margarine in large skillet. Add potato sticks and fried onions, stirring constantly until hot. Add egg mixture, stir. Allow eggs to set, then fold into an omelet. Serve with sliced tomatoes.

MINI FRITTATAS

Dairy/Passover   *Serves 8*

1½ cups chopped fresh
    asparagus
1   cup shredded Gruyère
    cheese
1   cup goat cheese

1   cup shredded white
    Cheddar cheese
9   large eggs, beaten
¼   teaspoon kosher salt
    Pepper
    Butter

Preheat oven to 350°. Blanch asparagus by boiling for 1 minute. Immediately plunge into ice water, drain. Combine cheeses, eggs, salt and pepper. Melt butter and coat sides of mini muffin pans. Place asparagus in bottom of each muffin cup. Spoon egg mixture over asparagus until muffin cup is ½ full. Bake 20 minutes until golden brown. Invert pans to remove frittatas. Arrange on a warmed tray or serving platter.

This can be made 1 day ahead. Refrigerate overnight, reheat 10 minutes at 350°.

Try other combinations of cheeses, substitute chopped spinach, tomatoes or peppers for asparagus.

SMOKED SALMON MATZAH BREI

Salmon and dill put "wow" in this traditional Passover dish.

Dairy/Pareve/Passover   *Serves 4*

6   tablespoons unsalted butter
    or pareve margarine,
    divided
2   large onions, diced
3   matzahs, crumbled

6   large eggs
1½ cups diced smoked salmon
    Salt and pepper
¼   cup finely chopped fresh dill

Melt 4 tablespoons butter or margarine in large pan over low heat. Sauté onions very slowly about 45 minutes to 1 hour until soft, golden brown and caramelized. Soak matzah in warm water 30 seconds, press out excess water. In a large bowl, beat eggs and fold in matzah. Add onions, salmon, salt and pepper. Melt 2 tablespoons butter or margarine in same skillet over medium heat. Pour in eggs, cook, stirring occasionally, until done. Fold in dill.

PINK PERFECTION SALAD

My mom makes this all the time and it is always a hit. It looks happy.
That may sound odd, but it does look happy and it tastes great.

Dairy/Pareve/Passover   *Serves 8*

24	ounces herring bits in wine, drained	2	stalks celery, finely diced
½-1	(16-ounce) jar pickled beets, drained, liquid reserved	1	large apple, finely diced
½	cup dairy or pareve sour cream	½	cup slivered almonds, toasted

Cut herring bits into bite size pieces and place in a medium bowl. Pat beets dry, dice and add to herring. Stir in ½ reserved pickled beet liquid. Cover, refrigerate overnight. When ready to serve, fold in sour cream, celery, apple and almonds.

WHITEFISH SALAD

A splendid dish for any holiday gathering, Sunday brunch or summer lunch.

Dairy/Pareve/Passover   *Serves 8 to 12*

4	stalks celery, finely diced	3	tablespoons dairy or pareve sour cream
2	tablespoons fresh lemon juice	3	cups smoked whitefish, bones removed
3	tablespoons mayonnaise		White pepper

Stir together celery, lemon juice, mayonnaise and sour cream. Gently fold in whitefish. Season with white pepper. Refrigerate until ready to serve.

A GRAND GRANOLA

Store this yummy cereal in single serving containers for easy snacking.

Pareve   *Serves 6 to 8*

3   cups rolled oats
1   cup slivered almonds
1   cup cashews
¾   cup sweetened coconut flakes
¼   cup plus 2 tablespoons
    firmly packed dark
    brown sugar

¼   cup plus 2 tablespoons
    maple syrup
¼   cup vegetable oil
¾   teaspoon salt
1   cup raisins

Preheat oven to 250°. In large bowl, toss oats, almonds, cashews, coconut and brown sugar. In separate bowl, whisk maple syrup, oil and salt. Combine both mixtures, spread onto 2 baking sheets. Bake 1 hour, stirring every 15 minutes to achieve an even color. Remove from oven. Transfer into large bowl. Stir in raisins, mix well. When cooled, store in airtight container at room temperature.

PASSOVER GRANOLA

Dairy/Pareve/Passover   *Serves 8 to 10*

2½ cups matzah farfel
1   cup sweetened coconut flakes
1   cup chopped fresh pecans

½   cup chopped dates
½   cup chopped dried apricots
1   cup raisins
¼   cup butter or pareve
    margarine, melted
1   teaspoon cinnamon
¼   cup firmly packed brown
    sugar
¼   cup honey
½   teaspoon salt
1   cup chocolate chips,
    optional

These recipes are so simple, a child would love to prepare them!
Children dressed for Carneval in Wiesbaden, Germany, c. 1926.

Preheat oven to 350°. Combine farfel, coconut, pecans and dried fruit. Add margarine or butter, cinnamon, brown sugar, honey and salt. Toss well. Put mixture on parchment lined baking sheet. Bake 15 minutes, turning frequently. Cool completely then add chocolate chips, if desired. Store in airtight container.

GOAT CHEESE AND ASPARAGUS ORECCHIETTE

In Italian, orecchiette means "little ears."
These small discs are perfect vehicles for this tangy sauce.

Dairy   *Serves 4*

1	pound orecchiette pasta	3	tablespoons fresh lemon juice
½	cup olive oil	1½	teaspoons finely grated lemon zest
1	medium onion, finely diced		Salt and pepper
1	pound medium asparagus spears, cut into ½-inch lengths	4	tablespoons goat cheese
½	teaspoon crushed red pepper	2	tablespoon minced chives
			Freshly grated Parmesan cheese

In large pot of boiling water, slightly undercook the orecchiette. Drain, reserving ⅔ cup of the cooking water. In large skillet, heat oil, add onion and cook over moderately low heat until soft. Add asparagus and crushed red pepper, cook over medium heat until crisp tender, about 2 minutes. Add juice, zest, salt, pepper and reserved cooking water to skillet. Add pasta, cook until al dente, slightly chewy to the bite, and asparagus is tender, about 2 minutes. Add goat cheese and chives, stir until melted. Serve with Parmesan cheese.

For a slightly different twist, try substituting fresh peas, quartered artichoke hearts or small broccoli florets for asparagus.

Choosing a wine accompaniment to pasta should be guided by what is on the pasta. A tangy red tomato sauce pairs well with dry reds while most cheeses work well with Chardonnays.

CHEESE TORTELLINI TOSS

Dairy   *Serves 8*

DRESSING

¼ cup fresh basil leaves
2 green onions, cut into 2-inch lengths
2 tablespoons chopped fresh parsley

1 tablespoon minced fresh dill
½ teaspoon salt
¼ teaspoon pepper
½ cup olive oil
¼ cup white wine vinegar

PASTA

2 (10-ounce) packages frozen cheese tortellini
2 medium tomatoes, chopped

8 ounces feta cheese
½ cup sliced black olives

In food processor, pulse basil, onions, parsley and dill. Add salt and pepper. Combine oil and vinegar, add to processor with motor running. Process until well blended.

Cook tortellini according to package directions, drain and cool. In large bowl, toss tortellini with dressing, tomatoes, cheese and olives. Refrigerate until serving.

MEDITERRANEAN PENNE PASTA

For pasta lovers, this penne with artichokes and Kalamata olives is a true delight.

Dairy   *Serves 6 to 8*

8 ounces penne pasta
⅔ cup crumbled feta cheese, divided
¼ cup grated Parmesan cheese, divided
1 medium red onion, halved, sliced
2 tablespoons olive oil

1 (14-ounce) can artichoke hearts, cut in large cubes
1 (16-ounce) can crushed tomatoes
¼ teaspoon salt
½ teaspoon pepper
8 ounces pitted Kalamata olives

Preheat oven to 350°. Cook pasta al dente, chewy to taste, drain. Place in lightly greased 11x7-inch baking dish. Sprinkle with ½ feta and Parmesan cheeses, set aside. In large skillet over medium high heat, sauté onion in olive oil, stirring constantly, until tender. Add artichokes and tomatoes, cook 2 to 3 minutes. Stir in salt, pepper and olives. Cover and reduce heat, simmer 10 minutes. Pour over pasta, sprinkle with remaining cheeses. Bake 15 to 20 minutes or until cheese melts.

If a pasta sauce is very thick, thin it with a little of the hot cooking water from the pasta.

For more flavorful baked pasta dishes, rub the baking pan with butter or pareve margarine, then sprinkle with grated lemon or orange zest. The pasta will come out of the oven infused with a hint of citrus flavor.

VODKA PENNE PASTA

So easy to prepare, Vodka Penne Pasta is a perfect weekday dish.
Serve with Italian bread, Avocado and Hearts of Palm Salad (page 72)
and Martini Trifle (page 230) for a complete meal.

Dairy   *Serves 2 to 4*

½	pound penne pasta or rigatoni	1½	cups heavy cream
2	tablespoons olive oil	½	cup tomato sauce
8	ounces sliced mushrooms		Salt and pepper
1-3	garlic cloves, minced		Freshly grated Parmesan cheese
¼	cup vodka		

Cook pasta according to package directions, drain and set aside. In large skillet, heat olive oil, sauté mushrooms and garlic for 30 seconds. Add vodka, allow to flame slightly, cooking until flames disappear. Stir in cream, bring to boil, reduce heat to simmer. Stir frequently until mixture is reduced by half. Add tomato sauce, season with salt and pepper. Fold in cooked pasta, stirring until coated, heat thoroughly. Sprinkle with Parmesan cheese.

Tomato lovers will enjoy adding diced canned tomatoes, up to 1 cup, or sliced sun-dried tomatoes, up to ½ cup, with cream.

MATZAH LASAGNA

Mangia, mangia...something Italian for Passover.

Dairy / Passover   *Serves 8*

3	tablespoons vegetable oil		Salt and pepper
2	large onions, chopped	5	matzahs, divided
2	minced garlic cloves	1	(8-ounce) can tomato sauce, divided
8	ounces Portobello mushrooms, diced	1	cup grated Monterey Jack cheese, divided
1	(14½-ounce) can diced tomatoes	½	cup grated Parmesan cheese, divided
½	teaspoon oregano		

Preheat oven to 350°. Grease 8-inch square pan. Heat oil in large skillet. Sauté onions, garlic and mushrooms until soft. Stir in tomatoes, oregano, salt and pepper. Simmer 10 minutes. Soak matzah in warm water 30 seconds, press out excess water. In prepared pan, layer matzahs, mushroom sauce, tomato sauce and Monterey Jack cheese. Repeat with second layer, ending with tomato sauce and Parmesan cheese. Bake 45 minutes.

When boiling pasta, do not add oil to the water as it makes pasta slick. Sauce does not adhere well to slick pasta.

Brunch, Dairy & Pasta

ROASTED VEGGIE LASAGNA

TOMATO SAUCE

1½	tablespoons diced white onion	½-1	cup water
2	minced garlic cloves	2	baby carrots
1	tablespoon olive oil		Pinch of kosher salt
2	(28-ounce) cans crushed tomatoes	½	tablespoon dried oregano
		1	teaspoon dried basil
1	(6-ounce) can tomato juice		Splash of red wine

VEGETABLES

1	large zucchini, diced	1	small red onion, diced
1	large carrot, peeled, diced		Olive oil
½	medium eggplant, peeled, diced		Kosher salt and pepper
¼	bunch fresh broccoli, diced	4	minced garlic cloves

PASTA

8 ounces lasagna noodles

CHEESE AND EGG MIXTURE

15	ounces ricotta cheese	8	ounces mozzarella cheese, thinly sliced
3-4	ounces creamy goat cheese		
1	large egg, beaten	2	teaspoons grated Parmesan cheese

In medium saucepan, sauté onion and garlic in olive oil until golden. Add tomatoes and tomato juice, simmer 10 minutes. Add water, carrots, salt, oregano, basil and red wine. Cover, simmer 10 to 15 minutes, stirring occasionally. Remove and discard carrots.

Preheat oven to 325°. Place all diced vegetables into large mixing bowl, coat lightly with olive oil. Sprinkle with salt, pepper and minced garlic. Spread onto a baking sheet. Bake 20 minutes or until golden brown.

Increase oven temperature to 350°. Fill large bowl with very hot water, add lasagna noodles, soak 20 minutes to soften. In medium bowl, stir ricotta cheese, goat cheese and egg until smooth and creamy. Pour small amount of tomato sauce in bottom of 12x9-inch lasagna pan. Layer noodles, mozzarella cheese, cheese and egg mixture, roasted vegetables, then sauce. Repeat layers, sprinkle Parmesan cheese on top. Bake 1 hour. Allow to set 10 minutes before serving.

One in a Million Kugel

Kugel

8	ounces butter, melted, divided	4	ounces cream cheese
1½	cups graham cracker crumbs	½	pint sour cream
8	ounces extra fine egg noodles	¾	cup sugar
½	pound creamed cottage cheese	5	eggs
		1	tablespoon vanilla

Optional Filling Ingredients

2 cups raisins, nuts, chopped pineapple, chopped dried fruits or chopped peaches or any combination of ingredients

Preheat oven to 350°. Mix 4 tablespoons butter with graham cracker crumbs, set aside. Cook, then drain egg noodles. Add remaining butter to noodles. Combine with cottage cheese, cream cheese, sour cream, sugar, eggs and vanilla. Fold in optional ingredients. Pour into greased 13x9-inch baking dish, top with graham cracker crumb mixture. Bake 1 hour.

To freeze, bake kugel 45 minutes. Cool and freeze. Defrost 4 hours, bake 30 minutes at 350°.

Sesame Noodles

A change of pace from potatoes and rice.

Pareve   *Serves 4*

1	(16-ounce) package angel hair or udon noodles	¼	cup tamari
2	tablespoons sugar	¼	cup toasted sesame oil
2	tablespoons balsamic vinegar	2-4	tablespoons toasted sesame seeds
			Green onions, chopped

Prepare noodles according to package. Whisk together sugar, vinegar, tamari and sesame oil. Pour over noodles, mix well. Toss with toasted sesame seeds, garnish with green onions.

Non-Dairy Sour Cream Substitute

2 cups silken tofu

¼ cup vegetable oil

3 tablespoons lemon juice

½ teaspoon salt

1 teaspoon sugar

Combine all ingredients and refrigerate. Or use one that is commercially available.

PINEAPPLE PEACH KUGEL

This Bundt-shaped beauty tastes as good as it looks.

Dairy/Passover   *Serves 12 to 15*

8	ounces butter, divided	1	(15-ounce) can crushed
1	pound wide noodles,		pineapple, drained
	cooked, drained	6	eggs
1	pound cottage cheese	1	cup sugar
1	pint sour cream	2	teaspoons vanilla
1	(15-ounce) can sliced		Dark brown sugar
	peaches, drained	½	cup pecan halves

Preheat oven to 325°. Add 1 stick of butter to hot noodles, stirring until butter melts. In large bowl, combine cottage cheese, sour cream, peaches and pineapple. Mix with noodles. In medium bowl, beat eggs with sugar and vanilla, add to noodles, mix thoroughly. Coat Bundt pan with 1 stick of butter. Pat dark brown sugar around sides and bottom of pan. Place pecan halves along creases of pan, embedding into butter and sugar. Pour in noodle mixture. Bake 1 hour. Immediately after removing from oven, place serving plate on top of the pan, flip it over to release from mold.

SAVORY VEGETABLE KUGEL

Frozen vegetables make this a year-round favorite.

Dairy/Pareve/Passover   *Serves 8*

KUGEL

4	ounces butter or pareve	1	(1-ounce) package onion
	margarine, melted		soup mix
8	ounces milk or pareve soy	3	large eggs, beaten
	milk	8	ounces fine noodles, cooked,
			drained

VEGETABLE CHOICES

1	(10-ounce) package frozen	2	(8-ounce) cans sliced
	chopped broccoli		mushrooms
1	(10-ounce) package frozen	16	ounces mushrooms, sliced,
	chopped spinach		sautéed

Preheat oven to 350°. In large bowl, combine butter or pareve margarine, milk, onion soup mix and eggs. With large wooden spoon, stir in cooked noodles and defrosted, drained vegetables. Pour into greased 2-quart casserole. Bake 1 hour or until firm to the touch. Serve immediately or refrigerate up to 2 days and reheat before serving.

Eastern European Jews were making kugels over 1000 years ago in the same manner as cholent. Kugels were cooked in a round covered pot that was dropped into the center of the cholent pot, taken to the baker on Friday and collected on Saturday afternoon. In 1950, at the request of members of the Hadassah Society in Minneapolis, a special pan was designed just for noodle kugels, so that a new generation could recreate the recipes their parents lovingly recalled. They called the pan a "bund" pan, which means "a gathering of people." It was trademarked a "Bundt" pan and has sold well ever since.

RABUN GAP CHOCOLATE COFFEE

Dairy / Pareve   *Serves 6*

½ pint dairy or pareve   2 tablespoons unsweetened
    whipping cream   cocoa powder
½ cup coffee liqueur   2 tablespoons sugar
4 cups hot coffee   Ground cinnamon

In saucepan, heat whipping cream and coffee liqueur, stirring until bubbles are just forming. In 2 to 3 batches, pour into blender with remaining ingredients, except cinnamon, blend 30 seconds. Garnish cups with sprinkling of ground cinnamon.

FAMOUS FAMILY HOT CHOCOLATE

Dairy / Passover   *Serves 6*

4   cups whole milk   10   ounces bitter chocolate
1½ cups heavy cream   2-8 ounces coffee or chocolate
½   cup sugar   liqueur

In a medium saucepan, combine milk, cream and sugar, bring to boil. Lower heat, simmer 3 minutes. Melt chocolate in the top of double boiler, pour milk mixture over chocolate. Strain through fine strainer. Add coffee or liqueur.

Executive Chef Gary Mennie, Canoe Restaurant, Atlanta, Georgia

WINTER NIGHT WHITE HOT CHOCOLATE

This will warm you up quickly.

Dairy   *Serves 4*

6	ounces white chocolate, grated	4	tablespoons brandy
1	cup heavy cream	2	tablespoons coffee liqueur
3	cups whole milk	1	(1.55-ounce) bar dark chocolate
1	teaspoon vanilla		

Place white chocolate in medium bowl. In medium saucepan over low heat, cook heavy cream and milk just until bubbles begin to form around edges of pan, being careful not to boil. Pour over white chocolate, allowing it to melt. Stir to combine. Whisk in vanilla, brandy and coffee liqueur, until light foam forms. With vegetable peeler, shave dark chocolate into curls to garnish each cup.

Opening night of the Mayfair Club outside the Biltmore Hotel, Atlanta, Georgia, 1930.

PEACHTREE SMOOTHIE

Dairy/Passover   *Serves 4*

2	cups peach nectar	1	cup peach yogurt
1	cup vanilla frozen yogurt	1½	cups frozen peach slices

Blend all ingredients until smooth.

BERRY BLAST SMOOTHIE

Dairy/Pareve/Passover   *Serves 4*

1	cup apple juice	1	cup frozen strawberries
1½	cups ready to drink lemonade	1	cup dairy or pareve raspberry sherbet
1	cup frozen raspberries		

In blender, purée all ingredients until smooth.

MANGO NECTAR ICED TEA

Pareve/Passover   *Yields 2 quarts*

2	quarts cold water		Sugar
9	herbal or black tea bags	6	slices mango
2½	cups mango nectar		

Bring water to rolling boil, remove from heat, add tea bags and steep for 5 to 6 minutes. Remove tea bags, add mango nectar. Add sugar and mango slices, stir well. Refrigerate for several hours to allow flavors to blend.

BREAKING *Bread*

BREADS

CZERNOWITZER CHALLAH

This recipe, adapted from a classic European challah (pronounced "CHERN-o-vitzer"), came from the late Lotte Langmann, a survivor of Auschwitz, via her great niece Sabina Gapany. It is almost foolproof and perfect for beginning bakers.

Pareve   *Yields 2 loaves*

1	envelope or 2¼ teaspoons instant yeast	
3¾	cups bread flour (17.6 ounces), divided	
¾	cup warm water	
3	large eggs, divided	

½   cup vegetable oil
1½   teaspoons salt
¼   cup sugar
     Poppy or sesame seeds, optional

In large bowl, whisk together yeast and ¾ cup flour, then whisk in warm water to make smooth slurry. Let mixture ferment uncovered 10 to 20 minutes, or until it begins to puff up slightly. Whisk in 2 eggs, oil, salt and sugar. When eggs are well incorporated plus salt and sugar have dissolved, stir in remaining 3 cups flour all at once, using hands or wooden spoon. When mixture resembles a shaggy ball, scrape it onto work surface, knead until smooth and soft, no more than 10 minutes. If dough is too firm to knead easily, add 1 to 2 tablespoon of water. If dough seems too wet, add 1 to 3 tablespoons of flour. Dough should feel smooth and firm, kneading easily without sticking to work surface. Place dough in clean warmed bowl, cover with plastic wrap. Let rise until doubled, about 2 hours.

Cover large baking sheet with parchment paper. Divide dough in ½ for 2 medium loaves. Braid or shape as desired. Position on prepared sheets. Cover with plastic wrap. Let loaves rise until tripled in size, about 1½ hours.

30 minutes before baking, place oven rack in lower third position, remove other racks. Preheat oven to 350°. Beat remaining egg with pinch of salt. When loaves have tripled and remain indented when gently pressed with finger, brush them with egg glaze. Sprinkle loaves with optional poppy or sesame seeds. Bake 25 to 35 minutes. After 20 minutes, switch breads from front to back. If loaves are browning too quickly, tent with foil. When loaves are well browned, remove from oven. Cool on wire rack.

Adapted from Maggie Glezer, A Blessing of Bread, Atlanta, Georgia

Bread for Friday night Shabbat dinner has been called challah for the last few hundred years. Challah has biblical roots as the portion of bread meant to be given to God.

Unbleached flour makes bread less airy, less chewy, yet tender and flavorful. Whole wheat flour adds texture, taste and color. The best flour choice contains at least 4 grams protein per 30 gram serving, or 13% protein. White whole wheat flour appears lighter and tastes sweeter than ordinary whole wheat, making breads and baked goods more flavorful.

BREAD MACHINE CHALLAH

Dairy/Pareve   *Yields 2 loaves*

WET INGREDIENTS

1 cup warm water
2 tablespoons butter or pareve
    margarine

1 large egg and 2 egg yolks,
    whites reserved
⅓ cup honey

DRY INGREDIENTS

3½ cups bread flour
1   teaspoon salt
½   cup sugar

¾ tablespoon instant active
    dry yeast

TOPPING

Honey

¼ cup poppy seeds

Active dry yeast in envelopes is a poor carbon dioxide producer. Instant active dry yeast is superior-quality yeast that can be added directly to the dough without proofing. It ferments better than active dry yeast, thus less is used. Use about ⅓ teaspoon active dry yeast or ¼ teaspoon instant yeast per cup flour in dough with little sugar or fat, in richer dough, this amount can be doubled. Instant active dry yeast is sold under names such as "Perfect Rise," "Bread Machine Yeast," "Rapid Rise," and "Quick Rise" in groceries.

Place wet ingredients in large bread machine in order listed. Add dry ingredients except yeast in order listed. Make well in center of dry ingredients, add yeast. Set machine for white bread, using manual setting, about 2 hours. When machine stops, remove dough, allow to rest 15 minutes. Flatten dough on floured board, divide into 2 equal parts, set aside 1 part. Separate other part into 3 medium rounded rope sections. Press tops of 3 ropes together. Braid and press ends together at bottom. Prepare 2 loaf pans with nonstick spray. Place braid in loaf pan. Follow same procedure for second loaf. Allow to rise in warm place 1½ hours or until dough rises to top of pans. Preheat oven to 325°. With wet pastry brush, brush tops with egg whites. Drizzle small amount of honey on top, cover with brush. Sprinkle with poppy seeds. Bake 28 to 35 minutes until tops and sides are golden brown. Remove from oven, cool 30 minutes before serving.

For one large challah, braid all the dough together. Bake on large cookie sheet.

Challah, the best part of Shabbat! Hebrew Academy kindergarten, Atlanta, Georgia, 1954.

Fruit-Filled Challah

Pareve   *Yields 2 loaves*

Bread

1	package active dry yeast	3	tablespoons honey
1	tablespoon sugar	¼	cup vegetable oil
1½	cups warm water, 110°-115°, divided	4	large egg whites
1	tablespoon salt	6-7	cups flour, divided
			Vegetable oil

Apple Filling

5	Rome or Gala apples, peeled, cored, diced	½	cup or more golden raisins or dried cranberries
	Juice of 1 lemon	¼	cup honey
		¾	teaspoon cinnamon

Glaze and Topping

1	large egg white	Cinnamon sugar

Dissolve yeast and sugar in ½ cup warm water, set aside until foamy. In large bowl beat remaining warm water, salt, honey, oil and egg whites. Stir in yeast mixture. Add 4 cups flour, 1 cup at a time, blending after each addition. Sprinkle work surface with flour. Knead dough 5 to 10 minutes, incorporating enough flour to make dough smooth and elastic. Place dough in greased bowl, turn dough over so there is grease on top. Cover with warm damp towel or plastic wrap, let rise in warm place until doubled in size, about 1½ hours.

Combine filling ingredients, cover and chill 1 hour. Drain, divide into six equal parts. Punch down dough, divide in half. Divide each half into 3 equal parts, for a total of 6 pieces. On floured board, roll each piece into a rectangle, covering remaining dough with plastic wrap. Brush with oil, top with even layer of apple filling to 1-inch from edges, roll into rope. Repeat with 2 other pieces of dough. Seal ends of 3 ropes together. Braid ropes, tucking sealed ends under, place on greased cookie sheet. Repeat with remaining dough and filling. Brush challahs with oil, cover with towel, allow to rise 45 minutes or until doubled in size. Preheat oven to 350°. Brush loaves with egg white, sprinkle with cinnamon sugar. Bake 30 to 40 minutes, cool on rack.

Having bread ingredients at room temperature before blending allows for quicker rising.

To proof dough, warm the oven to 175°, less than a minute. Turn off oven, put in dough and turn on oven light to maintain warmth. To use a microwave, heat 1 cup of water to boiling, turn off microwave and place dough inside. Preheated water keeps dough warm and allows proofing in a moist, draft-free environment.

ONION AND POPPY SEED PURIM RING

Start with the Chernowitzer Challah (page 193) recipe,
add onions and poppy seeds to make a crown fit for a queen.

Dairy/Pareve   *Yields 2-pound ring*

BREAD

1   recipe Czernowitzer Challah, rising (page 193)

FILLING

1½	cups very finely chopped yellow onions	6	tablespoons melted unsalted butter, margarine or oil
½	cup poppy seeds	1	egg
½	teaspoon salt		

Cover pizza pan with foil, grease generously or use parchment paper. Combine filling ingredients, divide in half.

When dough has doubled in bulk, do not punch down, cut into 2 pieces. Roll each piece into 30-inch strand. Using rolling pin, roll ropes into 30x4-inch rectangles. Heap in ½ filling down center of each strand. Pull long edges up over filling and pinch together. Place 2 ropes side by side, seams down. Start in middle, cross 1 rope over the other keeping seams facing down. Pinch ends together. Repeat with other half. Bring ends together to form ring. Pinch ends together to complete circle.

Carefully pick up ring. Place seam side down on prepared pan, cover with plastic wrap. Ring may be refrigerated up to 24 hours, and proofed after refrigerating.

Let ring rise until very soft and expanded, about 1 to 2 hours if previously refrigerated. 30 minutes before baking, place oven rack on lower position. Preheat oven to 350°.

Beat egg with pinch of salt. When ring has tripled and remains indented when gently pressed with finger, brush with egg glaze. Bake ring 45 to 50 minutes. After 30 minutes of baking, switch pan front to back. Continue baking 15 to 20 minutes. When well browned, remove from oven and cool on rack.

Adapted from Maggie Glezer, A Blessing of Bread, Atlanta, Georgia

The twisted ring of the Purim Ring looks like Queen Esther's crown, and the onions and poppy seeds are not only delicious, but also honor this Queen's bravery and piety. Queen Esther observed the rules of kashruth in King Ahashuarus' palace by eating only fruits, vegetables, nuts and seeds.

Dough can be mixed quickly in a food processor. Using the metal blade, combine all dry ingredients, including yeast, pulse a few times, then process for 2 minutes. Slowly add wet ingredients while the machine is running, process until dough forms a ball. Knead on a floured surface to smooth dough. Continue with the recipe.

CRANBERRY PECAN WHOLE WHEAT BREAD

This award-winning bread will rise to your expectations.

Pareve   *Yields 2 loaves*

3⅓	cups white whole wheat flour	1	tablespoon plus ½ teaspoon salt
3⅓	cups flour	1½	cups dried sweetened cranberries
1	tablespoon instant yeast	2	cups raw pecans
2⅔-3	cups warm water, divided		

Mix flour, yeast and 2⅔ cups water until just combined, dough will be soft and very sticky. Add remaining water only if the dough seems too firm, let dough rest 15 to 20 minutes. Turn dough out onto lightly floured work surface, knead briefly to smooth, dough should be very sticky. Do not add more flour. Use a spatula to knead in salt, cranberries and pecans. Dough will tighten and dry considerably. Cover dough, allow to rise in warm place about 2 hours or until dough triples in volume and becomes very soft.

Line baking sheet with parchment paper. Place dough on floured surface. Cut into two pieces. Shape into flat ovals, fold like envelope and turn over so seam side is down. Shape into either 9-inch loaf or longer thin roll. Place loaves seam side down on baking sheet, cover with plastic wrap. Refrigerate overnight or up to 24 hours.

Remove dough from refrigerator, let sit 2 hours or more. Loaves should be very soft and rebound very slowly or not at all when gently pressed. 30 minutes before baking, place oven rack in bottom third position. Place extra baking sheet on rack. Remove all other racks, preheat oven to 400°.

Brush loaves with water. Cut ½ inch deep slash down length of loaves. Place loaded sheet onto hot sheet, bake about 35 to 40 minutes, until dark brown and crusty. After 25 minutes of baking, turn the breads from front to back. Fully cool on rack.

Judaism proscribes the recitation of a variety of blessings to acknowledge that all the fruits of the earth come from God. The blessing over bread, hamotzi, gives thanks to God for bringing forth bread "from the earth". Bread in this blessing symbolizes all other foods to be eaten during the meal.

ROSEMARY FOCACCIA BREAD

Delicious as a snack or with a soup or salad.
For a treat, try it with Slow-Roasted Vidalia Onion Soup (page 91).

Dairy   *Serves 8 to 10*

1	pound frozen bread dough, thawed	½	cup grated Parmesan cheese, divided
3	tablespoons olive oil, divided	6	Kalamata olives, quartered
1	tablespoon chopped fresh rosemary	2	large garlic cloves, thinly sliced
	Pepper	4	oil packed sun-dried tomatoes, cut julienne
			Fresh rosemary

Preheat oven to 450°. Place dough in bowl, sprinkle with 1 tablespoon olive oil, rosemary and pepper. Knead dough until ingredients are combined. Roll into 9x6-inch rectangle on floured surface. Transfer to baking sheet. Flatten and shape into 12x9-inch rectangle. Brush with 1 tablespoon olive oil and sprinkle with ¼ cup Parmesan cheese, pressing into dough. Bake 12 minutes or until almost done. Top with olives, garlic, sun-dried tomatoes, remaining Parmesan cheese and olive oil. Garnish with fresh rosemary. Lightly cover, bake 5 more minutes. Cool slightly, cut.

For a change, substitute black olives and thyme for Kalamata olives and rosemary. Use thinly sliced yellow onions, oregano, garlic, fresh sage leaves, roasted red peppers and/or sautéed fennel. Substitute 1 teaspoon dried rosemary for fresh.

To freshen bread, preheat oven to 325°. Place bread in paper bag, close tightly and sprinkle outside of bag with water. Heat 5 to 10 minutes.

SWISS CHEESE FRENCH BREAD

An easy and versatile bread that can be served as an appetizer or with a dairy or pareve entrée.

Dairy   *Serves 6 to 8*

1	medium onion, finely chopped	1	long loaf French or sourdough bread
8	ounces butter	12	ounces Swiss cheese, shredded
2	tablespoons poppy seeds		
⅛	teaspoon salt		

Preheat oven to 350°. Sauté onion in butter until translucent. Add poppy seeds and salt. Cut bread in 2-inch slices ¾ way down, keeping loaf intact. Between each slice, place 1½-2 tablespoons Swiss cheese and 1½ tablespoons onion mixture. Wrap in foil. Bake 15 to 20 minutes.

TENDER BUTTERMILK BISCUITS

Dairy   *Yields 12 biscuits*

2	cups plus 2 tablespoons flour	2	tablespoons sugar
2	teaspoons double acting baking powder	4	tablespoons shortening
½	teaspoon salt	½	cup cold cream
½	teaspoon baking soda	1	cup cold buttermilk
			Flour
			Melted butter or margarine

Preheat oven to 450°. Generously grease baking sheet or cover with parchment paper. Sift first 5 ingredients into large bowl. Add shortening, rubbing it in with fingertips until mixture resembles coarse crumbs. Add cream and buttermilk, gently work into dry ingredients until wet dough forms. Place flour in bowl. Use nonstick spray to coat ¼ cup measuring cup. Flour hands, scoop out dough, gently roll in flour, shape dough into 2-inch balls and shake off excess flour. For very soft biscuits, place dough balls next to each other. For crustier biscuits, set them 2 inches apart on baking sheet. Brush tops with butter. Bake until golden brown, about 12 to 14 minutes.

For uniform biscuits roll out dough to 1-inch thickness. Using 2-inch diameter biscuit cutter or a drinking glass, cut out biscuits. Gather scraps and roll out to 1-inch thickness and cut out additional biscuits.

White Lily Flour makes biscuits very tender. Other flours produce chewier biscuits.

Once shortening has been added, this biscuit mixture can be stored, refrigerated in an airtight container up to 1 month.

Thanksgiving dinner, Fort Benning, Columbus, Georgia, 1942.

BEER-Y GOOD HUSHPUPPIES

There are scrumptious when served with warm peach preserves.

Pareve　　　　　　　　　　　*Yields 16 to 18 pieces*

1	cup self-rising white cornmeal mix	1	tablespoon sugar
½	cup self-rising flour	1	large egg, lightly beaten
½	cup finely diced onion	½	cup beer
			Vegetable oil for frying

In large bowl, combine cornmeal, flour, onion and sugar. Slightly mix egg and beer together, pour into dry mixture. Mix until just moistened, being careful not to over mix. Allow to rest 10 minutes. Pour 2-inches of oil into deep heavy iron skillet. Heat to 375° or until drop of water sizzles. Drop dough by spoonfuls into hot oil a few at a time, frying until brown on both sides, 2 to 3 minutes. Remove with slotted spoon. Drain on wire rack set over paper towels. Hushpuppies can be kept warm in oven up to 30 minutes before serving.

Beer in hushpuppies? You bet!
Super Saving Store, Beer & Wine, Atlanta, Georgia, c. 1960.

SPEAKING OF CORNBREAD

*I treasure my mother's old cast iron skillet that was
handed down to me along with our prized family cornbread recipe.*

Dairy   *Serves 6 to 8*

2   cups yellow stone ground
     cornmeal
1   cup flour
¾   tablespoon baking soda
½   teaspoon salt
¾   cup buttermilk
2   jalapeño peppers, finely
     chopped, optional

2   cups fresh corn, cut off cob,
     optional
1   cup grated Cheddar cheese,
     optional
2   very ripe tomatoes, finely
     chopped, optional
3   tablespoons vegetable oil

Preheat oven to 450°. In large bowl, sift together dry ingredients. Stir
in buttermilk plus sufficient water to make soupy mixture. Fold in any
combination of optional ingredients. Pour oil into cast iron skillet. Place
skillet in oven to preheat. When hot, remove skillet from oven and pour
in mixture. Bake 20 to 30 minutes until brown.

They'll be cooking southern in no time.
Soviet émigrés arrive in Atlanta, Georgia, 1979.

SOUTHERN SPOON BREAD

Serve this recipe's pareve version with Mouthwatering Beef Ribs (page 121) or Southern Fried Chicken (page 134) for an old-fashioned southern supper.

Dairy/Pareve   *Serves 8 to 10*

SPOON BREAD

1	quart milk or pareve soy milk	1	teaspoon baking powder
1	cup cornmeal	4	tablespoons butter or pareve margarine, softened
1	teaspoon salt	4	large eggs, separated
1	tablespoon sugar		

ZUCCHINI

2	shallots, finely minced	2	tablespoons butter or pareve margarine
2-3	zucchini, grated		

CORN

2-3 ears of corn, kernels removed

MUSHROOM

½	pound mushrooms, chopped	2	tablespoons butter or pareve margarine

Scald milk in top of double boiler. Combine cornmeal, salt, sugar and baking powder. Stir into hot milk. Add butter or margarine. Cook 10 to 15 minutes, until thickened, stirring frequently. Slowly stir into egg yolks, whisking well. Beat egg whites to stiff peaks, fold into spoon bread. Bake in greased 2-quart casserole 45 minutes.

To prepare Zucchini Spoon Bread, sauté shallots and zucchini in butter or margarine. Add to batter before folding in egg whites.

To prepare Corn Spoon Bread, add corn kernels to batter before folding in egg whites.

To prepare Mushroom Spoon Bread, sauté mushrooms, in butter or pareve margarine. Add to batter before folding in egg whites.

To scald milk, heat until it almost boils. There will be bubbles around the side of the pan.

PESACH ROLLS

These rolls are the answer to bread cravings during Passover.

Pareve/Passover   *Serves 6*

⅓   cup vegetable oil   1   tablespoon sugar
⅔   cup water   1   cup matzah meal
1   teaspoon salt   3   large eggs

Preheat oven to 375°. In medium pot boil oil, water, salt and sugar for 1 minute. Remove from heat, stir in matzah meal. Beat in eggs, 1 at a time. Drop by heaping tablespoons onto well greased cookie sheet. Bake 30 minutes.

Eat your bread with joy, drink your wine with a merry heart.

~Ecclesiastes, 9:7

Passover seder, Atlanta, Georgia, 1944.

PUMPKIN RAISIN NUT BREAD

*My great aunt gave me her most treasured
recipes when I was a young bride. This one's my very favorite.*

Dairy/Pareve   **Serves 12 to 15**

1	cup butter or pareve margarine	½	teaspoon baking powder
2½	cups sugar	1	teaspoon cinnamon
4	large eggs	1	teaspoon ground cloves
2	cups puréed pumpkin, not pie filling	1	teaspoon salt
3	cups flour	½	cup water
2	teaspoons baking soda	½	cup chopped nuts, any kind
		½	cup chopped raisins

Preheat oven to 350°. Grease and flour 2 loaf pans. Cream butter or margarine with sugar until fluffy. Beat in eggs, 1 at a time. Stir in pumpkin. Sift flour, baking soda, baking powder, cinnamon, cloves and salt. Fold dry mixture into pumpkin mixture, alternating with water. Stir in nuts and raisins. Pour batter into pans. Bake 50 to 60 minutes or until tester inserted in center comes out clean. Remove from oven. Invert to remove from pans. Cool on rack.

For that finishing touch, frost with Butter Cream Cheese Frosting found with Pineapple Carrot Cake (page 254).

"I treasure all my mama's old recipes, but especially those stained with flour, egg yolks and brown sugar."

SCHNECKEN

Schnecken, German for "snails", is a rich yeast roll that originated in Europe, immigrated to Pennsylvania and became the American sticky bun.

Dairy   *Yields 36 pieces*

DOUGH

2	tablespoons or 2 packages active dry yeast	1	cup milk
½	cup lukewarm water	3	large eggs
½	cup sugar, divided	6-6½	cups unbleached flour
8	ounces unsalted butter	1	teaspoon salt

BOTTOM OF PANS

4	ounces unsalted butter	¾	cup honey, divided
1½	cups firmly packed dark brown sugar, divided	⅛	cup whole blanched almonds

FILLING

1	cup chopped walnuts, divided	½	teaspoon cinnamon, divided
1	cup currants, divided		

In large mixing bowl, dissolve yeast in water with 1 teaspoon sugar, set aside 10 minutes. Melt butter with milk in saucepan over low heat, remove and cool to lukewarm. Beat milk, remaining sugar and eggs into yeast. Gradually stir in flour and salt. Dough will be very sticky. Cover with plastic wrap in bowl, refrigerate overnight.

Melt butter, generously brush on bottoms and sides of 36 muffin cups. Put ½ teaspoon firmly packed brown sugar and 1 teaspoon honey in each cup. Top with 3 almonds.

Preheat oven to 350°. Divide dough into 3 portions. On floured board, roll each portion into 12x7-inch rectangle. Brush dough with melted butter remaining from greasing muffin tins. Combine remaining sugar, walnuts, currants and cinnamon. Sprinkle with ⅓ of mixture. Roll tightly, like a jelly roll. Repeat with other portions. Cut each roll into 12 slices. Place slices in muffin cups, cut side down. Let rise, uncovered, 30 minutes. Brush tops with melted butter, bake 15 minutes. Reduce oven to 325°, bake 20 minutes until golden. Immediately invert onto parchment paper.

To prevent dough from sticking as it is rolled, use a heavyweight silicone rolling pin.

CHOCOLATE STREUSEL COFFEE BREAD

Dairy/Pareve   *Serves 8 to 10*

DOUGH

3 packages yeast	1 cup milk or pareve soy milk
½ cup warm water	1 cup sugar
1 cup plus 2 tablespoons sugar, divided	Dash of salt
6 cups flour	2 large eggs

FILLING

4 teaspoons unsweetened cocoa	2 teaspoons dairy or soy milk or pareve sour cream
8 teaspoons sugar	½ cup raisins
8 ounces butter or pareve margarine, softened	½ cup chopped nuts

Dissolve yeast in warm water and 2 tablespoons sugar, proof 5 minutes. Add flour, milk, 1 cup sugar, salt and eggs, mix well. Cover, let rise until double in size or refrigerate to rise overnight.

Preheat oven to 350°. Divide dough into 9 equal pieces. Roll each piece as thinly as possible into rectangle. Blend together cocoa, sugar, butter or margarine and 2 teaspoons milk or pareve sour cream in food processor. Spread chocolate filling, raisins and nuts down center of each rectangle. Roll lengthwise to cover filling, set aside. When 3 rectangles are filled and rolled, twist into braid, tucking ends under. Place on baking sheet, cover and let rise until doubled in size, about 1 to 1½ hours. Bake about 30 minutes.

This recipe calls for either dairy or soy milk!
Milk provided by the Jewish Ladies Aid Society Milk Fund,
Columbus, Georgia, 1932.

In 1924 in Columbus, Georgia, Laura Rosenberg, later known as the "Milk Lady", witnessed the "pinched faces and undernourished bodies" of children in a local school. A member of the Jewish Ladies Aid Society, Rosenberg was instrumental in opening the first of seven stations in Columbus supplying milk and crackers daily to more than 530 needy children.

STRAWBERRY SUNRISE BREAD

*It is traditional to take bread and salt as a house
warming gift. This one would be appreciated and enjoyed.*

Dairy/Pareve   *Yields 3 loaves*

1 cup water	2 packages dry yeast
¾ cup vegetable shortening	½ cup lukewarm water
8½ cups sifted unbleached bread flour, divided	Vegetable shortening for pans
1 cup cold water	4 ounces butter or pareve margarine
2 large eggs, beaten	1 (18-ounce) jar strawberry preserves
2 teaspoons salt	
¾ cup sugar	

In small saucepan, boil 1 cup water. Add shortening, stirring until melted,
cool. Sift 7½ cups flour into large bowl, set aside. In another large bowl,
beat cold water with eggs, salt and sugar. Beat in cooled shortening mix.
In small bowl, dissolve yeast in ½ cup lukewarm water, set aside to proof
5 to 7 minutes. Add to egg mixture. Slowly add flour, 1 cup at a time,
until completely incorporated and wet dough forms. Cover, refrigerate
overnight.

Remove dough from refrigerator. Grease 3 round glass or metal baking
pans. Knead dough with about 1 cup flour until well mixed, divide dough
into 3 portions. Knead one piece on well floured board, roll out to ½-inch
thick rectangle. Melt butter or margarine, brush small amount on flattened
dough. Spread preserves evenly. Roll up like a long jelly roll then twist
to fit into baking dish. Repeat with remaining 2 balls of dough. Brush
extra melted butter evenly across top of dough. Allow bread to rise 1 to
½ hours. Preheat oven to 350°. Bake 45 minutes or until tester inserted
in center comes out clean.

*Love tastes sweet,
but only with bread.*

~Yiddish proverb

CRANBERRY ORANGE QUICK BREAD

*Resist the urge to cut and taste this fragrant bread when
it is hot out of the oven. The texture and flavor improve as it cools.*

Pareve   *Yields 1 loaf*

2 cups sifted flour	¼ cup halved fresh cranberries
¾ cup sugar	½ cup chopped walnuts or
1½ teaspoons baking powder	pecans
1 teaspoon salt	2 teaspoons grated orange zest
½ teaspoon baking soda	1 large egg, beaten
1 cup coarsely chopped fresh	¾ cup orange juice
cranberries	2 tablespoons vegetable oil

Preheat oven to 350°. Grease 9½x5-inch loaf pan. Sift together dry ingredients. Stir in cranberries, nuts and orange zest. Whisk egg, orange juice and oil. Stir into dry ingredients until just moistened. Pour mixture into pan. Bake 50 minutes or until tester inserted in center comes out clean. Remove from pan and cool.

LIGHT LEMON POPOVERS

*Light and airy, these popovers are quite easy to prepare.
They have a crisp brown crust and moist interior that is delectable.*

Dairy   *Yields 6 large popovers*

2 eggs, beaten	3 tablespoons very finely
1 cup whole milk	chopped pecans
1 cup flour	2 tablespoons unsalted butter
½ teaspoon salt	or margarine, softened
1 teaspoon finely grated lemon zest	

Preheat oven to 475°. Grease popover or muffin pans. Beat together eggs, milk, flour and salt. Stir in zest and pecans. Let batter rest 30 minutes. Stir once to distribute pecans. Place popover pans or deep muffin tins in oven until very hot. Put ½ teaspoon butter in each cup. Pour batter equally into cups. Bake 15 minutes, reduce temperature to 350° and bake 20 to 25 minutes more until puffed and brown. Serve immediately.

For garlic Parmesan popovers, omit pecans and lemon zest. Mince and mash 1 garlic clove to a paste with the salt, whisk into batter with the flour. Pour ½ of the batter into pans, then sprinkle with ¼ cup Parmesan cheese. Cover with rest of batter and sprinkle another ¼ cup cheese over tops. Bake as directed.

Successful bread baking requires precise oven temperatures. Check temperature with a good oven thermometer.

ORANGE RAISIN SCONES

These scones are fabulous with marmalade, fruit preserves, lemon curd or honey.

Dairy   *Yields 12 scones*

3	cups flour	½	cup cold vegetable shortening, cut into pieces
⅓	cup sugar		
2½	teaspoons baking powder	1	cup plus 2 tablespoons cold buttermilk
¾	teaspoon salt		
½	teaspoon baking soda	¾	cup golden raisins
½	cup cold unsalted butter, cut into pieces	1	tablespoon grated orange zest
			Sugar

Preheat oven to 425°. Line large baking sheet with parchment paper. Blend flour, sugar, baking powder, salt and baking soda. Add butter and shortening. Rub together, using fingertips, until coarse meal forms. Add 1 cup buttermilk, raisins and zest. Stir gently until dough comes together in large moist clumps. Do not over mix. Gather dough into ball. Transfer dough to lightly floured work surface. Gently knead 3 or 4 turns just to combine. Divide into 2 pieces, flatten into ¾-inch thick rounds. Using floured knife, cut each round into 8 wedges. Transfer wedges to baking sheet, brush with remaining buttermilk and sprinkle with additional sugar. Bake scones until light golden brown, about 15 minutes. Serve warm or at room temperature.

For lemon scones, substitute lemon zest for orange zest and add 1 teaspoon vanilla to buttermilk. For fruit scones, substitute halved cranberries, chopped pineapple, dried diced apricots, blueberries or currants for raisins. To make chocolate scones, substitute semisweet chocolate mini chips for raisins.

If a recipe calls for unsalted butter and only salted butter is available, reduce the salt listed in the ingredients; ½ pound salted butter contains ¾ teaspoon salt.

H. Lander Grocery & Market, Atlanta, Georgia, 1935.

The Breman's Best Blueberry Muffins

Very tender and bursting with blueberries, these will become a summer morning tradition.

Dairy/Pareve   *Serves 10 to 12*

½ cup butter or pareve margarine	½ cup milk or soy milk
1 cup sugar	1 teaspoon vanilla
2 large eggs	2½ cups blueberries, divided
2 cups flour	Butter or pareve margarine, to coat
2 teaspoons baking powder	2 teaspoons sugar
½ teaspoon salt	

Preheat oven to 375°. On low speed, cream butter or margarine and 1 cup sugar until fluffy. Add eggs, 1 at a time, blending well after each addition. Sift together dry ingredients. Combine milk and vanilla. Blend milk and dry ingredients, alternately, into butter mixture. Mash ½ cup blueberries, fold into batter. Gently stir in remaining 2 cups whole berries. Grease muffin tins and top of muffin pan or use paper liners. Pile mixture high in each cup. Sprinkle tops with 2 teaspoons sugar. Bake 30 minutes. Cool in pan at least 30 minutes before inverting to remove.

Before adding fruit to batter, spoon a tablespoon or so of batter into each greased muffin cup. Stir the fruit into the remaining batter, then divide the batter among the muffin cups.

Over mixing muffin batter results in a tough muffins with tunnels and a compact texture. Do not use electric mixer. Only 10 to 15 strokes by hand are needed to moisten ingredients, batter should be lumpy with traces of flour.

Pass this one along to the next generation.
Family photograph, Atlanta, Georgia, c.1900.

CHEESE-Y MUFFINS
WITH BLUEBERRY SAUCE

These light flavorful muffins are just right with scrambled eggs.

Dairy/Pareve   *Serves 6 to 8*

COTTAGE CHEESE MUFFINS

16	ounces cottage cheese	⅛	teaspoon salt
2	large eggs, beaten	1	cup flour
3-6	tablespoons sugar	1	teaspoon baking powder
4	ounces unsalted butter, melted		

BLUEBERRY SAUCE

1	teaspoon cornstarch, or more	1	cup fresh blueberries
¾	cup plus 2 tablespoons water, divided	3	tablespoons orange juice
		½	cup sugar

Preheat oven to 350°. Whisk cottage cheese, eggs, sugar and butter. Combine dry ingredients, stir into cottage cheese mixture. Pour into 16 well greased nonstick muffin tins. Bake 25 minutes or until done. To prepare sauce, dissolve cornstarch in 2 tablespoons water. Bring remaining water and ingredients to boil. Add enough cornstarch mixture to thicken sauce slightly. Serve muffins with Blueberry Sauce.

Occasionally, one muffin will stick to its cup. Use a curved grapefruit knife to gently free the bottom of the muffin from the cup.

An easy way to grease muffin and loaf pans with butter is to use a pastry brush, since it can reach corners.

MINI CARROT MUFFINS

Pareve   *Serves 12 to 18*

¾	cup sugar	1	cup flour
¾	cup vegetable oil	2	large eggs, beaten
½-1	teaspoon lemon juice	1	teaspoon vanilla
1	teaspoon baking powder	½	teaspoon salt
1	cup grated carrots		

Preheat oven to 375°. Whisk sugar with oil and add remaining ingredients. Coat 2 mini muffin pans with nonstick spray. Spoon in mixture until pans are half full. Bake 12 to 15 minutes or until just brown. Cool 10 minutes and remove from pans.

GEORGIA PEACH STREUSEL MUFFINS

These gorgeous muffins are as beautiful as a perfectly ripe peach.

Dairy   *Serves 12 to 15*

STREUSEL

¾	cup flour	¼	cup unsalted butter
⅓	cup sugar		

MUFFINS

⅔	cup sugar	½	cup milk
¼	teaspoon salt	⅓	cup unsalted butter, melted
¼	teaspoon mace	1	teaspoon lemon juice
2	cups flour	1	teaspoon vanilla
1	tablespoon baking powder	2	fresh peaches, peeled,
1	large egg		pitted, finely diced
½	cup heavy whipping cream		

Preheat oven to 350°. In food processor, process streusel ingredients. Add more flour, if needed, to keep mixture crumbly, set aside. Sift dry ingredients into bowl. In separate bowl, whisk wet ingredients. Add to dry ingredients and stir to just combine. Stir in peaches. Grease and flour 18 muffin tins, fill ⅔ full with batter, sprinkle tops with streusel. Bake approximately 20 minutes.

Raphael Moses, a leading member of an established Jewish family in South Carolina, moved to Columbus, Georgia. A plantation owner and Confederate officer, in 1851, he was among the first to market peaches within Georgia. Credited with being the first to ship and sell peaches successfully outside of the South, Moses developed the method of packing them in champagne baskets, which preserved their flavor until they reached their destination.

Checking for ripeness, Dublin, Georgia, c.1925.

Almost any fruit works in this recipe. Good choices include chopped cranberries, blueberries, diced apples, banana chunks, pitted halved cherries, diced strawberries or raspberries. When using highly colored frozen fruits like raspberries, cranberries and blueberries, defrost only partially to prevent mashing the fruit or discoloring the batter.

RISE AND SHINE BRAN MUFFINS

These muffins are best made, refrigerated, then served 2 days later.

Dairy   *Yields 12 muffins*

½	cup unsalted butter, softened	½	cup raisins
¼	cup firmly packed light brown sugar	1	cup flour
		1	teaspoon baking soda
1	large egg, beaten	¼	teaspoon salt
1	cup sour cream	1	cup wheat bran
¼	cup dark molasses	2	tablespoons sugar

Preheat oven to 400°. In large bowl of electric mixer, cream butter and brown sugar until light and fluffy. Beat in egg, sour cream and molasses. Stir in raisins. In another bowl, whisk together flour, baking soda, salt and bran. Stir mixtures together until just combined. The batter should be lumpy. Spoon batter into 12 well buttered ⅓-cup muffin tins. Bake on middle rack of oven 15 to 20 minutes until golden brown and springy to the touch. Turn muffins out onto rack, sprinkle with sugar and cool.

For a change of pace, substitute chopped apples, bananas, dried apricots, fresh blueberries or sweetened coconut flakes for the raisins.

For uniform size, use an ice cream scoop to fill muffin tins. When baking less than a full tin, fill empty compartments with water to ensure that heat is evenly conducted.

CINNAMON MAPLE BUTTER

Dairy/Pareve/Passover   *Yields ½ cup*

½	cup unsalted butter or pareve margarine, softened	2	drops vanilla
		¼	teaspoon cinnamon
2	tablespoons maple syrup	⅛	teaspoon salt

Cream together all ingredients until smooth.

FRESH HERB BUTTER

Dairy/Pareve/Passover   *Yields ¾ cup*

½	cup butter or pareve margarine, softened	2	tablespoons minced green onions
1	tablespoon milk	1	teaspoon dry dill weed
		½	teaspoon dry tarragon

Cream together all ingredients until smooth.

CITRUS HONEY BUTTER

Dairy/Pareve/Passover   *Yields ¾ cup*

½   cup butter or pareve
      margarine, softened

⅓   cup honey
1   teaspoon grated orange or
      lemon zest

Cream together all ingredients.

GINGER PEACH BUTTER

Dairy/Pareve/Passover   *Yields 1 cup*

½   cup butter or pareve
      margarine, softened
¼   cup sugar
¾   teaspoon chopped
      crystallized ginger

⅛   teaspoon salt
¼   cup mashed ripe peeled
      peaches

Beat butter until fluffy. Stir in remaining ingredients until combined.

KUMQUAT MARMALADE

Fresh kumquats are found from November through March like their cousin, the orange.
They are tart and sweet at the same time, making exotic marmalades.

Dairy/Pareve   *Yields 12 jars*

2   pounds kumquats, seeded,
        sliced into strips
6   cups water
1   (2-ounce) package
        powdered fruit pectin
½   cup fresh lemon juice
½   teaspoon unsalted butter or
        pareve margarine

12   whole cloves
6   cinnamon sticks, broken in
        pieces
4-6   whole star anise
9½   cups sugar
¼-½ cup brandy, optional
½   tablespoon brandy extract,
        optional

Combine prepared kumquats and water in 2½-quart heavy saucepan, bring to boil uncovered. Simmer 1 hour or until fruit is tender. Measure kumquats and liquid. Add water, if needed, to make exactly seven cups. Return to saucepan with pectin, lemon juice and butter or margarine. Put cloves, cinnamon and star anise in cheesecloth bag, tie with thread. Bring kumquat mixture with spice bag to boil. Stir in sugar, return to full rolling boil. Cook 4 minutes, stirring constantly. Remove from heat, cool slightly. Add brandy or extract. Stir 5 minutes to prevent floating fruit. Remove spice bag. Ladle into twelve 8-ounce sterilized jars or store in plastic containers in refrigerator or freezer.

AND *Everything* NICE

DESSERTS & PIES

SACHER TORTE

In the 1970s and 1980s, when my husband was the Austrian Consul in Atlanta, we served this Viennese torte to our dinner guests. Sometimes I made 16 or more for a dinner party.

Dairy/Pareve   *Serves 12 to 15*

CAKE

1	cup butter or pareve margarine	6	ounces semisweet chocolate chips
1	cup sugar	1	cup flour
8	large eggs, separated	1	teaspoon baking powder

ICING AND FILLING

3	ounces semisweet chocolate chips	½	cup sugar
1	teaspoon water	1	(6-ounce) jar apricot preserves
1½	teaspoons butter, pareve margarine or vegetable oil	½	cup dairy or pareve whipped cream

Preheat oven to 350°. Cream butter or margarine. Add sugar then egg yolks, 1 at a time, continuing to beat. Melt chocolate chips. Very slowly fold chocolate into butter or margarine mixture. Mix flour and baking powder together, fold into batter. Beat egg whites until stiff. Fold into mixture. Pour into greased, floured 10-inch springform pan. Bake 1 hour. Allow cake to cool before removing pan sides.

Melt chocolate chips in double boiler. Add water and butter, margarine or oil, stirring until smooth. Stir in sugar, bring to boil. Add up to 1 teaspoon water if icing is too thick, stir well. Remove from heat.

Cut cake horizontally into 2 layers. Spread apricot preserves on bottom layer. Replace top layer. Spread icing over sides and top of cake. If desired, freeze at this point. To serve, top each slice with whipped cream.

Wedding, Columbus, Georgia, c.1900.

"When my son was in the Vietnam War, I mailed him a Sacher Torte every single week. Unfortunately it never arrived at the base because he and his driver devoured it on the way back from the post office. When he got married, he asked me to make it for his wedding cake."

CHOCOLATE MINT TORTE

*If taste buds tingle at the thought of chocolate and mint, this
layered combination of chocolate, peppermint and ice cream is the answer.*

Dairy — *Serves 12*

2	(1-ounce) squares unsweetened chocolate	6	mini chocolate covered peppermint patties, chopped
4	ounces unsalted butter	6	cups chocolate or vanilla ice cream, softened
2	large eggs	12	hard peppermint candies, crushed
1	cup sugar	½	cup hot fudge topping
¼	cup flour		
1	teaspoon vanilla		

Preheat oven to 350°. Melt chocolate and butter in double boiler. In the bowl of electric mixer, beat eggs with sugar until well incorporated. Slowly pour in melted chocolate mixture. Add flour and vanilla. Spread batter in greased 9- or 10-inch springform pan. Bake 15 minutes or until just done. Sprinkle chopped peppermint patties over warm cake. Let stand 5 minutes. Spread melted patties over surface with small spatula or back of spoon. Cool in pan on wire rack. When completely cool, combine ice cream and peppermint candies in large bowl. Spread evenly over cake. Freeze until firm, at least 2 hours. Remove sides of pan. Place fudge topping in small heavy duty plastic bag. Snip tiny hole in corner of bag. Squeeze to drizzle fudge sauce over torte. Serve immediately, or cover and freeze.

To cut cheesecakes and tortes, start with a ruler and measure the slices. Create guide marks with the tip of a sharp knife. Use unflavored waxed dental floss to create neat slices.

Chocolate Mocha Roulade

Seder guests will ask, "Why don't we have this dessert on all other nights?"

Dairy/Pareve/Passover   *Serves 10*

Roulade

6	eggs, at room temperature, separated
1	cup sugar, divided
1	teaspoon vanilla

¼	cup flour or Passover cake meal
¼	cup cocoa powder
	Regular or Passover confectioners' sugar

Filling

1½	cups heavy cream or pareve whipping cream
¼	cup regular or Passover confectioners' sugar

2	tablespoons instant coffee powder

Whipped Cream Frosting

1	cup heavy cream or pareve whipping cream
2	tablespoons regular or Passover confectioners' sugar

1-2	tablespoons instant coffee powder
½	cup finely chopped pecans or almonds

Preheat oven to 325°. Prepare 15x10½-inch jelly roll pan or rimmed cookie sheet with wax paper covering bottom and extending slightly above pan on all sides. In the large bowl of electric mixer, beat egg whites until frothy. Add ½ cup sugar, whip until firm, set meringue aside. In another bowl, beat egg yolks. Add ½ cup sugar and vanilla, beat until thick, light yellow. In medium bowl, sift together flour and cocoa powder, gently fold into egg yolks. Fold ½ cup of meringue mixture, by hand, into chocolate mixture. Fold chocolate mixture into remaining meringue, until well blended, pour into prepared pan. Tap pan on counter to remove air bubbles. Bake 22 minutes. The roulade is done when firm, bouncing back to the touch. Immediately invert onto piece of wax or parchment paper, sifted with confectioners' sugar. Gently peel off wax paper, cool 30 minutes.

In small bowl, whip cream. Beat in sugar and coffee powder, refrigerate. When chilled, spread filling evenly on top of cooled roulade. Carefully roll up from the long side. Cover, freeze several hours or overnight.

For frosting, whip cream in chilled bowl, slowly adding sugar and coffee powder. Whip until stiff peaks form, frost roulade. Sprinkle with chopped pecans or almonds. To serve, set out to thaw 1 hour or place in refrigerator 2 to 3 hours.

Confectioners' sugar is made with cornstarch. For Passover, special confectioners' sugar is available, or it can be homemade. In a food processor, combine 1 cup less 1 tablespoon sugar and 1 tablespoon potato starch. Using a steel blade, pulse until very fine.

Desserts & Pies

PAVLOVA ON PEACHTREE

This delectable meringue, named in honor of the
Russian dancer Anna Pavlova, is a "light as a cloud" dessert.

Dairy/ Pareve/ Passover   *Serves 6*

4	large egg whites	2	tablespoons sugar
1	cup sugar	2	cups strawberries
1	teaspoon white vinegar	1	cup blueberries
1	teaspoon vanilla, divided	2	kiwi, peeled, sliced
2	cups dairy or pareve whipping cream		

Preheat oven to 300°. Line cookie sheet with parchment paper. Remove paper from cookie sheet, trace the outline of serving plate on sheet and replace on cookie sheet. Beat egg whites until stiff peaks are formed. Gradually add 1 cup sugar, continually beating until sugar is incorporated and stiff, glossy meringue forms. Gently fold in vinegar and ½ teaspoon vanilla. Spoon meringue mixture onto traced circle, spreading out to edges. Make slight depression in middle. Bake 45 minutes. Turn off oven, leave meringue in oven 1 hour. Remove and cool.

Whip cream, beat in 2 tablespoons sugar and ½ teaspoon vanilla. Fill meringue. Garnish with fruit.

Freeze egg whites individually in ice cube trays for future use. Once frozen, place cubes in a freezer bag. Defrost in refrigerator before using.

Meringue can be made early in the day. Add whipped cream and fruit just before serving.

A Baked Apple a Day...

A sweet refreshing accompaniment to any meal.

Dairy/Pareve/Passover   *Serves 6*

6	Rome or McIntosh apples, cored	½	teaspoon pumpkin pie spice or allspice
2	tablespoons reduced sugar preserves, any flavor	1	tablespoon butter or pareve margarine, divided
2	tablespoons raisins	1	(12-ounce) can diet black cherry soda or 1½ cups apple juice
1	tablespoon grated orange zest		
½	teaspoon cinnamon		

Preheat oven to 350°. Place apples in glass baking dish. In small bowl, combine preserves, raisins and orange zest. Spoon over apples. Sprinkle with cinnamon, pumpkin pie spice or allspice. Dot each apple with butter or margarine. Pour soda around apples. Bake uncovered 1 hour, basting several times during last half hour. Remove from oven. Cover with foil while cooling.

For a crunchy treat, stuff hollowed apples before baking, with chopped nuts or crunchy "nut" cereal. Personalize apples with choices of preserves.

Sunday night dinner, Atlanta, Georgia, 1910.

BANANA MERINGUE PUDDING

A dessert fit for royalty.

Dairy/Pareve   *Serves 8 to 10*

To beat egg whites, separate eggs while cold as the yolk is firm and less likely to break. Remove any flecks of yolk from whites with the moistened tip of a cotton swab. Let egg whites come to room temperature before beating to ensure high volume.

PUDDING

2	tablespoons cornstarch	3	tablespoons butter or pareve margarine
4	tablespoons flour		
½	teaspoon salt	1	teaspoon vanilla
3	cups milk or pareve vanilla soy milk, divided	1	(12-ounce) box vanilla wafers
3	large eggs, separated	4-5	bananas, sliced, divided
½	cup sugar		

MERINGUE

1	tablespoon cornstarch	3	egg whites, reserved from pudding
2	tablespoons sugar		
½	cup water	6	tablespoons sugar
	Dash of salt	1	teaspoon vanilla

Preheat oven to 350°. In medium saucepan, combine cornstarch, flour and salt. Add ¼ cup milk. Whisk in egg yolks and sugar, heat. Add remaining milk, stirring continuously until boiling and thickened. Remove pudding from heat. Add butter or margarine and vanilla. Line bottom of 2-quart round glass dish with ½ vanilla wafers, then ½ bananas. Cover with ½ the pudding. Repeat layers, ending with pudding.

Produce stand, Atlanta, Georgia, c. 1920.

Preheat oven to 325°. In small saucepan heat cornstarch, 2 tablespoons sugar and water, stirring until clear, set aside. Add salt to egg whites, whip until peaks form. Fold egg whites into cornstarch, beat until creamy. Gradually add 6 tablespoons sugar, beating until stiff peaks form. Add vanilla. Spread meringue over pudding. Bake 15 to 25 minutes until golden brown.

Peppered Strawberries

Classic strawberries and cream with a spicy twist.

Dairy/Pareve   Serves 6

2   ounces unsalted butter or
    pareve margarine
1   cup sugar
½   cup freshly squeezed orange
    juice
4   cups hulled strawberries
2   tablespoons orange liqueur
2½ teaspoons coarsely ground
    fresh black pepper

1   cup well chilled dairy or
    pareve whipping cream
3   tablespoons confectioners'
    sugar
1   teaspoon vanilla
    Vanilla ice cream or pareve
    soy ice cream, optional

In large skillet, melt butter or margarine over moderately high heat. Stir in sugar and orange juice. Stir mixture until sugar dissolves, approximately 3 minutes. Add strawberries. Cook 2 to 3 minutes until berries are heated through, add orange liqueur, heat. Remove from stove, ignite with long match or grill starter. Shake skillet until flames go out. Sprinkle in pepper, gently combine mixture. In chilled bowl, beat whipping cream to form soft peaks. Add confectioners' sugar and vanilla until just combined. Divide strawberry mixture among 6 bowls or champagne flutes. Top with whipped cream or serve over dairy or pareve vanilla ice cream.

The fruit should pray for the welfare of the leaves.

~Yiddish proverb

Vinings Fruit Compote

Serve this sherry-spiked compote ladled over Atlanta's Best Pound Cake (page 253) with vanilla ice cream.

Pareve   Serves 8 to 10

3   cups water
⅓   cup sugar
⅓   cup cream sherry
12 ounces pitted prunes
1   (6-ounce) package dried
    apricots
3   thick lemon slices

¼   cup dried cranberries
1   (6-ounce) package dried
    peaches
½   (5-ounce) package dried
    apples
½   (6-ounce) package dried
    pears

Bring water, sugar and sherry to boil. Add fruit, simmer, covered 10 minutes or until tender. Cool and refrigerate. Bring to room temperature before serving.

Personalize this compote by varying the proportions of the dried fruits.

*Desserts &
Pies*

AWARD-WINNING APRICOT STRUDEL

*I was chosen as a "Bride Winner" in the 1957 Pillsbury Contest for this recipe.
It was the 9th annual Pillsbury contest. I participated in the bake-off as one of the
100 finalists from all over the country. One of the hosts was Ronald Reagan!*

Dairy/Pareve   *Yields 48 pieces*

CRUST

8	ounces butter or pareve margarine
2	cups sifted flour

1¼	cups dairy or pareve sour cream

NUT FILLING

1½	cups chopped nuts
1	cup sweetened coconut flakes

½	cup chopped raisins
¼	cup chopped Maraschino cherries

APRICOT FILLING

1	cup apricot preserves

1	tablespoon lemon juice

Cut butter or margarine into flour until mixture is consistency of small peas. Add sour cream and stir until dough clings together. Wrap in wax paper. Chill 5 to 6 hours or overnight.

Combine nut filling ingredients, set aside. Stir together apricot filling ingredients, breaking up large pieces of apricots.

Preheat oven to 350°. Divide dough into 4 parts. Roll out 1 part on floured board into 14x12-inch rectangle, adding flour as needed to prevent sticking. Spread with ¼ cup of apricot mixture, sprinkle with ¼ of the nut filling. Roll as for jelly roll, starting with 14-inch side. With seam side down, fold ends under. Using the tip of a knife, make ½-inch slits every 2-inches on top of roll. Place on ungreased nonstick baking sheet. Repeat procedure with remaining dough. Bake uncovered 30 to 40 minutes. Cut in slices. Serve warm or cold.

If freezing strudel, do so before baking. Carefully seal in plastic wrap. Gently place on flat surface in freezer. Defrost 2 hours before baking.

Our grandmothers knew how to stretch this delicate dough paper thin by using their knuckles. Many of today's bakers substitute phyllo dough.

TROPICAL COCONUT STRUDEL

A tropical treat that can be unique each time it's made.

Dairy/Pareve   *Serves 18 to 24*

3   cups sweetened coconut
    flakes
2   cups ground nuts
2   cups fruit preserves

16 sheets phyllo dough, thawed
    in refrigerator
    Butter or pareve margarine,
    melted

Preheat oven to 350°. Mix together coconut, nuts and preserves for filling, set aside. Dampen 2 cotton dish towels. Place 1 towel on flat surface, stack phyllo sheets on top. While working with each sheet, keep remaining sheets covered with the second damp towel. For each strudel, brush each of 4 sheets with butter or margarine, layering 1 on top of the others. Spoon ¼ of filling along long edge of stack. Roll up, placing seam side down on lightly greased baking sheet. Brush with melted butter or margarine. Using sharp knife, score diagonally across tops. Bake 20 minutes or until golden brown. While strudel is still warm, cut each log into 1½-inch pieces with sharp knife. Cool to room temperature. Store lightly covered or freeze.

Some choices for ground nuts are: almonds, pecans, walnuts, macadamia or hazelnuts. To enhance the tropical flavor try guava, peach or pineapple preserves.

Ladies, it's time for dessert.
Charter members, Daughters of Israel, Augusta, Georgia. c.1950

GEORGIA PEACH COBBLER

Dairy/Pareve   *Serves 4*

PEACHES

3-4 cups peeled, sliced peaches   4 ounces unsalted butter or
     Sugar   pareve margarine

BATTER

1   cup sugar   1 cup flour
2   teaspoons baking powder   1 cup milk or pareve soy milk

To peel a peach, drop into rapidly boiling water. Remove after 30 seconds, plunge into ice water and peel.

Sprinkle peaches with sugar. Let sit 30 minutes. In cold oven, place butter or margarine into 2-quart casserole dish. Heat oven to 350°. Sift sugar, baking powder and flour into mixing bowl. Add milk and stir until well blended. When butter or margarine melts and oven reaches 350°, slowly pour batter evenly into dish. Top evenly with peaches and return to oven. Bake 1 hour or until top is golden brown.

For ease, use fresh or frozen peaches. For variety try fresh or frozen pears.

PROGRESSIVE LITERARY SOCIETY.
FIRST ANNUAL DINNER DANCE.
JESTER'S LAKE.
APRIL 17th. 1929.

*Try this southern tradition for dessert at your next book club!
Progressive Literary Society, 1st annual dinner dance, Jester's Lake, Jonesboro, Georgia, 1929.*

CRANBERRY APPLE CRUMBLE

So simple, yet so delicious.

Dairy/Pareve   *Serves 4 to 6*

CRUMBLE

½	cup flour	¼	cup chilled butter or pareve margarine, cut into small pieces
¼	cup sugar		
¼	cup firmly packed brown sugar		

FRUIT

6	tart apples, peeled, sliced	1	tablespoon cornstarch or flour
1	cup fresh cranberries		Milk, pareve soy or almond milk
⅓	cup orange juice		Dairy or pareve ice cream
2	tablespoons sugar		

Combine all crumble ingredients in processor. Pulse to make coarse meal, set aside.

Preheat oven to 375°. Combine apples with cranberries and remaining ingredients, except milk or ice cream. Pour apple mixture into greased 2-quart baking dish. Sprinkle with crumble. Bake 40 to 45 minutes until bubbly. Serve warm with milk or ice cream.

Braeburn, Fuji and Granny Smith apples are tart and wonderful for cooking.

Berries and Cream Shortcake

Everyone agrees that this shortcake is berry, berry good!

Dairy   *Serves 8 to 10*

Cake

1½	cups cake flour	½	cup milk
1½	teaspoons baking powder	1	cup sugar
¼	teaspoon salt	½	cup butter, softened
1	teaspoon vanilla	2	large eggs

Fruit and Whipped Cream Fillings

2	cups fresh blueberries	½	cup strawberry or raspberry jam
1	cup halved fresh strawberries	1	cup heavy cream, well chilled
1	cup fresh raspberries	1	tablespoon sugar
1	cup fresh blackberries		

Preheat oven to 350°. Grease and flour two 8- or 9-inch cake pans. In small bowl, whisk together flour, baking powder and salt, set aside. Add vanilla to milk, set aside. With mixer on high, beat sugar with butter until light and fluffy, about 5 minutes then reduce speed to low. Add eggs 1 at a time, mixing well after each addition. Slowly add flour mixture, alternate with milk mixture. Increase speed to high, beat 2 minutes. Pour into pans, bake 25 to 30 minutes for 8-inch pans or 20 to 25 minutes for 9-inch pans, until tester inserted in center comes out clean. Cool cake in pans, on rack, 10 minutes. Remove from pans and cool completely on racks.

In large bowl, toss all berries with jam. Beat cream in mixer at high speed until soft peaks form. Add sugar gradually, beating until stiff peaks form. To assemble, place 1 cake layer on plate. Spread with ½ the whipped cream and top with ½ the fruit mixture. Place second cake layer over fruit. Top with remaining whipped cream and remaining fruit.

To substitute flour for cake flour, sift flour 2 times. Gently spoon into dry measuring cup, level with straight edge.

DIXIE BREAD PUDDING

Kick the Bourbon Sauce up a notch with whipped cream
sweetened with confectioners' sugar and/or spiked with sherry.

Dairy/Pareve   *Serves 8 to 10*

BREAD

8	slices bread, cubed, about 7 cups	4	large eggs
3	cups milk or pareve soy milk	2	cups sugar
4	tablespoons butter or pareve margarine	1	teaspoon vanilla
		1	teaspoon cinnamon

BOURBON SAUCE

4	ounces butter or pareve margarine	¼	cup bourbon
1	cup sugar		Dairy or pareve whipped cream
1	egg, beaten		

To scald milk, heat almost to boiling point.

Preheat oven to 350°. Place bread cubes in greased 2-quart round casserole or 13x9-inch dish. Scald milk with butter or margarine. Whisk together eggs and sugar. Stir scalded milk into eggs, stirring constantly to combine. Blend in vanilla and cinnamon. Pour mixture over bread cubes. Bake 45 minutes or until knife inserted in center comes out clean.

In top of double boiler, melt butter or margarine and sugar. Stir until smooth, cool. Whisk in beaten egg, return to heat, stirring continually to warm. Add bourbon. Pour warm sauce over bread pudding. Serve immediately. Top with whipped cream.

Try adding either 1 cup raisins, 1 large peeled, diced apple with ½ cup raisins, 1 cup diced dried apricots or ½ cup toasted almonds to the bread mixture.

Dixie Bread Pudding, a regional favorite! A photo-op in Macon, Georgia, 1914.

Amaretto Bread Pudding

A new twist on an old favorite dessert.

Dairy   *Serves 10*

Bread Pudding

4	cups half-and-half
1	small loaf dry challah, cut into cubes
2	tablespoons butter
3	large eggs

1½	cups sugar
2	tablespoons almond extract
1	cup golden raisins
¾	cup sliced almonds

Amaretto Sauce

½	cup butter
1	cup confectioners' sugar

1	large egg, beaten
¼	cup amaretto liqueur

In medium bowl, pour half-and-half over bread cubes, let stand 1 hour. Preheat oven to 325°. Grease 13x9-inch baking dish with butter. Beat eggs, sugar and almond extract in small bowl. Stir into bread mixture. Fold in raisins and almonds. Spread evenly into prepared baking dish. Bake on middle rack 50 minutes or until golden brown. Remove from oven to cool.

Jewish Welfare Board, location unknown, c.1960.

Combine butter and sugar in double boiler. Cook, stirring constantly, over simmering water until sugar dissolves and butter melts, remove from heat. Add small amount of hot mixture to beaten egg. Stir egg back into hot mixture. Cook over simmering water until thickened, whisking constantly, with water not touching top pan. Remove from heat, stir in liqueur. Serve warm sauce over warm bread pudding.

Delmonico Macaroon Pudding

A southern interpretation of a New York dessert worthy
of a fine restaurant. Try with homemade Walnut Macaroons (page 260).

Dairy　　　　　　　　　　　　　　　　*Serves 8 to 10*

3	cups milk	1	(10-ounce) bottle Maraschino cherries, sliced, divided, juice reserved
2	tablespoons unflavored kosher gelatin		
4	large eggs, separated	1	teaspoon vanilla
1	scant cup sugar		Pinch of salt
18	crumbled almond macaroons	1	cup heavy cream, whipped
¼	cup sherry		

Pour milk in saucepan, sprinkle with gelatin, set aside. Beat egg yolks and sugar until light. Heat milk and gelatin over low heat until steaming hot, stirring constantly. Do not allow mixture to boil. Stir milk slowly into egg and sugar mixture until thoroughly blended. Return to low heat, stirring constantly, bring to boil. Do not allow mixture to curdle. It will be thick. Remove from heat.

Add macaroons, stirring until thoroughly broken up. Mix sherry and juice from cherries. Add ¾ cup of sherry mixture to pudding. Add vanilla and sliced cherries, reserving 8 cherry halves for garnish. As mixture cools, stir often. Beat egg whites with salt until stiff peaks form. When pudding begins to thicken, gently fold in egg whites. Rinse 6 cup mold with cold water, pour in pudding. Cover and refrigerate at least 2 hours. When ready to serve, invert onto serving plate. Garnish with whipped cream and cherries.

Out of Fresh Milk?

Use one 14-ounce can evaporated milk plus 1 cup water plus 2 ounces milk instead of 3 cups of milk.

MARTINI TRIFLE

A little bit of this, a little bit of that...there's a taste to please everyone in this dish.

Dairy/Pareve   *Serves 4*

1 cup heavy cream or pareve whipping cream	6 shortbread cookies, crumbled into bite size pieces
1 tablespoon sugar	
1 tablespoon orange liqueur	6 cream filled chocolate cookies, crumbled into bite size pieces
¼ cup quartered strawberries	
¼ cup raspberries	
¼ cup blackberries	Sliced strawberries and mint sprigs
¼ cup blueberries	

Whip heavy cream in chilled bowl until peaks form. Slowly add sugar and liqueur. Refrigerate 1 to 2 hours. To serve, carefully layer fruits, whipped cream and crumbled cookies in martini or parfait glasses, making 2 or more layers of each. Top each glass with strawberry slices or other berries and sprig of mint.

For family-style entertaining, fold berries and crumbled cookies into whipped cream mixture. Place in a large glass bowl.

Brandeis University National Women's Committee tea, Atlanta, Georgia, c.1960.

CHASTAIN CASSATA

A sweet confection that will light up guests' eyes with their first bite.

Dairy *Serves 8 to 10*

CASSATA

1	(1-pound) loaf pound cake	3-4	tablespoons chopped candied cherries or mixed candied fruit
1	pound ricotta cheese		
2	tablespoons heavy cream		
¼	cup sugar	2	ounces semisweet chocolate, coarsely chopped
3	tablespoons orange liqueur		
		½	cup pecans, optional

CHOCOLATE FROSTING

2	tablespoons instant coffee powder	8	ounces unsalted butter, chilled, cut into ½-inch pieces
¾	cup hot tap water		
12	ounces semisweet chocolate		

With serrated knife, slice crusts off ends and sides of pound cake, leveling top of cake if rounded. Cut cake horizontally into 4 slices, each ½ to ¾ inches thick. In large bowl, beat ricotta cheese, cream, sugar and orange liqueur for 1 minute. With rubber spatula, fold in candied fruit, 2 ounces chocolate and pecans, if desired. Center the bottom slice of cake on flat plate, spread with ⅓ of ricotta mixture. Place another cake slice on top, keeping sides and ends even. Spread with ⅓ more ricotta mixture. Repeat until all cake slices and filling are used, ending with plain slice of cake on top. Gently press loaf to compact it. Refrigerate 2 hours or until filling is firm.

Combine instant coffee powder with very hot water. Melt 12 ounces chocolate in hot coffee in double boiler, stirring constantly, until chocolate is completely melted, pour into large mixing bowl. Beat on low with electric mixer, adding butter, 1 piece at a time, until mixture is smooth. Refrigerate until thickened to spreading consistency. With metal spatula, spread frosting evenly over sides, ends, and top of cassata. Cover loosely with plastic wrap. Refrigerate 1 to 2 days before serving, or freeze. Remove from refrigerator 1 hour or from freezer 3 hours before serving.

Melt chocolate over hot, not boiling, water in double boiler over very gentle heat. Keep water below simmering to prevent steam from hitting the chocolate. Or, microwave chocolate in a bowl at 50 percent power, stirring every minute until melted.

SUFGANIYOT, JERUSALEM JELLY DONUTS

A Sephardic Chanukah tradition, great to serve year 'round.

Dairy/Pareve   *Serves 12*

16   ounces dairy or pareve sour
     cream
4   large eggs
3   tablespoons sugar
1   teaspoon vanilla
1   cup flour

1½   teaspoons baking powder
     Pinch of salt
     Vegetable oil for deep frying
     Confectioners' sugar
     Jelly of choice

Whisk together sour cream, eggs, sugar and vanilla. Sift flour, baking powder and salt. Beat into sour cream mixture until consistency of cake batter. Add oil to deep skillet, 2 to 4-inches deep and heat. Drop tablespoons of batter into hot oil. Batter will form into balls. Remove with slotted spoon onto paper towels to drain. Immediately sprinkle with confectioners' sugar, serve warm with jelly of choice.

Lighting the chanukiah, Augusta, Georgia, 1958.

NO-BAKE KEY LIME CHEESECAKE

*Need a dessert for a hot summer day? No need
to heat up the oven with this refreshing cheesecake.*

Dairy/Pareve   *Serves 8*

CRUST

1	cup graham cracker crumbs	⅓	cup butter or pareve
¼	cup sugar		margarine, melted

FILLING

1	cup fresh lime juice	½	cup butter or pareve
¼	cup water		margarine
2	(¼-ounce) envelopes	16	ounces dairy or pareve
	unflavored kosher gelatin		cream cheese, softened
1½	cups sugar	½	cup dairy or pareve
5	large eggs, slightly beaten		whipping cream
1	tablespoon grated lime zest		Whipped cream
			Lime zest ribbons

In medium bowl, combine crust ingredients. Press in bottom of greased
9-inch springform pan, set aside. In 2-quart saucepan, combine lime juice,
water and gelatin, let stand 5 minutes to soften. Add sugar, eggs and lime
zest. Cook over medium heat, stirring constantly, until mixture approaches
a boil. Reduce heat, simmer 7 to 8 minutes. In medium bowl, combine
butter and cream cheese. Beat at medium speed, gradually adding hot lime
mixture. Refrigerate 1 hour, stirring occasionally.

Beat whipping cream until stiff peaks form. Fold into cooled lime filling.
Pour into crust. Cover, refrigerate at least 3 hours. Loosen edge of cake
with knife, remove sides of pan. Garnish edges of cake with whipped
cream and ribbons of lime zest.

*Over-beating
cheesecake batter,
including mixing at high
speeds, incorporates too
much air, which can cause
the cheesecake to collapse.
Leave the oven closed until
fully baked or cake may
crack. It is best to remove
a cheesecake from the pan
after refrigerating
24 hours.*

PUMPKIN CHEESECAKE

There's more to pumpkin than pumpkin pie.

Dairy/Pareve   *Serves 12 to 15*

CRUST

½   cup plus 2 tablespoons butter or pareve margarine, divided

2   cups graham cracker crumbs

FILLING

20   ounces dairy or pareve cream cheese

1½   cups sugar

1   cup flour

½   teaspoon ground ginger

½   teaspoon nutmeg

2   teaspoons cinnamon

4   jumbo eggs

3   cups canned pumpkin

TOPPING

16   ounces dairy or pareve sour cream

6   tablespoons sugar

1   teaspoon vanilla

Melt ½ cup butter or margarine, add graham cracker crumbs and mix well. Grease sides of 10-inch springform pan. Pat crumb mixture into pan bottom.

Preheat oven to 350°. Cream the cream cheese with sugar until fluffy, scraping sides of bowl often. Sift together flour, ginger, nutmeg and cinnamon. Add to cream cheese. Beat until smooth. Mixture will be very thick. Beat in eggs, 1 at a time. Add pumpkin and mix well. Pour filling into prepared pan. Bake 50 to 55 minutes or until cheesecake is set.

Combine topping ingredients. Pour evenly over hot cheesecake. Let cool. Refrigerate at least 6 hours before serving.

LEMON SUNSHINE ICE BOX CAKE

Dairy/Pareve   *Serves 8 to 10*

2   (3-ounce) packages
       ladyfingers
3   large eggs, separated
2   cups sugar
4   lemons, juiced, grated zest

1   pint dairy or pareve
       whipping cream
     Sugar
1¾   (0.3-ounce) packages plain
       kosher gelatin
1   cup cold water, divided

Grease 9-inch springform pan. Line sides with ladyfingers. Beat egg yolks. Slowly add sugar, beating until light. Add lemon juice and zest, set aside. Beat whipping cream until stiff, sweetening slightly with sugar during whipping process, set aside. Soften gelatin in ½ cup cold water. Heat remaining ½ cup water, stir into gelatin to dissolve and add to egg mixture. Beat egg whites until stiff. Fold egg whites and whipped cream into egg mixture. Pour into prepared pan. Chill until firm.

ALMOND ICE BOX CAKE

A slice of melt-in-your-mouth perfection.

Dairy/Pareve   *Serves 10*

8   ounces unsalted butter
       or pareve margarine,
       softened
1⅓   cups confectioners' sugar
6   large eggs, divided
8   ounces unblanched almonds,
       ground

1   teaspoon vanilla
12   almond macaroons
2   (3-ounce) packages
       ladyfingers
     Sweetened dairy or pareve
       whipping cream

Cream butter or margarine with sugar. Beat in 3 whole eggs, 1 at a time plus 3 egg yolks, reserving whites. Add almonds and vanilla. In separate bowl, beat reserved 3 egg whites until fluffy, fold into nut mixture. Line 9-inch springform pan with macaroons on bottom and ladyfingers around sides. Fill with almond mixture. Refrigerate overnight. To serve, top with sweetened whipped cream.

For perfect whipped cream, begin with thoroughly chilled cream, bowl and beaters. Start on medium speed. Beat until soft peaks begin to form, then add sugar, two tablespoons at a time. Add any flavorings when soft peaks have formed. If whipped too long, cream will become butter.

Whipped cream can be made with partially frozen evaporated skim milk.

PAREVE ICE CREAM

4   large eggs, separated
2   cups pareve whipping cream
¼   cup sugar
1½   tablespoons instant coffee
¼   cup chocolate syrup

Beat egg whites in medium bowl. In another medium bowl, beat whipping cream until thick. Fold in egg whites. Stir in egg yolks, sugar, coffee and chocolate syrup, beat until smooth. Pour mixture into a container. Freeze at least 6 hours before serving.

A homemade ice cream treat, what could be better?
Ice cream stand, Atlanta Georgia, c.1939.

PUMPKIN ICE CREAM TORTE

A glorious confection for Thanksgiving or any other day of the year.

Dairy/Pareve   *Serves 8 to 10*

1½	pounds gingersnaps, divided	1	teaspoon cinnamon
8	ounces butter or pareve margarine, melted	½	teaspoon nutmeg
2	cups canned pumpkin	1	cup chopped pecans
1	cup sugar	½	gallon dairy or pareve vanilla ice cream, softened
1	teaspoon salt		
1	teaspoon ginger		

Crush gingersnaps, reserving ½ cup for topping. Mix remaining crushed gingersnaps with melted butter or margarine. Lightly coat 9-inch springform pan with nonstick spray. Press gingersnap mixture into pan to form crust. Combine pumpkin, sugar and spices. Fold in nuts. In large bowl, fold mixture into softened ice cream. Pour into prepared pan, cover lightly with foil. Freeze for at least 4 hours. Move mold to refrigerator 30 minutes before serving to soften slightly. Run thin knife around edge of pan for easy removal. Top with reserved gingersnaps.

To lighten this dessert, use low fat ice cream and sugar substitute.

Cinnamon and nutmeg are two fragrant spices often used during Havdalah, the ceremony that marks the end of Shabbat, the Jewish day of rest. During the ceremony, which also includes a blessing over wine and the lighting of a special braided candle, the spices are savored by all present so that the sweetness of the Sabbath will be carried over into the work week.

ALMOND TOFFEE ICE CREAM TORTE

A torte is a decorated cake with several layers. This one is a chocoholic's delight!

ICE CREAM TORTE

½ gallon chocolate ice cream, divided	1 ounce Crème de Cacao
½ gallon coffee ice cream, divided	1 ounce coffee liqueur
	12 ounces almond toffee bits, divided

MOCHA FUDGE SAUCE

30 ounces prepared fudge sauce	2 ounces coffee liqueur

DARK CHOCOLATE SAUCE

8 squares bitter sweet chocolate	2 (13-ounce) cans evaporated milk
8 ounces unsalted butter	2 teaspoons vanilla
3 cups sugar	

Soften ice creams in refrigerator. Stir Crème de Cacao into chocolate ice cream. Stir coffee liqueur into coffee ice cream, mixing thoroughly. Lightly spray 9-inch springform pan. Line bottom and sides with ½ almond toffee bits. Alternate layers of chocolate ice cream, candy and coffee ice cream. Return pan to freezer for a few minutes after layering so layers do not mingle. Put thick layer of almond toffee bits on top. Return to freezer for at least 3 hours to firm. Freeze up to 3 weeks. To serve, unmold and place slices on plates with choice of sauce.

For Mocha Fudge Sauce, combine fudge sauce and coffee liqueur. Heat, stirring to blend. For Dark Chocolate Sauce, melt chocolate and butter in top of double boiler. Alternately add sugar and milk. Cook slowly while stirring constantly until thick, 30 to 40 minutes, add vanilla.

Dinner at the Standard Club, Atlanta, Georgia, 1954.

BLACK BOTTOM BANANA CREAM PIE

This divine recipe comes from Nancy Cole's Southern Sweets Bakery.
Nancy is the master baker for many of Atlanta's finest restaurants.

Dairy   *Serves 8*

CRUST

4	ounces unsalted butter	¾	teaspoon vanilla
4	ounces semisweet chocolate chips	2	cups crushed chocolate cookie wafers
2	tablespoons heavy cream		

GANACHE

2	ounces butter	6	ounces semisweet chocolate chips
4	tablespoons light corn syrup		
4	tablespoons cream		

VANILLA PASTRY CREAM

1½	cups half-and-half	2	large eggs
½	cup sugar	1	egg yolk
2	tablespoons flour	2	teaspoons vanilla

TOPPING

1	cup heavy cream	½	teaspoon vanilla
1	tablespoon confectioners' sugar	3	ripe bananas, sliced

Butter 10-inch extra deep pie pan. In saucepan, melt butter. Stir in chocolate chips until smooth. Add cream, vanilla and crushed cookies, mix. Pat into pie pan. For ganache, melt butter in heavy saucepan. Add corn syrup and cream, bring to simmer, without boiling. Remove from heat. Stir in chocolate chips until smooth.

For pastry cream, bring half-and-half to simmer in heavy saucepan. In medium bowl, whisk sugar and flour together. Blend in eggs and yolk. Temper eggs by adding ½ cup hot half-and-half to egg mixture, blend. Gradually add remaining half-and-half. Place in double boiler over medium heat, whisk as mixture thickens. Remove from heat, add vanilla. Pour into 10-inch baking pan. Cover with parchment and chill. Whip heavy cream with confectioners' sugar and vanilla until stiff peaks form, chill.

To assemble, pour ½ cup ganache into pie shell. Layer sliced bananas over ganache. Cover with remaining ganache, chill until set. Mound pastry cream on top. Cover with whipped cream topping.

Nancy Cole, Southern Sweets Bakery, Decatur, Georgia

Tempering refers to the blending of ingredients of different temperatures. To temper eggs, add a small amount of a hot liquid into relatively cooler eggs in order to warm them up without cooking them. This method is used in making custards, egg-based sauces, and other foods where eggs are used to thicken a hot liquid. Adding eggs into hot liquids can cause scrambled eggs, which is not desirable in most recipes.

APPLE AND CRANBERRY PIE

Cranberries in a pie? Try it! Everyone will like it.

Dairy   *Serves 8*

PIE CRUST

2½	cups flour	1	cup chilled unsalted butter, cut into 1-inch pieces
1	tablespoon sugar		
1	teaspoon salt	7	tablespoons ice water, or more

FILLING

1	cup dried cranberries	2¼	pounds tart apples, peeled, quartered, cored, thinly sliced
⅔	cup sugar		
3	tablespoons flour		
¼	teaspoon ground allspice	1½	tablespoons brandy
		1	teaspoon vanilla

EGG WASH

1	large egg yolk	1	teaspoon whipping cream

Blend flour, sugar and salt in processor. Add butter in small pieces, pulse processor until mixture resembles coarse meal. Add 7 tablespoons water, blend until moist clumps form, adding more water by tablespoonfuls if dough is dry. Gather dough into ball, divide into 2 pieces. Flatten pieces into disks, wrap in plastic. Chill at least 30 minutes or 1 day. Let dough soften slightly at room temperature before rolling out. Preheat oven to 375°. Position rack in bottom third of oven. Combine cranberries, sugar, flour and allspice in large bowl. Mix in apples, brandy and vanilla.

Roll out 1 dough disk on floured surface to 13-inch round. Transfer to 9-inch diameter glass pie dish. Spoon in apple filling, mounding slightly in center. Roll out second dough disk on floured surface to 13-inch round. Drape crust over filling, trim overhang to ½ inch. Press crust edges together, fold under and crimp edge. Stir yolk and cream in small bowl to blend. Brush over top but not edge of pie. Cut slits in top crust to allow steam to escape. Bake pie until apples are tender and crust is golden, about 1 hour. Transfer to rack. Let stand 1 hour. Serve warm or at room temperature.

To ease clean up, place a cookie sheet or piece of aluminum foil on rack under pie plate to catch spills and overflows.

*Desserts &
Pies*

240

OLD-FASHIONED SOUR CREAM APPLE PIE

It may be called old-fashioned, but it tastes great any time!

PECAN CRUST

1	cup flour	½	cup finely chopped pecans
¼	cup sugar	¾	cup apricot jam, strained
4	ounces butter, softened		through a fine mesh sieve
1	large egg		

APPLE PIE FILLING

3	tart apples, peeled, thinly sliced	¼	cup sugar
		1	teaspoon cinnamon
½	cup yellow raisins	1¼	cups sour cream
¾	teaspoon lemon peel	1	large egg
¼	cup firmly packed brown sugar	4	tablespoons sugar

Preheat oven to 350°. In large bowl of electric mixer, beat together flour, sugar and butter until mixture resembles coarse meal. Beat in egg just until blended. Stir in pecans. Pat dough on bottom and ½-inch up sides of 10-inch springform pan. Bake 15 minutes. Remove from oven. Spread top with apricot jam.

In mixing bowl, toss together apples, raisins, lemon peel, sugars and cinnamon until blended. Spoon mixture evenly into prepared crust. Bake 20 minutes. Beat together sour cream, egg and sugar. Pour mixture over apples. Return pan to oven. Continue baking 35 minutes or until top begins to brown. Serve warm or at room temperature.

Ballyhoo, an annual get together for Jewish singles, Atlanta, Georgia 1947.

MACADAMIA CRUST KEY LIME PIE

*One of Atlanta's premier fish restaurants, Ray's on
the River, knows how to pair tastes from the South Seas and the Keys.*

Dairy   *Serves 8*

CRUST

½   cup whole macadamia nuts
1   cup graham cracker crumbs
⅔   cup sugar

1.3   ounces toasted sweetened
        coconut flakes
      Pinch of salt
2½ tablespoons butter, melted

FILLING

½   cup plus 2 tablespoons Key
      lime juice
1½ teaspoons kosher gelatin
6   ounces sugar
16 ounces sweetened
      condensed milk

12 ounces heavy whipping
      cream
    Slices of lime
    Fresh raspberries

Preheat oven to 325°. Finely grind macadamia nuts in food processor. In stainless steel bowl, combine nuts, graham crumbs, sugar, coconut and salt, mix well. Add melted butter, mix well. Press into 10-inch pie pan. Place in oven, bake 10 minutes, until light brown. Remove, cool to room temperature.

In small bowl, place 2 tablespoons of Key lime juice and gelatin. Stir and let gelatin soften, set aside. In small saucepan, place remaining Key lime juice and sugar over medium heat. Bring to light simmer, stirring well until sugar is dissolved. Remove from heat. Combine with gelatin mixture, mix well. Add condensed milk, mix well. Cool in refrigerator. With electric mixer, whip cream to stiff peaks. Fold gently into Key lime mixture until well combined. Fill crust to top with Key lime mixture, cover lightly. Freeze overnight. To serve, remove pie from freezer 1 hour before serving. Cut into 8 slices. Refrigerate until ready to serve. Garnish with slices of lime and fresh raspberries.

Ray's On The River Restaurant, Atlanta, Georgia

LOVE THAT LEMON PIE

If you like Key Lime Pie, here is its first cousin, made with lemons.

Dairy   *Serves 8*

1   (10-ounce) package lemon or lemon nut cookies
6-8   tablespoons softened butter
3   large egg yolks
½   cup lemon juice

1   (14-ounce) can sweetened condensed milk
1   tablespoon grated lemon zest
   Whipped cream

Preheat oven to 350°. In food processor, grind cookies. Add butter, process until mixture is crumbly. Press into 9-inch pie plate. Bake 10 minutes. Remove from oven. Gently pat crust down with back of spoon. Whisk together egg yolks and lemon juice. Slowly whisk in condensed milk until smooth. Stir in lemon zest. Pour into baked crust. Bake 15 minutes, cool. Refrigerate and top with whipped cream.

Refreshing after exercising.
Bicycling in Atlanta, Georgia, c.1900.

TANGO TANGERINE PIE

There should be more tangerine desserts, as the fruit is sweet, tangy and so refreshing.

Dairy   *Serves 6*

PIE CRUST

1   (15-ounce) package refrigerated pie crusts

PIE FILLING

1½ cups sugar	2½ teaspoons grated tangerine
1 tablespoon flour	zest
¼ teaspoon salt	⅓ cup fresh tangerine juice
1 tablespoon yellow cornmeal	1 tablespoon lemon juice
¼ cup butter, melted	4 large eggs, lightly beaten
¼ cup milk	

GARNISHES

Sweetened whipped cream   Tangerine slices

Preheat over to 450°. Unfold pie crusts, stack on lightly floured surface and roll into 12-inch circle. Fit pie crust into 9-inch pie plate. Fold edges under, gently press. Bake pie crust for 8 minutes, cool on wire rack. Reduce heat to 350°. Whisk together all filling ingredients until blended. Pour into pie crust. Bake 40 to 45 minutes or until center is set, protecting edges of crust with aluminum foil after 20 minutes, cool. Garnish with whipped cream and tangerine slices.

Can be made up to 2 weeks ahead and stored in freezer.

Honey Crunch Pecan Pie

Two southern comforts, pecans and bourbon, come together in this fabulous pie.

Dairy/Pareve   *Serves 8*

CRUST

1⅓	cups flour	4	ounces butter or pareve margarine
½	teaspoon salt	3-4	tablespoons cold water

PECAN FILLING

4	large eggs, beaten slightly	½	teaspoon salt
¼	cup firmly packed brown sugar	1	teaspoon vanilla
		1	tablespoon bourbon
¼	cup sugar	2	tablespoons butter or pareve margarine, melted
1	cup light corn syrup	1	cup chopped pecans

CRUNCH TOPPING

⅓	cup firmly packed brown sugar	3	tablespoons butter or pareve margarine
3	tablespoons honey	1½	cups halved pecans

Combine flour and salt in mixing bowl. Cut in butter or margarine with pastry blender or 2 knives until mixture resembles coarse meal. Sprinkle with water, 1 tablespoon at a time, until dough forms ball. On lightly floured surface, roll crust into circle ⅛-inch thick, about 1½ inches larger than inverted 9-inch pie plate. Gently ease dough into pie plate, being careful not to stretch dough. Fold pastry edge under to make a double thickness around rim. Flute as desired.

Preheat oven to 350°. Combine all filling ingredients except pecans, mix well. Fold in pecans. Spoon filling into unbaked pastry shell. Bake 50 to 55 minutes. During the last 30 minutes of baking, cover edge of pastry shell with foil to prevent over browning.

For topping, combine brown sugar, honey and butter or margarine in medium saucepan. Cook over medium heat until sugar dissolves, 2 to 3 minutes, stirring constantly. Add pecans, stirring to well coat. During last 10 minutes of baking, remove pie from oven, spread crunch topping evenly over top. Return pie to oven. Bake until topping is bubbly and golden brown.

PEAR TARTE TATIN

An Americanized version of a classic French upside-down caramelized tart.

Dairy/Pareve   *Serves 8*

1	sheet frozen puff pastry	6	ripe firm pears, peeled, cored, cut into wedges
4	tablespoons unsalted or pareve margarine butter, divided	1	(2.25-ounce) package sliced almonds, divided
½	cup plus 1 tablespoon sugar, divided	½	teaspoon almond extract

Put oven rack on bottom position in oven, preheat oven to 400°. Remove 1 sheet puff pastry to thaw. Melt 3 tablespoons butter in 9-inch ovenproof shallow skillet. Remove skillet from heat. Sprinkle with ½ cup sugar. Arrange pears in pan, on bottom and along sides. Cook over medium heat 30 to 45 minutes or longer until syrup is golden brown and thick, remove from heat. Sprinkle with 2 tablespoons almonds and almond extract. Spread out thawed pastry sheet. Round off corners with knife and place over pears in skillet. Turn under edges where needed. Melt remaining butter. Brush over top. Sprinkle with remaining almonds and 1 tablespoon sugar. Place in oven, bake 25 to 35 minutes or until pastry is golden brown. Let stand 10 minutes. Flip onto serving plate.

SWEET *Endings*

CAKES & COOKIES

CHOCOLATE CHIP APPLESAUCE CAKE

Baking this easy and deliciously moist cake is a great activity to do with children.

Dairy/Pareve   *Serves 12 to 15*

CAKE

½ cup butter or pareve margarine	2 cups sifted flour
1½ cups sugar	1½ teaspoons baking soda
2 large eggs	½ teaspoon salt
1 cup applesauce	2 tablespoons cocoa
	½ teaspoon cinnamon

TOPPING

2 tablespoons sugar	1 cup chocolate chips
½ cup chopped pecans	

Preheat oven to 350°. In large bowl of electric mixer, cream butter or margarine and sugar. Add eggs and applesauce. Sift dry ingredients. Add to creamed mixture, stir until incorporated. Pour into greased 13x9-inch pan.

Mix topping ingredients and sprinkle over top of cake. Bake 30 minutes.

Birthday celebration, Atlanta, Georgia, c.1944.

ALPHARETTA APPLE COFFEE CAKE

Pareve   *Serves 12 to 15*

FILLING

4	cups tart apples, peeled, sliced	2	tablespoons cinnamon
		5	tablespoons sugar

CAKE

3	cups flour	1	cup vegetable oil
2	cups sugar	4	large eggs
3	teaspoons baking powder	¼	cup orange juice
1	teaspoon salt	1	tablespoon vanilla

When using shortening or butter to grease a pan, keep hands clean inside a plastic sandwich bag. Wear the bag like a mitt to grease the pan. When finished, remove the bag by turning it inside out before discarding.

Combine filling ingredients, set aside. Preheat oven to 375°. In medium bowl, sift together flour, sugar, baking powder and salt. Make a well in middle of mixture. In small bowl, whisk oil, eggs, orange juice and vanilla. Pour into well of flour mixture. Mix together with spoon until smooth and shiny. Pour ⅓ of batter into greased 10-inch tube pan. Drain excess moisture from apple filling. Add ½ apple filling to pan. Repeat, pouring ⅓ of batter and ½ of apple filling. Pour remaining batter on top. Bake 60 to 75 minutes. If cake browns too quickly, cover top lightly with foil.

As a variation, use 3 cups blueberries or sliced peaches, 5 tablespoons sugar and 2 teaspoons lemon juice.

Twenty-fifth anniversary celebration for Rabbi Isaac E. Marcuson at Temple Beth Israel, Macon, Georgia, 1947.

Cakes & Cookies

248

Pecan Streusel Coffee Cake

An easy and impressive cake to whip up when the phone rings and company is on the way.

Dairy/Pareve   *Serves 12 to 15*

Cake

8	ounces unsalted butter or pareve margarine, softened	3	cups sifted flour
2	cups sugar	3	teaspoons baking powder
3	large eggs	1	(12-ounce) can evaporated or pareve soy milk
		1	teaspoon vanilla

Topping

1	cup firmly packed light brown sugar	1	cup semisweet chocolate chips, optional
1	teaspoon cinnamon	4	ounces diced butter or pareve margarine
1	cup chopped pecans		

Preheat oven to 350°. Cream butter or margarine with sugar in electric mixer. Add eggs, 1 at a time. Sift together flour and baking powder, add alternately to mixer with milk. Add vanilla. Pour into well greased 13x9-inch pan.

In medium bowl, combine topping ingredients, except butter or margarine, and mix well. Sprinkle evenly over cake. Dot top generously with diced butter or margarine. Bake 45 minutes to 1 hour until done. Check with tester after 40 minutes. Cover with foil if pecans begin to burn.

"We always ate cake with big crumbs on it for breakfast on Shabbat. Once I sneaked in and took some of the crumbs. My mama cried, 'A mouse!' I had to admit it was only me."

For a handy cake tester, use a piece of dried thin spaghetti or a toothpick. If it comes out clean, the cake is ready.

KILLER CHOCOLATE CAKE

Chocolate on chocolate is a guaranteed success.

Dairy   *Serves 12 to 15*

CAKE

2	cups flour	4	heaping tablespoons cocoa
2	cups sugar	½	cup buttermilk
1	teaspoon baking soda	2	large eggs, slightly beaten
1	teaspoon salt	2	teaspoons vanilla
1	cup water	½	cup chopped pecans,
5	ounces unsalted butter		optional

TOPPING

4	ounces unsalted butter	1	pound confectioners' sugar
⅓	cup milk	¼	teaspoon vanilla
4	heaping tablespoons cocoa		

Preheat oven to 350°. Sift first 4 dry ingredients into large bowl, set aside. In small saucepan, over low heat, bring water, butter and cocoa to boiling point. Pour over dry ingredients, stirring until smooth. Add buttermilk, eggs, vanilla and pecans, stir well. Pour into greased 13x9-inch baking dish. Bake 30 minutes, remove from oven. Prepare topping while cake is still hot.

Combine topping ingredients in medium saucepan. Heat on medium, stirring until smooth. Spread on top of warm cake.

When dealing with interruptions while cooking, tracking measurements can be a challenge. Picture the mixing bowl as the face of a clock. For example, when a distraction occurs after adding 3 cups of flour, place a spoon at the 3 o'clock position in the bowl.

FLOURLESS CHOCOLATE CAKE

Chocolate cakes are always a hit at any celebration.

Dairy   *Serves 10 to 12*

¼	cup prepared coffee	6	large eggs
¼	cup coffee liqueur	½	cup sugar
14	ounces semisweet chocolate, cut into ½-inch cubes	1	cup heavy cream
		1	tablespoon vanilla

Preheat oven to 350°. Grease 9-inch springform pan and line bottom with greased wax paper. In medium saucepan, heat coffee and coffee liqueur to boiling point. Remove from heat. Whisk chocolate into hot liquid, stirring until melted. In medium bowl, beat eggs and sugar 10 minutes or until tripled in volume. Fold in chocolate mixture. Whip cream, add vanilla and fold into batter. Pour into prepared pan. Place pan into larger pan filled with 1-inch of hot water. Bake 1 hour. Cool and serve at room temperature. Cake will rise, fall and crack. Serve with fresh berries and/or a dollop of whipped cream.

Substitute 1 tablespoon of prepared coffee for coffee liqueur during Passover.

Anniversary celebration at The Mayfair Club, Atlanta, Georgia, 1935.

CHOCOLATE CHIP BANANA CAKE

Bananas too ripe to eat? The best solution is to make this easy cake for the whole family.

Dairy/Pareve   *Serves 10 to 12*

½ cup butter or pareve
    margarine
1¼ cups sugar
2 large eggs
1 teaspoon baking soda
¼ cup dairy or pareve sour
    cream

1 cup mashed bananas
1½ cups flour
¼ teaspoon salt
1 teaspoon vanilla
6 ounces mini chocolate chips
1 cup chopped walnuts,
    optional

Preheat oven to 350°. Grease and flour 9-inch tube pan. Cream butter or margarine with sugar. Beat in eggs 1 at a time. Dissolve baking soda in sour cream, add to creamed butter or margarine and beat well. Add bananas, flour, salt and vanilla, mix well. Stir in chocolate chips. Pour into prepared pan. Bake 35 to 45 minutes.

Save ripe bananas by peeling them and freezing them in freezer bags. Always be prepared to make smoothies, banana bread or muffins.

EASIEST EVER BANANA POUND CAKE

Dairy/Pareve   *Serves 12 to 15*

1 pound unsalted butter or
    pareve margarine
1⅔ cups sugar
4 large eggs

4 cups self-rising flour, sifted,
    divided
2 cups mashed ripe bananas

Preheat oven to 350°. Heavily grease and flour 10-inch Bundt or tube pan. Cream butter or margarine with sugar. Beat in eggs, 1 at a time. Add 2 cups flour, a little at a time, bananas, and then remaining flour. Pour into prepared pan. Bake 1 hour. Let cool in pan 10 minutes. Remove from pan, cool completely on wire rack.

ATLANTA'S BEST POUND CAKE

Atlanta's Best Pound Cake is terrific for entertaining.

Dairy/Pareve   *Serves 12 to 15*

8 ounces unsalted butter or pareve margarine
3 cups sugar
6 large eggs
3 cups flour
¼ teaspoon baking soda
¼ teaspoon baking powder
1¼ cups dairy or pareve sour cream
2 teaspoons vanilla
1 teaspoon lemon extract, optional

Bring all ingredients to room temperature. Preheat oven to 350°. Cream butter or margarine with sugar until almost white. Add eggs 1 at a time with mixer on slow speed. In medium bowl, sift together flour, baking soda and baking powder. Alternately add flour mixture and sour cream to mixer in small portions, beating until fully incorporated. Add vanilla and lemon extract. Beat 2 to 3 minutes until smooth. Pour into greased Bundt or 10-inch tube pan. Bake 1½ hours or until tester comes out clean.

Entertaining friends, Atlanta, Georgia, 1944.

PINEAPPLE CARROT CAKE

So elegant, it could even be a wedding cake!

Dairy/Pareve   *Serves 24 to 30*

CAKE

2	cups flour	2	teaspoons vanilla
2	teaspoons baking powder	2½	cups grated carrots, peeled
1	teaspoon baking soda	1	(8-ounce) can crushed pineapple, drained
½	teaspoon salt		
2½	teaspoons cinnamon	½	cup sweetened coconut flakes
4	large eggs		
1¼	cups vegetable oil	1	cup chopped walnuts
2	cups sugar		

BUTTER CREAM CHEESE FROSTING

½	cup butter or pareve margarine, softened	1	teaspoon vanilla
8	ounces dairy or pareve cream cheese, softened	3	cups sifted confectioners' sugar

Preheat oven to 350°. In medium bowl, combine flour, baking powder, baking soda, salt and cinnamon. In large bowl, beat together eggs, oil, sugar and vanilla. Add flour mixture a little at a time. Stir in carrots, pineapple, coconut and walnuts. Pour batter into 2 greased 9-inch nonstick tube pans. Bake about 40 minutes, until cake tester inserted in center comes out clean. While cake is cooling, beat frosting ingredients until well blended. Frost when cool.

Double wedding, Atlanta, Georgia, 1948.

BLUEBERRY HILL CAKE

The fresh summer taste of blueberry is a thrill.

Dairy/Pareve   *Serves 12 to 15*

CAKE

1	cup butter or pareve margarine	1½	teaspoons vanilla
2	cups sugar	½	teaspoon salt
3	large eggs	1	teaspoon baking powder
1	cup dairy or pareve sour cream	2	cups flour
		1¾	cups fresh blueberries

CINNAMON SUGAR

½	cup sugar	1¼	cups chopped pecans
2	teaspoons cinnamon		

Preheat oven to 325°. Grease and flour 10-inch tube pan. Cream butter or margarine with sugar in large mixing bowl. Add eggs 1 at a time, mixing well after each addition. Combine sour cream with vanilla. Sift together dry ingredients. Add dry ingredients alternately with sour cream to butter mixture. Fold in blueberries.

Combine cinnamon, sugar and pecans. Spoon ⅓ of batter on bottom of prepared pan, top with ⅓ of cinnamon mixture. Repeat twice. Bake 1 hour 45 minutes.

The easiest way to remove a cake from a pan is to place a damp steaming hot towel over the cake for 10 seconds after it is removed from the oven. Then, holding a wire rack over the cake, invert the cake onto the rack. Or, line the pan before baking with strips of greased parchment or wax paper that extend beyond the rim. When inverting the cake after baking, it will slide right out.

DREAMY CREAMY COCONUT CAKE

Dreamy, creamy, dramatic crowd pleaser.

Dairy   *Serves 10 to 12*

CAKE

½	cup vegetable shortening	1	teaspoon baking soda
4	ounces butter, softened	¼	teaspoon salt
2	cups sugar	1	cup buttermilk
5	large eggs, separated, at room temperature	2	teaspoons vanilla
2	cups flour	⅛	teaspoon cream of tartar

COCONUT FILLING

1	(6-ounce) package fresh frozen coconut	1	cup sour cream
		2	cups sugar

WHIPPED CREAM FROSTING

16	ounces whipping cream	1	teaspoon vanilla
⅔	cup sugar	1	cup coconut filling

Preheat oven to 350°. Grease and flour three 9-inch round cake pans. Cream shortening and butter with sugar until light and fluffy. Add egg yolks 1 at a time, beating well after each addition. Combine flour, baking soda and salt. Add to creamed mixture alternately with buttermilk, beginning and ending with flour. Beat well after each addition. Stir in vanilla. Beat egg whites until frothy, add cream of tartar. Beat until stiff but not dry. Fold egg whites into batter. Spoon batter into prepared pans. Bake 25 to 30 minutes until tester comes out clean. Cool in pans 10 minutes. Remove from pans to cool completely. Split layers in half, making 6 layers. Set aside.

Centennial celebration at The Temple, Atlanta, Georgia, 1967.

Thoroughly combine filling ingredients, refrigerate 30 minutes. Reserving 1 cup, spread remaining filling between cake layers. Whip cream with mixer on high speed. When cream starts to thicken, slowly add sugar and vanilla. Beat until firm. Fold in reserved coconut filling, mixing thoroughly. Frost sides and top of cake. Store in refrigerator up to 2 days before serving.

To split cake layers in half horizontally, remove cooled cake from pan and place on a flat surface. Measure the cake with a ruler, mark a cutting line with toothpicks at intervals around the cake. Cut through the cake just above the toothpicks with a long serrated knife or unflavored dental floss.

HAPPY NEW YEAR HONEY CAKE

A sweet New Year for all with this traditional treat.

Pareve   *Serves 6*

⅓ cup finely chopped dried apricots	Juice of 1 orange and 1 lemon
¼ cup whiskey, Canadian whiskey or bourbon	¾ teaspoon baking soda
⅓ cup vegetable oil	1 teaspoon salt
¼ cup sugar	2 cups flour
2 large eggs	⅓ cup chopped almonds, walnuts or cashews
1 cup honey	Grated zests of 1 orange and 1 lemon
3 tablespoons applesauce	
⅓ cup apricot jam	

Soak apricots in whiskey for 1 hour. Preheat oven to 350°. Coat 10x5-inch loaf pan with nonstick spray, dust with flour. Cream oil and sugar together, add eggs. Combine liquid ingredients. Mix together dry ingredients. Add to egg mixture alternately with liquids. Stir in nuts, apricots, orange and lemon zest. Bake 45 minutes to 1 hour until tester inserted in center comes out clean.

PASSOVER SPONGE CAKE

"Passover was a family reunion! Why, people came from all over!
My aunt from Miami baked and brought at least 20 sponge cakes for all the
family to take home." This is her cherished recipe. Crown this creation with
cirtus-flavored whipped cream and serve with fresh strawberries.

Pareve/Passover   *Serves 8*

10 large eggs, separated, at room temperature	1 cup sugar
½ cup Passover cake meal	Juice of 1 lemon
½ cup potato starch	Juice of 1 orange
	½-1 cup chopped pecans

Preheat oven to 325°. Prepare 10-inch tube pan with nonstick spray. Beat egg yolks until light. Sift together cake meal and potato starch. Slowly add sugar, cake meal, lemon and orange juices to yolks. Mix well, set aside. Beat egg whites until stiff. Fold slowly into egg yolk mixture. Stir in nuts. Pour into prepared pan. Bake 1 hour 10 minutes. Invert immediately.

This sponge cake is also a delightful base for parfaits, tiramisu or trifle with layers of whipped cream and fruit.

When preparing sponge cakes, beat the egg yolks until light yellow before adding other ingredients. Carefully fold the egg whites into the egg batter to prevent loss of air and volume.

PASSOVER MANDEL BREAD

Pareve/Passover   Serves 10 to 12

1	cup Passover cake meal	4	large eggs
1	cup potato starch		Juice and grated zest of
1	cup vegetable oil		1 orange
1¾	cups sugar		Juice and zest of ½ lemon
1	tablespoon vanilla	1	cup chopped walnuts

Preheat oven to 350°. Grease 3 or more miniature loaf pans. Sift together cake meal and potato starch, set aside. Cream oil with sugar, add vanilla, eggs, juices and zest. Fold in dry ingredients, add walnuts. Fill loaf pans ½ full, bake 35 minutes, cool. Invert onto cutting board. Cut ½-inch thick slices. Place on cookie sheet. Lower heat to 325°. Return to oven 10 to 12 minutes, turn, bake another 10 to 12 minutes until lightly browned.

PASSOVER BROWNIES

*A very versatile and easy recipe. Layer leftover
brownies with pudding or mousse for a new dessert.*

Dairy/Pareve/Passover   Serves 12 to 18

4	ounces unsweetened chocolate	2	cups sugar
8	ounces unsalted butter or pareve margarine	¼	cup Passover cake meal
		¼	cup potato starch
4	large eggs	1	teaspoon vanilla

Preheat oven to 325°. Coat 13x9-inch baking pan with nonstick spray, dust with cocoa or additional cake meal. Melt chocolate and butter or margarine over low heat, cool completely. Beat eggs and sugar until very thick and light in color. Stir in melted chocolate, cake meal, potato starch and vanilla. Pour batter into pan. Bake 30 minutes or until just set. If over baked, these brownies are extremely dry. Test 2 to 3 minutes before suggested baking time is up, toothpick inserted in center should have wet crumbs clinging to it.

When freezing baked goods, put the item or items on a tray, separating cookies, brownies, etc. from each other, and into the freezer without packaging. After a few hours, wrap items fully in aluminum foil, sealing well and dating the label. Frozen baked goods keep up to 60 days. To defrost, unwrap while frozen and allow to thaw at room temperature, usually 1 to 2 hours.

Cocoa powder is unsweetened chocolate from which 76 to 90 percent of the cocoa butter has been removed. Cocoa gives huge chocolate flavor without adding fat, particularly in recipes that already contain a lot of butter, like cakes and cookies. Blend 3 tablespoons of cocoa powder with 1 tablespoon of vegetable oil to substitute for 1 ounce of unsweetened chocolate.

*Cakes &
Cookies*

PASSOVER RASPBERRY SQUARES

A Passover interpretation of a perennial favorite.

Dairy/Pareve/Passover   *Serves 8 to 10*

8	ounces unsalted butter or pareve margarine	1	cup sugar
2	large egg yolks	1	teaspoon vanilla
2	cups Passover cake meal	1	(12-ounce) jar raspberry preserves

Preheat oven to 325°. Cream butter or margarine. Mix in all ingredients, except preserves. Remove from mixing bowl, roll into ball. Place ¼ of mixture in plastic bag, freeze. Spray 11x8-inch or 9-inch glass baking dish with nonstick spray. Press remaining dough into bottom of pan, bake 20 minutes. Remove from oven, spread with preserves. Remove dough from freezer, crumble on top of preserves, pressing down gently. Bake 30 minutes longer, remove from oven. Cool, then cut into squares.

PASSOVER LADYFINGERS

Use these light pastries to make tiramisu or shortcake during Passover.

Pareve/Passover   *Serves 10 to 12*

3	eggs, separated	3	tablespoons sugar
⅛	teaspoon salt	½	cup potato starch
1	cup Passover confectioners' sugar	¼	cup Passover cake meal Passover confectioners' sugar
1	teaspoon vanilla		

Preheat oven to 350°. Prepare baking sheet or lady finger pans by spraying with cooking spray and dusting with matzah cake meal. Beat egg yolks, add salt, confectioners' sugar and vanilla at high speed until mixture becomes thick and very light in color. With clean, dry beaters, beat egg whites until they begin to thicken. Gradually add sugar, beating until stiff but not dry. Fold yolk mixture into whites. Sift together potato starch and cake meal, add ½ into egg mixture. Fold in remaining dry mixture, being careful not to over mix. Using pastry bag with ⅝-inch tip, pipe mixture into ladyfinger pans or in 4-inch lines on baking sheet. Lightly sift additional confectioners' sugar over top. Bake 8 to 10 minutes until golden. Remove from pans while still hot. Cool on racks. Freeze if desired.

Any recipe containing flour may be converted for Passover. Substitute ⅝ cup of potato starch or Passover cake meal, or a combination of cake meal and potato starch for 1 cup flour.

Cakes & Cookies

PASSOVER CHOCOLATE MACAROONS

Simplify Passover preparations by baking these macaroons ahead of time.

Pareve/Passover   *Yields 30 cookies*

5	ounces semisweet chocolate	1	teaspoon vanilla
2	large egg whites	7	ounces sweetened coconut
½	cup sugar		flakes
	Pinch of salt		

Preheat oven to 350°. Line 2 rimmed cookie sheets with parchment paper. Melt chocolate in top of double boiler or microwave. Cool to room temperature. With electric mixer, beat egg whites until firm. Slowly add sugar, salt and vanilla. Beat until whites are stiff and shiny, approximately 5 minutes. Fold in cooled chocolate and coconut with rubber spatula. Using approximately 2 tablespoons of dough per cookie, drop about 15 cookies on each sheet. Bake 16 minutes. Cool on racks. Freeze, if desired.

To prevent macaroons from sticking to parchment paper, lift a corner of the paper and drop a few tablespoons of water onto the cookie sheet immediately after removing from the oven. Steam will form and loosen the macaroons. Remove the macaroons from the paper at once. Place onto wire racks to cool.

WALNUT MACAROONS

Pareve/Passover   *Yields 12 cookies*

1	cup walnut pieces	1	egg white
1	cup plus 1 tablespoon superfine sugar, divided		

Preheat oven to 350°. Put walnuts on baking sheet, toast about 10 minutes until lightly browned, allow to cool. Line another baking sheet with parchment paper. In food processor, process nuts until finely ground, not pasty. In medium bowl, mix ground nuts with sugar and enough egg white to make a stiff paste. Spoon into pastry bag with ½ inch tip. Pipe small rounds or drop small mounds by teaspoonful onto prepared baking sheet. Space cookies ½-inch apart, lightly sprinkle with sugar. Bake 15 to 20 minutes until lightly browned. Remove from oven, transfer to wire racks to cool. Store in airtight container or freeze.

Toasted almonds or pecans can be substituted for walnuts.

Place ½ nut atop each cookie before baking to identify the nut used and to alert those who are allergic to nuts.

To make superfine sugar, use a food processor with a metal blade. Process sugar for 30 seconds with feed tube covered.

*Cakes &
Cookies*

RUSSIAN RUGALACH

Here is a yeast dough that doesn't need to be kneaded. Make lots, they disappear quickly.

Dairy/Pareve   *Yields 64 pieces*

3 cups sifted flour	3 large egg yolks, beaten
1 package dry yeast	1 cup sugar
4 ounces butter or pareve margarine, softened	1 cup finely chopped pecans
2 cups dairy or pareve sour cream	3 teaspoons cinnamon
	Dash of nutmeg

Mix flour and yeast in large bowl. Cut in butter or margarine with pastry blender. Add sour cream to egg yolks, stir into flour mixture. Wrap mixture in wax paper, chill overnight. Combine sugar, pecans, cinnamon and nutmeg. Set aside.

Preheat oven to 325°. Separate dough into 4 pieces. Roll each piece into large circle. Spread ¼ cup sugar mixture on work surface. Press 1 side of dough on top of sugar mixture and turn to coat other side. Cut circle into 16 wedges. Roll each wedge, beginning with the wide edge, creating crescent shape. Place on lightly greased cookie sheet. Bake 20 to 25 minutes or until browned.

As a variation for filling, try chocolate chips, nuts, canned fillings or preserves.

Sewing clothes for the needy in war-torn Europe,
Jewish Council for Russian War Relief, Atlanta, Georgia, c.1944.

HAMANTASCHEN

Haman's triangular hat inspired the shape of these fruit-filled favorites. This recipe has been used by Atlanta's Greenfield Hebrew Academy Student Council as a Purim fundraiser for many years.

Dairy/Pareve   *Serves 12 to 24*

6 tablespoons butter or pareve margarine	2 teaspoons baking powder
1 cup sugar	2 tablespoons milk or pareve soy milk
1 large egg	1-2 (12.5-ounce) cans fruit filling
2 cups plus 2 tablespoons flour	

Cream butter or margarine with sugar. Add egg and mix well. Sift together flour and baking powder, add to butter. Add milk, mix until dough forms. Wrap dough in plastic, refrigerate until cold. Roll out ⅓ of dough on lightly floured surface. Use glass rim or cookie cutter to cut 3-inch circles. Save scraps to roll again. Place 1 teaspoon fruit filling in center of each circle. Press up 2 sides in an inverted "V." Pinch corners and press up remaining side, to form triangular pastry showing filling in middle. Repeat process with remainder of dough and filling. Place on parchment lined cookie sheets without edges. Refrigerate 30 minutes.

Preheat oven to 375°. Bake 15 to 20 minutes until lightly browned, rotating sheets if necessary for even browning. Cool on wire racks.

Canned fruit filling comes in a variety of flavors including apricot, red raspberry, strawberry and prune.

Ready for a Purim celebration at Temple Beth Israel, Macon, Georgia, c.1911.

"SINSATIONAL" STUFFED BROWNIES

Dairy *Yields 3 to 4 dozen brownies*

4	ounces unsweetened chocolate		2	teaspoons vanilla
8	ounces unsalted butter		½	cup flour
4	large eggs		2	cups chopped candy or other fillings
2	cups sugar			

Grease and flour 2 foil lined 13x9-inch pans. Melt chocolate and butter or margarine in top of double boiler or in microwave. Set aside to cool slightly. In medium bowl, whisk together eggs and sugar. Stir chocolate mixture into egg mixture. Add vanilla and flour. Pour evenly into prepared pans. Cover and freeze 1 pan until firm or overnight, refrigerate the other.

Preheat oven to 350°. Prepare filling by chopping candy or measuring desired amount of any filling. Evenly layer filling on top of frozen unbaked brownies in pan by gently pressing down with finger tips. Spoon contents of other pan over candy layer. Let stand at room temperature 20 minutes. Bake 30 to 35 minutes or until just barely done, a tester inserted should have wet crumbs sticking to it. Cool, cut into squares.

Filling options include 2 cups of chopped candy bars, peanut butter mixed with sugar, nuts, chocolate covered raisins or use a variety and make wide strips of the chosen assortment.

To line a pan for brownies, flip the pan over, shape the foil over the pan, lift off and put inside the pan. This allows for easy removal and cutting of cooled brownies.

GIANT CHOCOLATE TOFFEE COOKIES

Outrageously huge, outrageously delicious and outrageously easy to make.

Dairy   *Yields 22 cookies*

½ cup flour
1 teaspoon baking powder
¼ teaspoon salt
½ pound chopped bittersweet chocolate
½ pound chopped semisweet chocolate
4 tablespoons unsalted butter
⅛ teaspoon cinnamon
1 tablespoon chocolate orange liqueur

1¾ cups firmly packed brown sugar
4 large eggs
1 tablespoon vanilla
5 (1.4-ounce) chocolate covered toffee bars, coarsely chopped
½ cup chopped macadamia nuts, lightly toasted
½ cup chopped slivered almonds, lightly toasted

To chop nuts quickly and with easy clean up, place nuts in a sealed airtight plastic bag and pound with the smooth side of a meat cleaver, large can of vegetables, or rolling pin.

Whisk flour, baking powder and salt in small bowl. Stir chocolates and butter in top of double boiler over medium heat until melted and smooth. Cool chocolate mixture to lukewarm. Stir in cinnamon and liqueur. With electric mixer, beat sugar and eggs until thick, about 5 minutes. Beat in chocolate mixture, vanilla and flour mixture. Fold in toffee and nuts. Chill batter until firm, about 45 minutes. Preheat oven to 350°. Line 2 large rimmed baking sheets with parchment paper. Drop batter by ¼ cupfuls onto sheets, spacing 2½-inches apart. Bake until tops are dry and cracked but cookies are still soft to the touch, about 15 minutes. Allow cookies to completely cool on pans. Store in airtight container at room temperature, up to 2 days.

RAVE REVIEW OATMEAL RAISIN COOKIES

*Everyone in our family lived in the neighborhood.
So if I wanted a cookie, I just went from house to house until I got one.*

Dairy/Pareve   Yields 24 large or 48 medium cookies

8 ounces unsalted butter or pareve margarine, softened	½ teaspoon salt
	¼ teaspoon nutmeg
1 cup firmly packed brown sugar	1½ teaspoons cinnamon
	1½ cups coarsely chopped walnuts, toasted
1 cup white sugar	1½ cups baking raisins
2 eggs	3 cups regular oats
1½ cups flour	1½ cups semisweet chocolate chips, optional
½ teaspoon baking powder	

Placing racks in middle and lower portion of oven, preheat to 350°. In electric mixer, combine butter or margarine with brown and white sugars. Beat until very creamy, about 3 minutes. Add eggs, 1 at a time, beating well after each addition.

Celebrating the Fourth of July, Atlanta, Georgia, c.1912.

Combine flour, baking powder, salt, nutmeg and cinnamon. Beat into butter mixture. Fold in walnuts, raisins, oats and chocolate chips, by hand, combining well. Form into 2½-inch balls. Place 6 on each parchment lined baking sheet. Bake 25 minutes, reversing sheets from middle to lower rack half way through baking time. Let cool 5 minutes. Carefully remove to wire racks to cool.

For chewier cookies, refrigerate the dough balls on the baking sheet for 10 minutes before baking.

Baking raisins are moister than regular raisins. However, regular raisins are time-honored in baked goods.

Oatmeal Lace Cookies

*This dainty cookie can be shaped to hold fruit or mousse or
rolled into a piroulline, a cigar-shaped wafer. Classic in taste and appearance.*

Dairy   *Yields 48 cookies*

8	ounces butter	1½	cups flour
6	tablespoons evaporated milk	1½	cups quick cooking oatmeal
6	tablespoons white corn syrup	1½	cups sugar
3	teaspoons vanilla	1	teaspoon baking powder

Preheat oven to 375°. Line cookie sheet with parchment. Melt butter in medium saucepan. Add evaporated milk, corn syrup and vanilla. Combine dry ingredients, gradually add to saucepan mixture on lowest heat. While keeping batter warm, drop by tablespoonfuls onto prepared cookie sheet, 3 inches apart. Bake 7 to 8 minutes, watching carefully to avoid burning.

To form a cup, drop by 2 tablespoonfuls on cookie sheet. When baked, remove from cookie sheet. While still warm and pliable, place over the back side of muffin pan.

For chocolate dipped piroullines, while still warm from the oven, quickly wrap baked cookie around wooden dowel to form cigar shape. In small saucepan, melt semisweet or bittersweet chocolate with 1-inch square of paraffin wax. Once rolled cookie is cool, dip ½ into chocolate mixture.

Silicone pastry brushes, spatulas, spoons and baking sheet liners are wonderful. They handle high heat, up to 500°, and are truly nonstick, so they are a cinch to clean.

Jewish War Veterans war bonds rally, Atlanta, Georgia, c.1943.

MEXICAN WEDDING COOKIES

*Whether it's congratulations, mazel tov or felicitaciones,
these cookies are delicious in any language.*

Dairy   *Yields 4 dozen*

1½	cups chopped pecans, toasted	1	cup confectioners' sugar
1½	cups butter, softened	2	teaspoons vanilla
¼	teaspoon salt	3	cups flour
			Confectioners' sugar

Preheat oven to 350°. Place pecans on cookie sheet, bake 7 minutes, watching until slightly browned. Cool, grind in food processor until fine. Using electric mixer, beat butter and salt in large bowl until light and fluffy. Add 1 cup sugar and vanilla. Beat until blended. Beat in pecans, then flour. Refrigerate dough 30 minutes.

Preheat oven to 350°. Shape into 1½-inch balls, place on cookie sheet ½-inch apart. Bake cookies 10 to 12 minutes. Remove cookies, roll in confectioners' sugar. Transfer to rack, allowing cookies to cool completely. Roll in sugar again when cool, if desired.

When substituting toasted ground almonds for pecans, use 1 teaspoon vanilla and 1 teaspoon almond extract.

To have homemade cookies in minutes, make and freeze dough, in a sealed plastic container up to 60 days. Defrost, covered at room temperature about 1 hour. Bake according to recipe directions.

ORANGE FRUIT CHEWIES

These cookies are packed with fruit, flavor and sunshine.

Dairy   *Yields 40 cookies*

COOKIES

3	tablespoons butter	1	teaspoon baking soda
2	teaspoons grated orange zest	½	teaspoons salt
⅔	cup orange juice	1	cup unsalted butter, softened
1⅓	cups chopped pitted prunes	1¾	cups firmly packed dark brown sugar
⅔	cup yellow raisins	1	egg
3½	cups flour	1	teaspoon vanilla
2	teaspoons cinnamon	1	cup chopped walnuts

GLAZE

3	cups confectioners' sugar	2	teaspoons lemon juice
½	teaspoon grated orange zest	¼	teaspoon vanilla
3½	tablespoons orange juice		

Preheat oven to 350°. Grease 3 baking sheets with butter. In large saucepan, combine zest, juice, prunes and raisins. Bring to boil, simmer 5 minutes, remove from heat. Combine flour, cinnamon, soda and salt in bowl. Cut butter into slices, add to fruit with brown sugar and stir until butter melts. Add egg and vanilla, stirring well. Stir in flour mixture and nuts.

Drop dough by plum sized mounds onto cookie sheets about 2 to 3-inches apart.

Bake 1 cookie sheet at a time 10 to 13 minutes until cookie edges start to brown and center is barely firm. Remove from oven, let sit for 1 minute then transfer to wire rack.

Combine glaze ingredients, stir well. Thin with more orange juice, if needed. Ice cookies with 1 to 2 tablespoons glaze using tip of table knife. Allow to dry before storing between sheets of wax paper.

CRANBERRY PECAN TASSIES

A tisket, a tasket, a tassie for Purim or picnic basket.

Dairy/Pareve   *Yields 2 dozen*

TASSIE SHELLS

1 (3-ounce) package dairy or pareve cream cheese, softened

½ cup unsalted butter or pareve margarine, softened

1 cup flour

FILLING

1 large egg

¾ cup firmly packed brown sugar

1 tablespoon melted butter or pareve margarine

1 tablespoon vanilla

2 tablespoons chopped pecans

⅓ cup finely chopped fresh or frozen cranberries

Confectioners' sugar

Blend cream cheese and butter or margarine until smooth. Stir in flour and mix until soft dough forms. Chill at least 1 hour or overnight. Shape into 2 dozen 1-inch balls. Place in ungreased 1¾-inch round tart pans. Press dough evenly against bottom and sides of pans.

Preheat oven to 350°. Beat together egg, brown sugar, melted butter or margarine and vanilla. Stir in pecans and cranberries. Spoon filling evenly into shells, less than 1 tablespoon per tart, filling to just below tops. Bake 18 to 25 minutes until filling is set and crust is light brown. Remove and cool. Run knife around edges to loosen, remove and dust tops with confectioners' sugar.

To substitute ⅔ cup dried cranberries for fresh or frozen, soak dried cranberries in hot tap water 15 minutes, drain.

Dressed for Purim, Atlanta, Georgia, c.1917.

RAZZMATAZZ RASPBERRY BARS

This may be the most raved about raspberry recipe in Georgia.

Dairy   *Yields 36 bars*

½	cup butter	½	teaspoon salt
2	cups white chocolate chips	½	teaspoon almond extract
2	large eggs	½	cup seedless raspberry jam
½	cup sugar	¼	cup chopped or sliced
1	cup flour		almonds

Preheat oven to 325°. Grease and flour 9-inch square pan. In small saucepan, melt butter over low heat. Add chips, but do not stir. Beat eggs in large mixing bowl until foamy. Add sugar, beat until lemon colored, 3 to 4 minutes. Stir in chocolate and butter mixture. Add flour, salt and almond extract. Mix on low speed until combined.

Spread ½ of batter in prepared pan and bake 15 to 17 minutes or until light golden brown. Remove from oven. Heat jam in bowl in microwave oven 30 seconds on full power, spread on baked crust. Drop spoonfuls of remaining batter evenly over the jam. Sprinkle with almonds. Bake an additional 25 to 30 minutes or until the edges are brown. Cool completely, cut into small squares.

Entertaining patients at the U.S. Army Hospital, Fort Benning, Georgia, c.1943.

TOASTED ALMOND BARS

Wonderful for hospitality suite baking. Guests from afar will go nuts about these bars.

Dairy/Pareve   *Yields 25 bars*

BARS

4	ounces unsalted butter or pareve margarine, softened		1	teaspoon vanilla
			¼	teaspoon almond extract
1	cup firmly packed light brown sugar		1	cup sifted flour
			½	teaspoon baking powder
1	large whole egg plus 1 egg yolk		½	teaspoon salt
			1	cup finely chopped almonds, toasted

ICING

3	tablespoons melted butter or pareve margarine, softened			Milk or pareve soy milk, as needed
1½	cups sifted confectioners' sugar		¼	teaspoon almond extract

Preheat oven to 350°. Cream butter or margarine with sugar until light. Beat in egg, egg yolk, vanilla and almond extracts. Sift dry ingredients together. Add to butter mixture. Stir in almonds. Spread into lightly greased and floured 9-inch square pan. Bake 20-25 minutes, cool and cut into bars.

For icing, beat butter or margarine with sugar. Add enough milk to make icing creamy. Stir in almond extract. Spread evenly over bars.

To soften butter quickly, put butter in a sealed plastic bag. Place bag in large bowl of warm water. In about 5 minutes, the butter will be ready to use.

SWEET AND SALTY NUT BARS

These crunchy bars taste just like candy.

Dairy   *Yields 36 bars*

CRUST

1½ cups flour	½ cup butter, softened
¾ cup firmly packed brown sugar	¼ teaspoon salt

TOPPING

¼ cup light corn syrup	1 tablespoon water
6 ounces butterscotch flavored chips	¼ teaspoon salt
2 tablespoons butter	1½ cups mixed nuts

Heat oven to 350°. Spray 13x9-inch baking pan with nonstick cooking spray, set aside. Combine all crust ingredients in large mixer bowl. Beat at low speed, scraping bowl often, until mixture resembles coarse crumbs, 1 to 2 minutes. Press crumb mixture into prepared pan, bake 10 minutes.

Place all topping ingredients except mixed nuts in saucepan. Cook over low heat, stirring constantly, until chips are melted and mixture is smooth, 5 to 7 minutes. Stir in nuts until well coated. Spread mixture onto crust. Bake 10 to 12 minutes or until golden brown. Cool completely, cut into bars.

"Can we sneak these Sweet and Salty Nut Bars into the theater?"
Orphans from the Hebrew Orphans Home attend the movies,
Atlanta, Georgia, c.1920.

MOM'S MARVELOUS MANDEL BREAD

My mom has to make these when my father isn't around so she can hide them in the freezer, otherwise Dad eats them all in one sitting!

Dairy/Pareve   *Serves 12 to 24*

3	cups sifted flour	2	teaspoons vanilla
2	teaspoons baking powder	3	large eggs
8	ounces butter or pareve margarine, softened	1	cup chopped pecans
1	cup sugar	1	large egg yolk, beaten

Preheat oven to 300°. Sift together flour and baking powder. In large bowl of electric mixer, beat butter or margarine 2 minutes. Gradually add sugar, beat well. Add vanilla and eggs, 1 at a time, mix well. Slowly fold in flour mixture, beat to mix well. Add pecans, mix. Pour into 2 greased 13-inch loaf pans. Bake 50 minutes, brush tops of loaves with beaten egg yolk, continue baking another 5 minutes or until golden. Remove from pans. Cool on wire rack. Refrigerate overnight.

Next day, preheat oven to 350°. Slice into ½-inch thick slices. Place slices flat on ungreased cookie sheet. Brown 7 minutes on each side.

As a variation, add chocolate chips, dried fruit or any type nut.

Before second baking, mandel bread may be frozen. When ready to bake, defrost, slice and bake according to directions.

Or VeShalom Sisterhood bazaar, Atlanta, Georgia, 1979.

Collaborative baking and cooking sessions, a local tradition since the early 1900s, have established a camaraderie among Sephardic Jews that mothers pass on to their daughters. Members of Atlanta's Sephardic shul, Or VeShalom, create elaborate, delicate Sephardic pastries and cookies when baking as a group several days a week in preparation for the much anticipated annual Chanukah bazaar and bake sale.

RASPBERRY FILLED MANDEL BREAD

Use any jam, preserves or filling. For Purim, try poppy seed or prune filling.

Pareve   *Serves 12 to 24*

3	large eggs	2	teaspoons baking powder
1½	cups sugar, divided	½	cup chopped almonds
1	cup vegetable oil	6	tablespoons raspberry jam, divided
2	teaspoons almond extract		
½	teaspoon vanilla	½	teaspoon ground cinnamon
4½	cups flour, divided		

Preheat oven to 325°. In large bowl of electric mixer, combine eggs, 1 cup sugar, oil, almond and vanilla on medium speed until well mixed, about 1 minute. In another large mixing bowl, combine 4 cups flour and baking powder. With mixer on low speed, slowly add flour to egg mixture until smooth, thick dough forms. Add additional flour, if needed, ¼ cup at a time, until dough forms a ball. Stir in almonds.

Remove dough to generously floured board, divide into 3 equal balls. Roll out 1 ball to form 8-inch log. Slice log in half lengthwise to create two 8-inch logs. Gently flatten each half until it is 2-inches wide. Place 2 tablespoons raspberry jam on 1 log, spread to cover surface. Place other log on top, pinching edges to seal in filling. Repeat with remaining dough and jam. Place logs onto greased baking sheet.

In small bowl, combine remaining ½ cup sugar and cinnamon. Sprinkle over logs. Bake until lightly browned, about 40 minutes. Remove from oven, increase temperature to 350°. While still hot, slice logs on diagonal into 1-inch pieces, return to baking sheets. Bake until lightly toasted, about 10 minutes. Remove to rack, cool completely. Store in airtight container.

Mandel bread is usually baked twice to dry both sides. To streamline the method lay the slices on a wire cooling rack. Set the rack on a cookie sheet and place it in the oven. The rack elevates the slices, allowing air to circulate all the way around them, drying both sides at once.

Praline Pecans

Pralines were invented in France, transported to
New Orleans and are now available to all.

Dairy/Pareve   *Yields 1 pound*

1   cup firmly packed brown   2   cups pecan halves, toasted
    sugar   1   teaspoon vanilla or maple
½   cup sugar   extract
⅔   cup dairy or pareve sour
    cream

Preheat oven to 350°. Lightly coat baking sheet with nonstick spray.
In medium saucepan, over medium heat, stir together sugars and sour
cream, bring to boil, reduce heat. Simmer syrup until it reaches 240° on
candy thermometer. Remove from heat, add pecans and vanilla, stirring
to coat. Spread mixture onto wax paper, separate nuts with forks, allow to
completely dry. Place in jar with tight fitting lid. Store in cool dry place.
Do not refrigerate.

Plains Georgia Peanut Brittle

Dairy/Pareve   *Yields 1 pint*

1   cup raw peanuts   1   teaspoon vanilla
1   cup sugar   1   teaspoon butter or pareve
½   cup light corn syrup   margarine
⅛   teaspoon salt   1   teaspoon baking soda

Spread out 15 inches of foil, coat with cooking spray. In non-reactive
medium to large bowl, mix peanuts, sugar, corn syrup and salt. Microwave
mixture on full powder for 4½ minutes. Stir, microwave for another
4½ minutes on full power. Add vanilla and butter or margarine. Microwave
on full power for 2 minutes. Add baking soda, stir quickly. Immediately
spread onto prepared foil. Cool and break into pieces.

The peanut is actually not a nut at all. It's a legume. Perhaps that's why boiled peanuts, cooked in the shell, in salt water, a cooking method typical of other beans, is such a popular snack in the South.

Georgia's official state crop is peanuts. Georgia produces 42 percent of the entire U.S. peanut crop and has 4880 peanut farmers. The most famous Georgia peanut farmer is Jimmy Carter, who ran his family peanut farm and business prior to being elected Georgia's governor in 1970 and president of the United States in 1976. Former President Carter and his wife, Rosalynn, still make their home in Plains, Georgia in the heart of the "peanut belt."

TOFFEE MATZAH CRUNCH

Try using coarsely chopped white chocolate or
a combination of chocolates and any variety of nuts.

Dairy / Passover   *Serves 15*

4-6 unsalted matzahs
2 sticks unsalted butter
1 cup firmly packed light
   brown sugar

¾ cup chocolate chips
¾ cup white chocolate chips
1 cup slivered almonds,
   toasted

Preheat oven to 375°. Line large jelly roll pan with foil, cover foil with paper parchment, to prevent sticking. Line pan evenly with matzahs, breaking extra pieces of matzah to fill spaces. Combine butter and brown sugar in 3-quart, heavy bottomed saucepan. Cook over medium heat, stirring constantly, until mixture comes to boil. Continue cooking 3 more minutes, stirring constantly. Remove from heat, pour over matzahs, spreading evenly with metal spatula. Place pan in oven, immediately reduce heat to 350°. Bake 15 minutes, watch closely to avoid burning, lowering heat to 325°, if necessary. Remove from oven, immediately sprinkle chocolate chips on matzahs. Let stand 5 minutes to soften. Using spatula, spread chocolate over matzahs, sprinkle with slivered almonds, pressing gently into chocolate. While warm, cut or break into squares or odd shapes. Chill in refrigerator until set, about 30 minutes.

KOSHER FOR
PASSOVER INDEX

*Many other recipes in this cookbook can be adapted
for Passover by substituting ingredients.*

Index

E

F

$\mathcal{T}$

SEASONED WITH LOVE

Culinary Treasures from The Breman, 1440 Spring Street NW, Atlanta, Georgia 30309
678·222·3700, www.thebreman.org

Please ship *Seasoned with Love* to:

Name _____

Address _____

City _____State _____Zip_____

Phone _____ E-mail_____

Enclosed please find my **CHECK** made payable to **The Breman** for _____ *Seasoned with Love* cookbooks.

Suggested Retail Price	$32.50 each	Quantity _____ $_____
Georgia Residents, please add appropriate sales tax		$_____
Shipping and Handling (if applicable)	$5.00 per first book	
	$3.00 each additional book	$_____
	TOTAL ENCLOSED	$_____

Or CHARGE to: (circle one)　　　Visa　　MasterCard　　American Express

Expiration Date _____ Account Number _____ Signature_____

* To receive a discount for an order of more than 5 cookbooks, please visit www.thebreman.org or contact The Breman at 678-222-3700.

All proceeds from the sale of Seasoned with Love benefit the educational programs at The Breman, teaching students of all ages the universal values of respect for difference and individual responsibility. Thank you for your support.

— —

SEASONED WITH LOVE

Culinary Treasures from The Breman, 1440 Spring Street NW, Atlanta, Georgia 30309
678·222·3700, www.thebreman.org

Please ship *Seasoned with Love* to:

Name _____

Address _____

City _____State _____Zip_____

Phone _____ E-mail_____

Enclosed please find my **CHECK** made payable to **The Breman** for _____ *Seasoned with Love* cookbooks.

Suggested Retail Price	$32.50 each	Quantity _____ $_____
Georgia Residents, please add appropriate sales tax		$_____
Shipping and Handling (if applicable)	$5.00 per first book	
	$3.00 each additional book	$_____
	TOTAL ENCLOSED	$_____

Or CHARGE to: (circle one)　　　Visa　　MasterCard　　American Express

Expiration Date _____ Account Number _____ Signature_____

* To receive a discount for an order of more than 5 cookbooks, please visit www.thebreman.org or contact The Breman at 678-222-3700.

All proceeds from the sale of Seasoned with Love benefit the educational programs at The Breman, teaching students of all ages the universal values of respect for difference and individual responsibility. Thank you for your support.

SEASONED WITH LOVE

Culinary Treasures from The Breman, 1440 Spring Street NW, Atlanta, Georgia 30309
678·222·3700,   www.thebreman.org

Please ship *Seasoned with Love* to:

Name _____

Address _____

City _____ State _____ Zip _____

Phone _____ E-mail_____

Enclosed please find my **CHECK** made payable to **The Breman** for _____ *Seasoned with Love* cookbooks.

Suggested Retail Price $32.50 each   Quantity ____ $_____

Georgia Residents, please add appropriate sales tax $_____

Shipping and Handling (if applicable) $5.00 per first book

                                                         $3.00 each additional book $_____

                                                                    TOTAL ENCLOSED $_____

Or CHARGE to: (circle one)   Visa   MasterCard   American Express

Expiration Date _____ Account Number _____ Signature_____

* To receive a discount for an order of more than 5 cookbooks, please visit www.thebreman.org or contact The Breman at 678-222-3700.

All proceeds from the sale of Seasoned with Love benefit the educational programs at The Breman, teaching students of all ages the universal values of respect for difference and individual responsibility. Thank you for your support.

— —

SEASONED WITH LOVE

Culinary Treasures from The Breman, 1440 Spring Street NW, Atlanta, Georgia 30309
678·222·3700,   www.thebreman.org

Please ship *Seasoned with Love* to:

Name _____

Address _____

City _____ State _____ Zip _____

Phone _____ E-mail_____

Enclosed please find my **CHECK** made payable to **The Breman** for _____ *Seasoned with Love* cookbooks.

Suggested Retail Price $32.50 each   Quantity ____ $_____

Georgia Residents, please add appropriate sales tax $_____

Shipping and Handling (if applicable) $5.00 per first book

                                                         $3.00 each additional book $_____

                                                                    TOTAL ENCLOSED $_____

Or CHARGE to: (circle one)   Visa   MasterCard   American Express

Expiration Date _____ Account Number _____ Signature_____

* To receive a discount for an order of more than 5 cookbooks, please visit www.thebreman.org or contact The Breman at 678-222-3700.

All proceeds from the sale of Seasoned with Love benefit the educational programs at The Breman, teaching students of all ages the universal values of respect for difference and individual responsibility. Thank you for your support.